Beyond Therapy

Beyond Therapy

The Impact of Eastern Religions
on Psychological Theory and Practice

Edited by Guy Claxton

Wisdom Publications London

First published in 1986

Wisdom Publications
23 Dering Street
London W1, England

British Library Cataloguing in Publication Data
Beyond therapy: the impact of eastern
    religions on psychological theory and practice.
    1. Psychology   2. Buddhism — Influence
    I. Claxton, Guy
    150   BF51

ISBN 0 86171 043 6

Set in Palatino 10.5 on 13
by Setrite of Hong Kong
and printed and bound in
Singapore by Eurasia Press
(Offset) Pte. Ltd.

Contents

6 *Contents*

Editor's Introduction

THE FADDISH WAVE of interest in the Eastern religions, especially in self-indulgent caricatures of Zen and Taoism, of the sixties and seventies has broken, leaving behind it a lasting, more serious swell of understanding and enquiry. The chapters in this book represent a summary of how the enquiry is going from one particular point of view: the impact that the spiritual traditions are having on the work of psychologists and psychotherapists.

The idea for the book arose out of a symposium on *Buddhism and Psychology* that I convened for the Annual Conference of the British Psychological Society in 1983. John Crook, David Fontana, Joy Manné-Lewis and I put together some papers and under the chairmanship of Martin Skinner, we prepared to display our, as we thought, minority interest. The enthusiasm, experience and sheer number of those who attended frankly astonished us. It turned out that literally hundreds of psychologists (mostly clinical, but educational and academic as well), psychotherapists and psychiatrists had been studying, meditating, and pondering on how to use the spiritual traditions in their work. Clearly their involvement had had an impact on them personally. Equally clearly they sensed strong implications for how to think about, and be with, other people, particularly those going through periods of distress or confusion. Yet they had been

7

tending to pursue their interest privately, feeling somewhat unsure about how colleagues would react if they knew, and suspecting that the ideas and practices of the spiritual traditions might not be accepted as 'respectable' psychology. They were, in many cases, probably right.

But things have changed rapidly over the last few years. In America the study of Buddhist psychology and its implications for our understanding of 'self' and even the cognitive processes of 'mind' has become accepted. The *Journal of Transpersonal Psychology* is now an institution. The Social Science Research Council has sponsored a conference on 'Buddhism and Cognitive Science.' Collections of articles have appeared discussing for example, the psychological ideas embedded in particular Eastern scriptures[1] or the implications of the spiritual traditions for psychotherapy.[2] And in Britain, too, the standing of such studies is no longer in question. Since that symposium in 1983, the British Psychological Society has offered at its conferences a workshop on meditation, and symposia on the social dimension of meditation, and on the so-called 'new religions' which claim to offer traditionally-based but contemporarily-clad forms of the spiritual path. 1986 sees a BPS sponsored 'International Conference on Eastern Approaches to Self and Mind,' as well as the publication of this book. Concern with the impact of the spiritual traditions on psychology and psychotherapy is now legitimate and psychological meditators can come out of the closet.

Part of the apprehension that has inhibited people from accepting the spiritual traditions as fit objects for psychological study stems from their usual designation as 'religions,' and for most Western psychologists, brought up within a predominantly Judeo-Christian culture, the word smacks of faith, belief, ritual and dogma. We might be able to talk about the psychology of *why* people need a concept of God, as Freud did. But a notion of God that is so strongly transcendent (outside ourselves), and transparently mythological, seems to offer no point of purchase for a psychological interpretation. The authorized, ritualized, dogmatised versions of Islam, Hinduism and Buddhism seem equally closed. However it is not to these 'Sunday Service' forms of religion that the expression 'the spiritual traditions,' as used here, refers. The lingering distrust that the word 'religion' may arouse is inappropriate in this context, and is better put aside. A sceptical attitude towards the spiritual traditions is well and good: it is the cynical one that now looks bigotted and dated.

If the spiritual traditions are not religions, as commonly conceived, then what are they? They are better thought of as systems for understanding and promoting deep personal change. And they derive from the teachings of individuals who have themselves undergone a lasting transformation of a particular kind. In this transformation their attitudes to the fundamental human questions that concerns life and death, change and bereavement, happiness and suffering, responsibility, relationship and identity have been altered irreversibly and radically. And by 'attitudes' I do not mean 'opinions,' but rather the basic personal stances that they have taken — that we all have taken — on these matters, often without even realizing that we have done so. The transformation (often called 'enlightenment') is something you do not get over. Once it has happened it permeates your actions and perceptions, feelings and motivations, completely. People who have been through it tend to be described by others as simple, natural, genuine and straightforward; serene and peaceful yet alert and full of life and vitality; wise in their words and economical and effective in their actions; kind, friendly, gentle and considerate in their dealings with people; perceptive and intelligent; at ease in their bodies and at home in the world. They seem to have shed the neurotic baggage that the rest of us reluctantly carry about: anxiety, irritation, resentment, regret, guilt, meanness, greed, jealousy, possessiveness, worry, confusion and the rest of the familiar catalogue. And while we look on with envy, or even disbelief, they assert that this transformation is available to all. What we see as the inevitable minuses that must come along with the plus of being alive, they see as being the unwanted and unnecessary by-products of some mistakes we have made in the way we look at things. The spiritual traditions explain very precisely what these mistakes are, and offer equally precise techniques for undoing them.

Ten years ago I would have poo-pooed all this. I was interested in semantic memory, paradoxical sleep, and the function of the frontal lobes — and that was what psychology was about. When I started interviewing students who wanted to read psychology at Oxford, I was told to weed out the ones who wanted to know 'what made people tick' or to 'understand themselves,' and I agreed this was a sound idea. But I've slowly changed my mind. I see psychology paddling around in the shallow waters of human experience and behaviour, often afraid to broach, or even acknowledge, the Big Questions, as if to do so were somehow embarrassing and naive. And I see philosophy and theology deliberately aiming off-centre as well. Yet there seems no good reason why these disciplines, which celebrate and exercise the mind, should not concern themselves with those deep enduring questions that matter most to everyone. And psychology has least excuse of all.

The literature of psychotherapy has made a good start, of course, though it often seems to accept that what is normal is *ipso facto* what is natural, and we are entitled to entertain some doubt about that. But there is one body of writing that seems to hit the nail on the head, and that does not shy away from, or apologise for, doing so: that of the spiritual traditions. Of course much of it, even when translated, is in a language that doesn't always ring a bell. It often uses concepts, analogies and examples that spoke to people living two millennia ago, and that are not common currency today. But with the help of modern teachers of the same ilk — the *roshis* from Japan, *lamas* and *rinpoches* from Tibet, *bhagwans* and *maharishis* from India — its essential psychology can be recast in modern form. These traditions seem to offer me what I had grown to miss in psychology, and it is in the hope that there will be other psychologists and psychotherapists who have been feeling the same way, that we have put this interim package of reports together.

So the contributors to this book are explorers of possibilities, applications, implications, parallels. We are not converts or adherents, but we share a sense that the spiritual traditions have a great deal to offer psychology and psychotherapy. As I say, most of us have been touched in our own lives by things we have read within these traditions, by the qualities of spiritual teachers we have come across, or by our own first-hand experiences with meditation. But we share too a caution about misinterpreting, misapplying or trivializing the theories and practices we are studying. We have to be very careful, for example, in reading Buddhist scriptures in translation, for there are some awful ones about, and unless we read Pali or Sanskrit it is hard to tell the good from the bad. We risk preferring and quoting the ones that simply confirm our preconceptions. There are as yet too few people around who are literate both in these ancient languages and in the languages of contemporary psychology.

Equally there are important issues to be discussed about the proper relationship between meditation and therapy. In this book there are quite clear differences of opinion about that, as there were as well between very experienced meditation teachers and therapists in John Welwood's excellent collection of pieces, *Awakening the Heart*. Clearly this is an area within which we need to listen carefully to each others' experiences, and proceed cautiously. So the book presents a variety of positions, experiences, debates, work-in-progress and current dilemmas. What the spiritual traditions have to teach us is problematic, but it is, we are convinced, a problem well worth tackling.

The chapters fall naturally, (though not entirely neatly) into two groups. The first is concerned with the ideas of the traditions and with explicating them in psychological terms. In the opening paper Colette Ray sets the scene with an overview of both Hinayana and Mahayana Buddhist teachings and the ways in which these have been picked up or paralleled by Western psychologists. She focuses particularly on Carl Jung and George Kelly. There then follow a set of three papers that home in on the crucial notion of *self*. David Fontana lays out the view that thought, to which we give such respect and special status in our mental lives, is more properly seen as another of the 'senses.' I attempt to show what our 'theory' of self actually consists of, what attributes it is supposed to have, whether there is in fact any good evidence for this theory, and where it comes from. Susan Blackmore caps this nicely by arguing that 'self' is not a theory we *have*, but a model that we constantly *create*, and that during experiences of 'altered states of consciousness' — or of *satori* — we may create a different model, or none at all.

Next there is a pair of chapters that explores in more detail the relationship between the spiritual traditions and two modern psychological thinkers. In the first Martin Skinner looks at G.H. Mead's ideas on self and relates them to Zen. And then Fraser Watts describes the 'spiritual psychology' of Rudolf Steiner, arguing that he was a pioneer of the new common endeavours to capture spiritual wisdom in a language accessible to the contemporary West. Another pair of papers follows that draw out the psychology from particular Buddhist teachings. Whilst most of the preceding chapters have tried to convey something of the broad spirit of the traditions, these two attend more carefully (and quite rightly) to the letter, making sure we do not get carried too far away from the original scriptures. Joy Manné-Lewis provides an admirably clear distillation of the 'psychology of enlightenment' to be found in the Pali canon. And Andrew Rawlinson gives us a strong feel for the intricate psychology of the Mahayana school.

The second major group of chapters is concerned with ideas, but with ideas in practice: with the *applications*, in other words, of spiritual techniques and notions to the 'treatment' of unhappy or disturbed people, and the search for betterment amongst ordinary 'normal neurotics.' The first four chapters all take as their focus of concern some form of clinical or psychotherapeutic situation, and explore the value of the spiritual traditions therein. Ian Wray gives us a scene-setting overview of the western therapeutic traditions before subjecting them to scrutiny from a Buddhist point of view. Stephen Parry and Richard Jones again look at a range of psychotherapists, but, picking up the theme of some of the earlier chapters, explore especially the importance and relevance of Buddhism's 'no-self' teaching for both therapy and therapists. Malcolm Walley outlines the Tibetan Buddhist approach to mental health, and describes some of his work using specific spiritual techniques with both patients and health professionals. Padmal de Silva focuses in on the behavioural approach to therapy, and finds many of the common techniques of behaviour change foreshadowed — and sometimes described in precise detail — in early Buddhist texts. And in order to rub the point in, David Brandon gives some nice examples of a seventeenth century Zen master, Bankei, giving ordinary people advice about their problems and worries that would not sound out of place in a modern Social Work department.

The attention of this section shifts with the next three papers to the influence of spiritual ideas and practices on the lives of people in the everyday world — people who are neither monks nor patients. Michael West gives us a brief review of research on the effects of meditation, points out some of the shortcomings of that research, and then gives us some fascinating excerpts from his own interviews with long-term meditators about their beliefs, experiences and motivations. The next two papers discuss the so-called 'new religions,' which purport to combine traditional spiritual, and modern psychotherapeutic techniques in the service of the growth or liberation of those who seek it. Guy Fielding and Sue Llewelyn take a cool look at the reactions of society to these groups, and at the way that some of the accusations that have been made can reflect uncomfortably on the more 'acceptable' institutions of both religion and psychotherapy.

While Paul Heelas and Rachael Kohn take a closer look at a few of the 'new religions', their practices, beliefs and clienteles.

And finally I contribute a few concluding thoughts to this second section, reviewing some of the issues, particularly to do with the place of spiritual techniques in the therapeutic context, that have emerged.

Guy Claxton
London,
February, 1986

Part One
Ideas

1

Western Psychology and Buddhist Teachings: Convergences and Divergences

Colette Ray

Colette Ray is a Lecturer in Psychology in the Department of Human Sciences, Brunel University, where she teaches clinical psychology. She has researched and written widely on psychological aspects of health care, and particularly on the treatment of cancer.

'WHAT ARE WE, and what might we be?' This is the most challenging question that human beings can ask of themselves, and Western Psychology presents us with an apparently bewildering array of answers from which to choose. To the radical behaviourist, we are a cluster of mechanisms geared to a particular environmental history and a particular set of current contingencies. The thoughts, feelings, values and longings which seem at an intuitive level to characterise what is essentially human are peripheral; they are mere epiphenomena and we are primarily objects in a world of objects. It is only recently that behaviourists have acknowledged that we are agents as well as acted upon, and that cognitions play a role in shaping both the environment, as it affects us, and our responses to that environment. Psychoanalytic theory shares the behaviourist's scepticism of naive views of what we are, but its insights point in a different direction. It describes an unconscious substratum of everyday experience and behaviour, a depository of forces which give rise to emotional conflict and confusion and which we tend to deny because of their base nature. Humanistic and existential psychologies, in contrast, emphasise our creative functions. Human nature is potentially active rather than reactive, benign rather than base. We can do more than merely seek an equilibrium, by reforming maladaptive behaviour patterns or reconciling conflicting forces. We can strive to actualise self and to create meaning in a chaotic and often hostile world, and we are free to define the terms of our being and to develop toward wholeness and fulfilment. No one of these perspectives is necessarily truer than the others. Each gives emphasis to a facet of human nature, to disposi- tions or possibilities that are neglected elsewhere.

HINAYANA TEACHING

Early Buddhist Psychology incorporates similar themes and it is possible to draw parallels in broad and general terms at least. Firstly, some of its ideas are echoed in behavioural psychology. The world is depicted as an intermeshing of *dharmas*, psychological and external events which arise and fall away under the influence of past causes *(hetu)* and present conditions *(pratyaya)*. This continuous and ever changing flux of events is the *dharma santana*, which is itself orderly but which, in our experience, can seem like a torrent sweeping us along. We are locked into *karma* to the extent that we fail to realise and take hold of this stream of causality. The Buddhist practitioner is encouraged to develop insight into the nature of the flow; the *santana* can be steered by attention to the conditions without which *dharmas* will not arise: beneficial *dharmas* can be encouraged and maintained, and undesirable *dharmas* prevented or suppressed. Secondly, Buddhism stres- ses, as do dynamic psychologies, the importance of the 'fires' or passions as determining forces. Through these we remain attached to and immersed in the flood; only with their suppression can we escape. Unlike Western psychology, however, Buddhism includes ignorance as a passion along- side craving and fear. Thirdly, like humanistic and existential psychologies, Buddhism claims that human beings can be different from what they often are; that they have untapped potentials to be developed and that conventional and accepted meanings are arbitrary in themselves and limiting in their effects. Finally, Western psychology is sometimes claimed to be 'obsessed' with pain, to focus upon the negative rather than the positive aspects of our experience. Buddhism takes as its starting point the problem of *dukkha*. This covers the spectrum of suffering from acute distress to the general unsatisfactoriness of existence and the confusion, agitation and upset that can typify our experience in the world. *Dukkha* has its roots in craving, fear and ignorance and Buddhism prescribes a path which leads to the elimination of suffering.

However, the Buddhist orientation in tackling such themes is different from a western one. Western models emphasise the importance of predictability and control. The well-adjusted person develops realistic expectations of outcomes, and has a sense of self efficacy in achieving these.[3] Strength rather than vulnerability is valued, activity is preferred to passivity, and a perception of control over outcomes is the hall-mark of adjustment.[4,5] From a Buddhist viewpoint, however, all worldly outcomes are transitory and insubstantial *(anitya)*. Buddhism encourages a detachment from everyday concerns, and an acceptance of and openness to all experience. The task is not to engineer positive outcomes and avoid negative ones, but to transcend all attachments and aversions. Needs and desires are themselves barriers to enlightenment, to the extent that we identify with them. Rather than seeking their expression and satisfaction, they should be acknowledged and set aside. Western psychology makes much also of the importance of a coherent self-image and of high self-esteem. It is healthy to have a clear sense of one's own identity and a feeling of autonomy, and to value oneself and one's achievements. Buddhism denies the existence of self as a distinct entity *(anatman)*; we are no more than form, feelings, percep-tions, impulses and consciousness and these are transient. The self is merely a construction, and yet it refers everything to itself and distorts experience. The goal is thus not to try further to enhance the self, but to undermine it. Clinging to the illusions of self and permanence, the world can never, finally, meet our expectations and we are prey to *dukkha*.

Suffering can cease only with the realisation that all substantive adaptations of self and strivings for security are worthless. Furthermore, Western psychology views as healthy the person who is free from symptoms and is functioning efficiently and happily in the world. The Buddhist viewpoint portrays this conventional adjustment, to the extent that it can be realised, as complacency, since it is based upon delusion. We live fictional lives, and the specific nature of the roles and drama these involve make little difference. True spiritual health begins with a feeling of disgust with this superficial way of being, a recognition of the intrinsic hollowness of the fiction and an abandonment of its pretensions.

These ideas are not totally alien, and at an intellectual level we may be able to accept their logic. In the west, however, an implicit distinction is maintained between philosophical ways of understanding the world and systems of understanding which form a basis for action. From a Buddhist point of view, theory and practice are inextricably linked. It is all too easy for 'students' of Buddhism to adopt the former without the latter, thus creating yet more intellectual games to play. If the import of the teaching is to be fully realised, then this requires a dedicated struggle, with constant attention to the workings of consciousness and a gradual wearing away of its delusions. Traditions may differ as to whether enlightenment is gradually developed or suddenly achieved, but all are agreed that the path is an arduous one. There are no half measures. If one is not prepared to make the final sacrifice and uproot the self, then the teaching may be appropriated by it. Understanding can become yet another defence, serving to distance self from pain without challenging its integrity. The teaching becomes a strategy for coping rather than a path to transformation.

MAHAYANA TEACHING

Later developments of Buddhism argued that the Hinayanist

goal, based upon a suppression of *dharmas* and on escape from *samsara*, is provisional only. *Anuttara samyak sambodhi*, the supreme and perfect enlightenment, goes beyond even *nirvana*. The *bodhisattva* who treads this path does not try to engineer a way out of *samsara*, but to transcend the world of appearance. There is a truth which encompasses the whole, including *samsara*. The *Arhat*, it is claimed, by opting for *nirvana* robs himself of this final realisation. Like the *Arhat*, the *bodhisattva* quietens the passions, cultivating generosity, moral discipline, patience, devotion, mindfulness and insight. However, unlike the *Arhat*, he clings to no view. *Hinayana* teachings deny the reality of the everyday world as we perceive it; the Heart Sutra, the core sutra of *Mahayana* teaching, denies also the doctrines of the *Hinayana*. It denies the existence of skandhas; of sense organs, sense objects and consciousness; of the twelvefold chain of causations. It even denies the reality of suffering and the attainment of wisdom. The emphasis is on the abandonment of all conceptual attachment, rather than on the abandonment of samsaric activity.

The abdication of all viewpoints is epitomised in *Madhyamika* philosophy, and in the teaching of *Sunyata* or the void. The *pratitya-samutpada* of the *Abidharma*, the causal law governing the rise and fall of dharmas, is directly challenged by Nagarjuna. He argues that if *dharmas* are conditioned and dependent, then they are not entities; they can have no abiding nature. Self essence and contingency are not compatible. It follows, according to Nagarjuna's argument, that if we cannot assume the existence of entities, then causation in turn is meaningless. It is said that *dharmas* are subject to origination, maintenance, decay and destruction, but if *dharmas* are empty then what is there that is originated, maintained, subject to decay and destroyed? Nagarjuna thus states the eight resounding negations: no stopping, no arising, no destruction, no permanence, no sameness, no difference, no coming, no going. *Dharmas* are non-arising and quiescent.

As *upaya* or skilful means we can use the concept of

dharmas and causation to cut through common sense views and divorce ourselves from the world of egocentricity and desire: its emptiness is realised and we are freed from its constraints. Yet if we do not recognise the essential emptiness of these alternative ways of construing the world, their provisional and relative nature, then we find ourselves in another, though different trap. They are no more and no less true than the constructs they replace. *Sunyata* cuts through these views in turn. Furthermore, *Sunyata* is a sword which is then turned against itself. *Sunyata* is itself *Sunyata*, and to cling to it has been described as the greatest and most damning error. Just as it is erroneous to conceive of *dharmas* or causation, so it would be wrong also to put in their place a principle of no-*dharmas* or non-causation. This too is but a view, and any such stance is an error. Murti, in The Central Philosophy of Buddhism,[6] quotes the *Kasyapa Parivarta* (p.164):

> Those, Kasyapa, that (mis) apprehend *Sunyata* as a negative fact, I consider them the forlorn, the irrevocably lost. ∴. Better it is to entertain the substance view (*pudgala-drsti*) of the magnitude of the Mount Sumeru than the *Sunyata*-view of the nihilist (*abhavabhinivis-inah*). Why is it so? Of all theories, Kasyapa, *Sunyata* is the antidote. Him I call the incurable who mistakes *Sunyata* itself as a theory (*drsti*). It is as if a drug, administered to cure a patient, were to remove all his disorders, but were itself to foul the stomach by remaining therein. Would you Kasyapa consider the patient cured? . . . Likewise, Kasyapa, *Sunyata* is the antidote for all dogmatic views; but him I declare incurable who misapprehends *Sunyata* itself as a theory.

Sunyata is the all-encompassing view which clings to no view and excludes no view. It points to the suchness of things, a direct seeing which emerges of itself when we can stand aside from our conceptual attachments. This is the 'Wisdom

Gone Beyond' that cannot be apprehended intellectually but only intuitively, and at the culmination of the path. No teaching can convey this realisation. It can only point toward it and do so, at that, indirectly. It is beyond the scope of analysis and systematisation and, as such, beyond the scope of psychological theorising. By definition, the latter can hinder development along the path. Mind-created meanings, no matter how sophisticated and 'insightful' in a relative sense, cannot provide a stable ground of experience. They merely substitute one framework for another, in an attempt to disavow the void. *Mahayana* Buddhism does not try to fill the emptiness but to deepen it, to develop a state of 'meaning-free-ness' where one is open to all experience and can act spontaneously.

EAST AND WEST

To the western way of thinking, it is difficult to imagine what is left of value if both emotional attachments and the power of reason are invalidated, and Buddhism is sometimes described as nihilistic. This is an unjust charge. With a realisation of one's Buddha-nature, passion becomes compassion and intellect becomes wisdom. There is an alternative and positive way of being. One is grasping, the other receptive; one seeks to stamp itself upon the world, the other is open and responsive; one tries to assimilate all to itself, while the other recognises no divide and can thus accommodate to all. A more serious issue is whether teachings developed in the East can provide useful guidelines for people in the West. While it would be wrong to stereotype too rigidly the 'western mind' and the 'eastern mind,' there are traditional and cultural differences which cannot be ignored. Buddhist texts talk of *upaya* as skilful means in the context of teaching: no theory can have absolute truth; any specific teaching has value only in that it can point the way to development; and different teachings may be appropriate in different contexts.

Carl Gustav Jung is the psychologist who has gone furthest in attempting a synthesis between eastern and western models, but he cautions against an over-enthusiastic adoption of the former. Western consciousness, he claims, has been uprooted from the unconscious and the latter is suppressed. In the East, the unconscious is manifest in experience, and in that context it is appropriate to seek to control the influence of the passions by detaching from them. In the West, a similar path can lead to a further and undesirable suppression: '...since one cannot detach oneself from something of which one is unconscious, the European must first learn to know his subject (the unconscious).'[7] The initial task is thus to assimilate unconscious contents into consciousness and, only then, to seek an emancipation from them. These contents are no more real than those of ego consciousness. They are fragments of the whole, and in this fragmentary form are fantasies and illusions, but we need to express the fantasy and the illusion if we are to extract meaning from it and achieve a realisation of the whole. It is premature to seek liberation from something we have no contact with; one cannot set down something one does not know one is carrying. To attempt to do so is to foster an even greater separation rather than a movement toward wholeness, and the result can be hollow: 'For the European, it is sheer poison to suppress his nature, which is warped enough as it is, and to make of it a willing robot.'[8]

These sentiments are similar to those expressed in *Mahayana* teachings. *Hinayana* sees as the goal the stopping (*nirodha*) of samsaric activity; *Bodhisattvas* of the *Mahayana* pledge themselves to remain in the world for the value of other beings. Furthermore, in the *Vimalakirtinirdesa*,[9] Manjusri is portrayed as saying that it is only among the mud of the passions and false views that the *bodhicitta* or will to enlightenment can be produced and brought to fruition. The seeds of enlightenment need to germinate over time, and it is the trials and tribulations of existence that provide their nourishment. The fire of the passions themselves are the Buddha-nature. In their crude form, when harnessed to the self, they obscure this nature; if they are gentled, rather than suppressed, they are transformed and marry with the Buddha nature. All extremes are to be avoided. Vimalakirti says '...although a Bodhisattva should thus subdue his mind, he cannot adhere *(sthatavyam)* to either the control of the mind *(cittaniyama)* or the license of the mind *(cittaniyama)*. And why? Because to adhere to the license of the mind is characteristic of fools *(bala)* and to adhere to the control of the mind is characteristic of the listeners *(sravaka)*.'

Jung's concern about the transposition of Eastern ideas to the West lies not only with what he sees as the Westerner's underdeveloped awareness of the unconscious and its forces. While he maintains that the West errs in its exclusive emphasis on the intellectual, the rational and the scientific, he implies that the path to development lies in the broadening of this consciousness rather than in setting it aside.

> ...it is sad indeed when the European departs from his own nature and imitates the East or 'affects' it in any way. The possibilities open to him would be so much greater if he would remain true to himself and evolve out of his own nature all that the East has brought forth in the course of the millennia.[10]

and similarly 'Only by standing firmly on our own soil can we assimilate the spirit of the East.'

Here again, the conflict between this and Buddhist views is more apparent than real. The *Hinayana* presents a detailed and analytical account of psychological phenomena and even *Madhyamika* philosophy, which aims to undermine all intellectual constructions, presents its position via sophisticated logical arguments. Reason can point the way to enlightenment although it cannot itself represent it. The intellect is a resource; our error is in identifying with our thoughts and theories and treating these as reflections of reality. As Jung himself says, 'The intellect does, in fact, harm the soul when it dares to possess itself of the heritage of the Spirit.' Reason can become a cage, dictating our actions, channelling them in accordance with preconceptions, and stifling spontaneity and creativity. Yet through reason we can challenge old assumptions and explore new possibilities, and even express in part a knowledge which is beyond reason.

A major source of confusion in psychological theorising is in identifying intellectual reasoning with knowledge. Knowledge is assumed to exist only to the extent that it is cognitively framed and articulable. Yet knowledge is reflected in action also. For example, the Personal Construct Theory of George Kelly is generally interpreted as giving a central role to the intellect and rational functions. Yet Kelly, in his later writings, challenged this interpretation.[11] Actions themselves are a way of construing: the individual 'knows the event through his own art of approach to it.'[12] For Kelly, there are an infinite number of ways in which an event can be so construed, and the human quest lies in elaborating our constructions, in the light of experience, toward a closer approximation to the truth, even though absolute truth may not in itself be realisable:

> What we think we know is anchored only in our own assumptions, not in the bedrock of truth itself, and that world we seek to understand remains always on the horizons of our thoughts.[13]

Each experience is a fresh experiment, and Kelly cautions against logical thought as a framework for action since it seeks to interpret the present in terms of the past. Nor is it enough to throw oneself mindlessly into experience, since in this way too one will be driven by past influences. Kelly argues instead for commitment, which he defines as involvement together with anticipation while remaining open to the possibility of new subsequent constructions. Only by constantly reconstructing experience in this way can 'obvious' meanings be challenged and new perspectives created.

Meaning is implicit in action, but no meaning is absolute. It evolves and is continuously transformed through living in the world; life can be meaning-free without being mean-ingless. Neither reason nor feeling are separate from the Buddha-nature. They can be expressions of this nature, to the extent that they flow from the situation and one's engage-ment with it. They distort and are a corrupting influence if they are allowed to determine experience, shaping it in accordance with our preconceptions, attachments and avers-ions. Both the intellect and the passions are manipulative, but if this grasping aspect can be set aside then the one becomes wisdom and the other compassion. This in itself is not a matter for the intellect or the will. On the face of it, it is the simplest of things but, as Jung often said, simple things are always the most difficult.

2
Mind, Senses and Self

David Fontana

David Fontana is a Senior Lecturer in
Educational Psychology at University
College, Cardiff. His recent books include
The Education of the Young Child
(Blackwell, 1984) and *Teaching and Personality*
(Blackwell, 1986)

THE IMMEDIATE PROBLEM for Westerners, trying to find their way into the vast and subtle field of Buddhist thought and practice, is that Buddhism defies the kind of categorization so popular with the Western mind. It is a religion, yet it is not a religion. It is a philosophy yet it is not a philosophy. And, although I shall use the term 'Buddhist psychology' freely in this chapter it is a psychology and yet it is not a psychology. Not surprisingly, this elusiveness lends to Buddhism a somewhat disturbing quality, rather in the way that Surrealism or Dadaism in art are disturbing. Like Surrealism or Dadaism, Buddhism demands that we either re-shape our categories or abandon them altogether and replace them with direct experience rather than thoughts *about* experience. Don't relate to Buddhism solely as a religion or as a philosophy or as a psychology we seem to be told; just relate to Buddhism as Buddhism. The very attempt to categorise it is to limit it and to approach it with preconceptions that act as insuperable obstacles to appreciating what it actually is.

But Buddhism does not simply present us with material that cannot easily be fitted into our existing categories, it often presents us with material that appears to contain insuperable contradictions. In Buddhism there are experiences of God yet no God to be experienced. In Buddhism we each have an individual self yet we do not have an individual self.

33

And in Buddhism we live in a world that is real yet in a world that is unreal. How seriously, you may ask, should we take something that deals in ambiguities and paradoxes of this kind? Can it provide us with any sort of cognitive map to allow us to find our way around? Does it give us anything upon which the mind can take a hold? I can only answer these questions by saying that Buddhism demands that we abandon the disjunctive thinking to which we have become accustomed and replace it with inclusive thinking. We must abandon the rigid notion of '*either* this *or* that' and replace it with the much more flexible notion of '*both* this *and* that.' If we revert to our statement of a moment ago about God, the self and reality this means we can re-phrase them as 'In Buddhism there is both a God and there is not a God, there is both a self and there is not a self, in Buddhism the world is both real and it is unreal.[14]

Once having made these statements and proved ourselves capable of tolerating the apparent ambiguity which they contain (and toleration of ambiquity is a feature of the creative person is it not?) we then find, after a period that may take weeks or months or years, that they contain a subtle inner meaning capable of taking us beyond the limits of simple linear thought. They are not, in other words, merely what they seem, the muddled statements of men and women who cannot make up their minds. They are a challenge to our view of reality as we see it, a leap into another form of thinking that takes us beyond the structures of thought that we have come to believe represent reality.

But why, the Westerner may ask, bother to take that leap? Why not stay with our own logical, linear thinking? It seems to serve us well enough for most purposes. It allows us to invent science, to use words with precision, to hold our own at seminars and dinner parties. Why chase after illogicalities? There is, in all conscience, enough confusion in the world without looking for any more.

BUDDHISM AND HUMAN BEHAVIOUR

At its simplest level, the answer for the psychologist lies in the profound effect that Buddhism appears to have upon human behaviour, an effect that many of us would accept is highly beneficial in that it promotes psychological health. That is, if by psychological health we mean the ability to live in harmony with oneself and nature, to show tolerance and compassion to one's fellow human beings, to endure hardship and suffering without mental disintegration, to prize non-violence, to care for the welfare of all sentient beings, and to see a meaning and purpose in one's life that allows one to enter old age or to face death with serenity and without fear. What psychotherapist could wish more for his client?[15]

C.G. Jung, one of the first Western psychologists to make a deep study of Buddhism, wrote that 'it was neither the history of religion nor the study of philosophy that first drew me to the world of Buddhist thought, but my professional interests as a doctor.'[16] And a few sentences later Jung emphasises the matter further when he states that '...in our sphere of culture the suffering of the sick can derive considerable benefit from...the Buddhist mentality, however strange it may appear.' Again, a little later, Jung comments that it is no wonder the doctor, concerned as he is to alleviate psychological suffering, should value 'religious ideas and attitudes so far as they prove helpful as therapeutic system,' and should single out the Buddha as one of the supreme helpers since the essence of his teaching 'is deliverance from suffering through the maximum development of consciousness.'

The most obvious reason for psychologists to interest themselves in Buddhism, therefore, is the issue of psychological health (their own as well as their clients'!). In addition, however, Buddhist thought has considerable implications for our psychological models of humans. For although Buddhism cannot be neatly categorised as a 'psychology,' it nevertheless, in the complete picture of human beings that it represents, subsumes even the most rarefied and specialised concerns of the Western psychologist. So much so in fact that no scientific or analytical psychologies have developed in the cultures of the East. There has been no need. Buddhism together with Hinduism, Taoism and Confucianism have satisfactorily provided all the answers to the questions that Easterners ask about their mental life.

But this still leaves us with the problem of where Western psychologists can best find their way into the vast and subtle panoply of Buddhism, a task rendered ostensibly more difficult by the variety of different groupings that make up this panoply, ranging from the apparent austerities of the Theravadin schools of Sri-Lanka and South-East Asia through the colourful kaleidescope of Tibetan Tantric Vajrayana Buddhism to the Mahayana schools of the Far East, the theism of Japanese Pure Land Buddhism and the baffling mental hygiene of Rinzai and Soto Zen. Perhaps the answer to this is that we must each find our own way in, conscious that the way we find will, like our responses to a projective technique, reflect something of the stage of personal development we happen to be in at the time. Nevertheless, it seems to me that one aspect of Buddhism that remains reasonably consistent across the different schools, and that offers an immediate stimulus to the thinking of the Western psychologist, is the group of Buddhist concepts that have to do with the mind in general and the mind as the receptor of experience in particular. Something of the importance to Buddhism of our chosen starting point is evidenced by a statement taken from Govinda (incidentally one of the Westerners who gets closest to the heart of Buddhism), namely that the purpose of Buddhist psychology is to enable you to find out what is going on in your own mind.[17]

Note that Govinda says in your *own mind*. Buddhist psychology is essentially something to try out on yourself, and the Buddhist has little sympathy with the Western idea that psychology is primarily the study of other people's behaviour rather than one's own. As we shall see shortly, Buddhism teaches not so much facts about people, as a method by which within one's own life one can find out what these facts are for oneself.

BUDDHISM AND THE MIND

Let us therefore take *mind* as our starting point. To the Western psychologist the mind is a rather vague notion, which we would perhaps define loosely as the totality of the individual's psychological life, or perhaps as the succession of mental processes that we describe as thinking. Either way, the identification of the mind with thinking is clear, and is made even clearer when we go on to talk about the conscious mind, which we take to be the repository of all those thoughts that can be readily called into consciousness as required. To Buddhism, however, this identification of the mind with thinking is regarded as a fundamental error. We can see why if we introduce at this point the Buddhist teaching on sensory experience. Buddhism speaks of six not five senses (*sadaya-tana*), namely seeing, hearing, smelling, tasting, touching and *thinking*. Thus at the practical level Buddhism accords thinking no necessarily separate status from the other forms of sensory experience. It is simply one of the six ways in which we experience what the Buddhist refers to as the external world.[18]

To the Western psychologist, such an idea may seem preposterous. We make a clear distinction between sensory events and cognitive events. The former are essentially response events, triggered off by external stimuli, while the latter are personal events, capable of higher level processes such as abstractions and generalizations, and therefore of a certain functional autonomy. The closest we allow the process of thinking to approach the processes of sensory experience is to see the former as associations to the latter or as mental representations of them. Philosophers also make a clear cognitive/sensory distinction when they talk of thinking as possessing intentionality,[19] while sensory experience

requires the prompting of cognitive or instinctive processes
before it can function with intent.

Yet preposterous as it may look at first sight, we can
nevertheless make sense of the Buddhist idea within the
confines of Western scientific thought, since it does not
appear to violate any demonstrable law. Buddhism arrives at
this idea through an insistence that it is not the sense organ in
itself that perceives an external object, rather it is that portion
of the brain handling perception which does so. Seeing is
therefore done by the visual cortex: the eyes are simply the
channel, just as the ears are the channel for sound perception
and the skin the channel for tactile perception. Thus vision,
hearing, feeling, smelling and tasting are located firmly
within the realm of mental events. We cannot be directly
aware of the essence of material objects and happenings, only
of the essence of the sense-perceptions and experiences
which create within us the representation and idea of matter.
Thus sensory experiences and thoughts cannot be other than
constituents of the same psychological category, namely the
category of mental events.

Space does not allow us to develop this model any further,
but even in this abbreviated phenomenological form it does
not do particular violence to Western psychological, philosophical or physiological theories. And if senses can be
identified in this way with thoughts, so thoughts can be
identified with the senses. We can for example visualise or in
extreme cases hallucinate sensory sensations. We can also
dream them, often with disturbing force. And such experiences allow us to appreciate, if not to replicate, the clarity of
visualisation achieved by students of Tantric Buddhism as
well as by Raja Yoga adepts and by masters of Tai Chi Chuan,
of Chi Kung, and of related exercises.

However, even if we grant that a reasonable case can be
made against the notion of a clear functional dichotomy
between sensory and cognitive experience, we are left with
the question of the utility of such a case. Models in science are
abandoned not so much through the discovery of facts that

fail to accord with them as by the erection of other models which prove themselves of greater use. So what, if any, are the psychological advantages of the Buddhist model over that traditional to Western psychology? We have already made the claims that Buddhist psychology appears of value in fostering the development of psychological health and in providing us with an alternative model of humans. We now need therefore to indicate how this model might be used in the substantiation of these claims.

The first point we have to make is that if thinking is seen as of the same functional order as sensory experiences then it loses something of its special status. In the West, as we have already said, when we discuss the mind we tend to identify it with conscious and pre-conscious thought processes. Similarly, and perhaps by extension, when we discuss the *self* we also show this cognitive identification, in this case with special categories of cognition that have to do with concepts about ourselves as unique, separate individuals. Though certain writers such as Mead[20] have suggested that a single notion of the self is inadequate, and that in its place we must postulate the dual notion of the self as subject and the self as object (that is, as somebody who knows concepts about himself as well as somebody to whom these concepts apply), most self theories have preferred to ignore what looks suspiciously like a metaphysical abstraction.

However, in the Buddhist model, if thoughts are of the same functional order as sensory experiences, then it follows that there must be some receptor of these experiences, some receptor moreover who is capable of unifying them in a way that has both meaning and practical value to the individual. As Guy Claxton says in Chapter 3, Buddhism does not confuse this receptor with the 'self as subject' notion advanced by Mead or indeed with any of the models that postulate the existence of an enduring, individual (and therefore limited) self. Some authorities consider that Buddhism refers to it instead as consciousness, but here we run into complexities since in Buddhism there are various different forms of consciousness (that is, intuitive, reflective and receptive), each of them linked in some way to thought and to sensory experiences, with no distinction recognised between consciousness and the content of consciousness. Instead, it should more properly be referred to as *awareness*. Awareness is simply that quality (or perhaps more properly process) that attends to incoming signals. The Western psychologist is familiar with this mechanism in so far as it relates to the attention we afford to sense data, but the Buddhist goes further and sees the same mechanism at work when it comes to attending to thoughts. Thus he will talk of watching one's thoughts come and go in precisely the same way that he will talk of watching one's visual experiences come and go.

He will proceed further and insist that if we watch closely enough we will see not only that thought experiences and sensory experiences are of the same order, but that even within that order the boundaries between these two sets of experiences are illusory, just as they are illusory between each of the other five senses themselves. Again the Western psychologist should not find this view impossible to understand. Many people report 'seeing' music as colours, or feeling crawling sensations on their skin when they see snakes or certain insects, or 'tasting' substances when they are smelling them. Even more familiar is the notion that cognitive expectations influence the way in which we see, hear, taste, touch and smell things.

The only difference between attending to thoughts and attending to the other five senses, argues Buddhism, is that we tend to identify with thoughts and not with other kinds of sense data. This gives us the illusory impression that we *are* our thoughts and, perhaps worse still in terms of healthy psychological functioning, that we have no control over them. The waking mind is almost continually attending to a train of discursive thinking, as if it is helpless to do anything else. Not for nothing is a chattering monkey used in the East as the symbol for the mind. By its apparently uncontrollable chattering the mind dominates our attention, preventing us from experiencing what the Buddhist calls 'things-in-themselves,' that is the true essence of things uncontaminated by concepts about them. And worse still, it prevents us from experiencing that pure awareness that remains when thinking and all other sensory data are excluded. A pure awareness which is in fact what we are in ourselves, uncontaminated by mental chatter. The Buddhist psychologist is, therefore, asking us to experience what we really are instead of what we think ourselves to be.

MEDITATION AND THINKING

Lest anyone should argue that experiencing what we are is an impossibility, let me say that this is simply a way of describing meditation, or rather a particular kind of meditation known to the Buddhist as vipassana or insight meditation.[21] In vipassana, the mind initially attends to one simple sensation (such as the intake and exhalation of the breath, or to the rise and fall of the abdomen as one breathes), and all other sensations including thinking are ignored. This initial stage, which is really the concentration stage, is then superseded by meditation proper, in which even the breathing is ignored and the individual experiences only awareness, a state in which the person who is aware and the act of awareness itself merge and become one. Buddhism sometimes refers to it as a state of pure being. In other words, just as we experience things-in-themselves if we look at them without concepts *about* them, so do we experience being-in-itself if we still the process of thinking and of the thought forms that usually dominate the centre of our awareness. Such a state has to be experienced rather than talked about, but of modern Western psychologists Wilber[22] has probably been most successful in describing it and in showing how it relates to and exceeds Western psychological paradigms.

Before discussing the implications of this for psychological health, we should clarify something of what it means for our model of human beings. Clearly Buddhism has no time for the Cartesian view of *cogito ergo sum*. Nor has it time for the notion that we can arrive at a workable apprehension of reality and of what it means to be human either by studying the behaviour of others or by submitting to the authority of so-called experts. There is no substitute for direct personal experience, since we each of us, as the Western phenomenologist would agree, carry reality around with us inside our own heads. What matters is experience, not other peoples' experience but our own, and not our thoughts about experience but experience itself. Govinda[23] puts it that 'Every individual must himself tread the path of realization, for only the knowledge that is won by experience has living i.e. life-giving value.' And the Pali Canon, the earliest collection of Buddhist literature that runs to some eleven times the length of our own Bible puts it even more emphatically:[24]

> Watchfulness is the path of immortality: unwatchfulness is the path of death. Those who are watchful never die: those who do not watch are already as dead.

For those who object to the introduction of the term 'immortal' in the above quotation, I should say that you can substitute the term 'self-mastery' without distorting (though not without limiting) the sense of what is being said. The word 'death' you would have to leave as it stands.

As a consequence of its stress upon awareness or watchfulness, Buddhism offers us not a clear-cut model of humans but a set of techniques for each of us to find the model (or better still experience that model) for ourselves. This is one reason why Buddhism cannot be classified as a philosophy or even perhaps as a religion in the strictest Western sense. It does not teach us about ultimate reality so much as teach us a method for experiencing that ultimate reality, or (more accurately though more perplexingly) for experiencing the fact that we ourselves *are* that ultimate reality.

Thus Buddhism places no special reliance on faith or upon

taking things on trust from the teachings of others. The Buddha tells us to check up for ourselves. Faith is the first step, not the last. And it need be no more than the faith that takes us to a physician in the vague hope that he may help us, and that prompts us to give his advice a fair try. Once we try the methods of Buddhism, we find ourselves sustained by the results that accrue from them rather than by any blind faith in the person who first revealed them to us. Buddhism teaches us what to do in order to be enlightened (or to obtain salvation or mental health or whatever we prefer for the moment to call it), not what enlightenment actually is. And by following this teaching Buddhists appear to pass beyond questions about God or ultimate reality or the final purpose of life. The Buddha maintained what the Buddhist scriptures call a 'noble silence'[25] when he was asked by his disciples about these things. They none of them can be expressed in words. They are accessible only to experience. Those of us with an interest in these matters will notice a parallel with Christ's teachings here. In contrast to the endless speculations entered into by Western theologians and philosophers in the 2,000 years since his death Christ nowhere encourages fundamental questions about the nature of reality or of Heaven or of the Almighty. Instead his message is much simpler, 'Seek and ye shall find, knock and it shall be opened unto you.' Again the emphasis is upon direct experience. Stop talking *about* religion, and go away and try living it instead.

With its emphasis upon experience, and its refusal to grant a distinction in kind between thoughts and other sense data, it is perhaps not surprising that Buddhists, and in particular Zen Buddhists, insist that as long as we can stop substituting thoughts about experience for experience itself, then we can gain enlightenment not only by experiencing pure being when we turn inwards but also by experiencing things-in-themselves when we turn outwards. Thus the literature[26] tells us of men and women who, at the appropriate stage in their development, suddenly achieved enlightenment through

seeing plum trees in blossom or on hearing the notes of a
musical instrument, or even on being struck a blow or having
their nose tweaked by the Zen master (I must emphasise that
hitting people or tweaking noses is not to be recommended
as a way of helping them to enlightenment unless they are at
the point where they are able to appreciate the experiences
for what they are).

BUDDHISM AND PSYCHOLOGICAL HEALTH

But why should these Buddhist methods have benefits for
psychological health? And do these benefits only accrue
when the individual reaches the enlightened state? To take
the second question first, the answer is that thankfully no (I
say 'thankfully' since full enlightenment seems to take a long
time coming in most cases!). Indeed, if some benefits were
not apparent fairly early on, the individual could hardly be
expected to carry on using the methods, since as we have said
he is not expected to take them simply on faith. As to the first
question and the benefits themselves, the most obvious one
is that individuals are enabled to assume increasing control
over their thoughts and in consequence over the emotions to
which these thoughts give rise. In essence all psychological
ill-health, whether we are discussing neuroses, psychoses or
simple anxiety appears to involve at some point the individual's inability to gain mastery over his or her own thought
processes. Negative and fear-provoking thoughts constantly
intrude, contributing to depression, anxiety states, feelings of
inadequacy and so on. One identifies with one's thoughts,
and although one may 'know' that they are irrational and
counter-productive, one is unable either to prevent their
occurrence or to engage in effective cognitive restructuring.

Through Buddhist methods of meditation, the individual
learns not to attend to thoughts, but to treat them instead
with the same detachment given to other sensory signals.
This is quite different from fighting or repressing one's

thoughts, since there is no psychic effort involved. One simply keeps the awareness centred upon the breathing or upon another chosen focus and allows thoughts to arise and disappear again without becoming involved in them and without allowing the discursive train of free associations usually consequent upon thinking to get under way. Over a period of time, thoughts that are treated in this manner begin to lose the power to force their way into our attention. A point is reached in meditation where thoughts arise with decreasing frequency, and where they seem to flit across the background of the mind without power to produce associations or emotional reactions. And eventually even these thoughts fail to arise, and one can go through a whole session of meditation without afterwards recollecting the occurrence of a single distracting influence.

One cannot, of course, spend all one's time in meditation, but the control one gains over one's thoughts during meditation appears to be directly generalisable to normal states of consciousness. Thoughts lose their power to intrude unwanted, and the discursive thinking in which we normally indulge becomes much more subject to conscious control.

The second benefit of Buddhist techniques, closely allied to the first, is that concentration, which Buddhism describes as the optimal relationship of awareness to each moment of experience, becomes enhanced. The calm focused attention practised during meditation, referred to in Buddhism as mindfulness, like the thought control to which we have just made reference, also generalises to normal states of consciousness. In fact a degree of mindfulness is taught in Buddhism quite independently of meditation, and involves keeping the mind focused upon the present moment, the present action, the present sensation. Through mindfulness one optimises the processes of memory (many of the things that elude recall do so because we were not properly attending to them when we first experienced them), one takes in far more of what is happening around one, and one acquires the relaxation that comes from being in the present moment instead of always thinking about the next task to be tackled or the reasons why we find the present one uncongenial to us. Through mindfulness in fact comes that total absorption in whatever it is we happen to be doing that is sometimes referred to as the Zen state, a state in which consciousness of the self disappears, and like a child at play the distinction between the actor and the act disappears.

The third benefit of Buddhist methods is that by freeing ourselves from the dominance of thinking and of the objects associated with thought we can also gradually free ourselves from undue attachment to these objects. Again this is a Buddhist technique that can be taught independently of meditation, but again it involves something of the same processes. Since in Buddhism external reality is not apprehended directly but only through our responses to it, there is a sense in which the external world is an illusion created by these responses. It is also impermanent, subject to a constant process of birth and death, of change, decay and renewal. Attachment to this impermanence is a root cause, indeed the root cause, of suffering. The present moment, good times as well as bad, the people and things we love are all changing, · moment by moment. Through attachment we try to cling to them in the form which we perceive them to have now, and inevitably we suffer as they change and as we change along with them. Non-attachment is not, as some people take it to be, indifference to the outside world. Indeed at the heart of Buddhism, as at the heart' of Christianity, is the concept of love or compassion for all sentient beings. But non-attachment means accepting people and things as they are, from moment to moment, rather than attempting to force their development into pre-conceived moulds, or attempting to keep them fossilised in the form which they took when we first met them or first fell in love with them. Thus the Buddhist can accept change without regret, knowing it to be inevitable, and can accept with equanimity the end of a happy experience or a happy relationship. Since everything will end, why attempt to cling to it? Such clinging is the result, Buddhism argues, of ignorance, of failing to recognise things as they are.

And with non-attachment also comes a lessening of desire for sensual experiences. Desire, Buddhism claims, is simply another form of attachment, as indeed is fear. Fear is an example of a kind of negative attachment, with the individual just as surely dominated by the things he fears as he is by the things for which he feels sensual desire.

Far from being a pessimistic outlook, non-attachment is a way towards calmness and serenity. Why even fear death, ask the Buddhists, since we are each of us dying and being re-created at each moment of our lives, from the bodily cells that die and are replaced, to the sensations (including thoughts) that arise and disappear. Physical death is simply another example of the passing away of all things, to be followed by re-creation as surely as our bodies are being re-created at the present moment. Life is the cause of death, and death is the cause of life. Those who most fear death are also those who most fear life, in the sense of fearing the constant changes and challenges that life brings with it. Thus fear of death indicates a dual attachment, firstly an attachment to the transient things of the present moment, and secondly a negative attachment to the prospect of the series of changes that we call death.

CONCLUSION

The three major benefits that we have discussed in this paper subsume a wide range of other psychological advantages which space does not allow us to pursue. But each of these can be seen to follow from our central theme, that is, that thoughts are of the same order as sense experience and can be attended to and controlled in the same way. If this seems to make Buddhism anti-intellectual then so be it, though anyone who cares to research the vast literature will find in Buddhism as in Hinduism an amazingly subtle edifice of

abstract thought rivalling and often surpassing in its richness and complexity anything produced by the Western
mind. But Buddhism is adamant that rational thinking of this
kind, though it is a valuable tool, is limited when it comes to
the realities of individual psychological and spiritual experience. If it is used to try and probe these realities, rational
thinking becomes a hindrance rather than a help, an obstacle
on the path to enlightenment or salvation or self-transcendence.

This recognition of the limitations of rational thinking
will, I hope, make it clear why we said at the outset that
Buddhism is a religion yet not a religion, a philosophy yet
not a philosophy, a psychology yet not a psychology. It is
said that Buddhism is not a religion because it contains no
God. If I have explained myself adequately, you will perhaps
now see that it would be truer to say that Buddhism contains
no concepts *about* God. If you want to know God you must
experience God for yourself. It is said that Buddhism is not a
philosophy because Buddhism shows a distrust of the kind
of thinking upon which philosophy depends. It would be
truer to say that Buddhism shows the limitations of the kind
of thinking upon which philosophy depends. It is said that
Buddhism is not a psychology because it rejects the notion
that we can explore others in a scientific sense. It would be
truer to say that Buddhism shows we can only explore others
if we first explore and know our own individual self. But be
prepared for the fact that such exploration, as Guy Claxton
discusses in Chapter 3, may throw up the paradoxical finding that ultimately there is no individual self to explore, and
no individual person to do the exploring.

3
The Light's on but there's Nobody Home: The Psychology of No-Self

Guy Claxton

Guy Claxton is a Lecturer in the Psychology of Education at King's College London, and the author of *Wholly Human: Western and Eastern Visions of the Self and its Perfection* (Routledge and Kegan Paul, 1981)

The central assertion of Buddhism is that we are all living our lives on the basis of mistakes, and that, because we have not spotted these mistakes, we create for ourselves unnecessary suffering. The experience of the 'enlightened ones' – the Buddhas – down the ages, is that it is possible for anyone and everyone to see through these mistakes, to become 'disillusioned,' and thereby to achieve a moment-to-moment serenity and intelligence that had previously been only a dream or a desire. Thus while we in the West see disillusionment in a negative light, connoting disappointment, or a bitter and cynical attitude to life, for Buddhism disillusionment is of central value, and it is what the Buddhist seeks. We grow up, so Buddhism says, with a model of the world in which we put our trust, yet which is in countless ways false. Our beliefs lie to us constantly, causing us to see as important, necessary or real that which is not, and to reject as unimportant or unreal experiences that are not sanctioned or condoned. Thus misery is created: our blind adherence to these illusions leads us to struggle with our lives, to see ourselves and others falsely, to keep trying to put things right that are only wrong in theory, not in fact. Like a children's game, or someone with a post-hypnotic suggestion,[27] we dream up monsters and princesses, baddies and goodies, and expend our energies on fleeing from, or grasping for, these fantasies. But, says Buddhism, peace of mind arises only in the letting go of our illusions. It is disillusionment that brings tranquillity and equanimity.

One of these conceptual mistakes — or rather one cluster of them — is seen as being crucial, for it functions as the lynch-pin that keeps all the others locked in place. One of the optimistic aspects of the Buddhist way is its claim that we do not have to weed out all our errors individually. Rather if we focus our efforts on pulling out this pin, then other illusions will *of themselves* begin to break up or burst. It is here that the spiritual way goes beyond, and differs from, the way of psychotherapy, for whilst therapy prunes the branches of our misconceptions about what it means to be a 'normal,' 'sane' or a 'worthwhile' person, Buddhism and meditation aim at cutting the roots, namely our deep, unexamined and fallacious premises about what it means to be a person at all. Through constant training in early childhood, all the more effective for being implicit — dissolved in the way others relate to us, rather than spelt out directly — we acquire an unnecessary view of ourselves. Mostly we are unaware of holding this view, or *any* view, at all, and to the extent that we do notice it, it seems natural and inevitable. But if our 'sense of self' is *second* nature to us, we might wonder what was the *first*: what Zen calls our 'original face?'

The sense of self is hard to examine because it forms the stage on which all our actions are performed, the screen onto which all our experience is projected; and if it is untrue, warped or slanted, then the whole drama of a life is distorted. Meditation is the turning of attention away from, or perhaps beneath, the drama of the production to a detailed inspection of the stage itself. As we shall see, those who pursue this critical examination to the end are, like 'those who go down to the woods today,' sure of a Big Surprise — there is no stage, no screen, no ground, no experiencer, no knower, no self. It is all going on in mid air. It is the purpose of the rest of this chapter to render this assertion somewhat less preposterous, to help the mind make sense of it so that it can at least be entertained. Buddhist psychology does not of course create the state of which it treats, anymore than reading the menu gives you the taste of the dish, but it does prepare the way, helping the mind to become more amenable to its transformation.

Specifically I want to use my space here to open up three questions. First, what are the premises that give rise to the sense of self? Secondly, are the ideas that we hold about self well-founded? Is there good evidence for them in our experience? Thirdly, how does the sense of self come about?

The premises that self inhabits

Let us look first at what the concept of Self consists of: what are the features by which we seem to know it? The first and most fundamental is *separateness*. Our sense of Self is individual, localised, personal. It belongs in this little bit of space right here, and what is not right here is not Me. For there to be a Me there must be a Not-Me, and a boundary that separates the two. This boundary may not be sharp, or always well-defined, but it must be there. For instance the experience of perceiving, feeling, doing and especially thinking seem very central. 'I' see, feel, act, decide. Just as we suppose an electron behind the track, a disease behind the symptoms, a God behind the experience of grace, so we construe thought as evidence for a thinker, acts as evidence for an actor, feeling and perception as evidence for an experiencer. Thus the general tendency to reify our concepts, to grant them existence and reality is manifest in the way we view our Selves.

The other side of Me is Not-Me: if I *am* this, then I cannot also be that. Clearly I am not this table, nor the unfinished hotel I can see from the window, nor you. Much of my experience seems to impinge on me from without. It happens *to* me, but it isn't me. But our attitude to the substance of which we are composed is somewhat ambivalent. *Am* I a body, or do I *have* one? We allow ourselves to say 'I am tired' and 'I am ill' − but baulk at saying 'I am measles' or 'I am my stomach.' We keep the body at a distance, so to speak, relating to it via possession rather than identification. I *have* a brain and a headache. They are not quite Me, but are certainly Mine, and it is hard (at least in some cultures) to imagine that 'I' continue to exist when the body does not.

Curiously, one of the effects of creating this boundary around our Selves, and splitting our experience into Me and Not-Me is to make ourselves vulnerable. Whatever we put inside the stockade, whatever we write into the definition of our individual selves, a threat to that is a threat to Me. Identified with wealth, poverty is a threat. Identified with control, chaos is a threat. Identified with the body (although with some misgivings), disability and death are threats. Thus − and this is where Buddhism swoops so naturally from the philosophical to the mundane − it is the very act of seeing our Selves as separate and as *this* and not *that*, which creates anxiety like a shadow.

The second characteristic of Self is *persistence*. Separateness defines Me as limited in space and content; persistence defines Me as limited in time. 'I' was born; 'I' will die; in between 'I' exist and persist, and some essence continues through my life unchanged, like a thread. Today I am in a different room thinking different thoughts; my body is bigger that it was when I was seven; and yet in some way I am the same Guy Claxton as I was yesterday or thirty years ago.

And the third characteristic, the one most readily observable perhaps, is *autonomy*. Much of my experience seems to happen to me: I construe my Self as a recipient of anger, the baby's cry, and the smell of seaweed. I don't identify closely with some internal processes: 'I am beating my heart' is not an assertion we would want to defend. But over Thought and Action in particular I claim to have some control. 'I am walking the dog,' 'I thought it over and decided not to go,' 'I want to go to the zoo tomorrow' all point to an 'I' that is a producer, an author, as well as a spectator. This sense of a Self that is the cause, and therefore in control, of at least some of what I think and do, is crucial. I reason, I choose, I decide, I intend, I initiate, I evaluate, and sometimes I change my mind. Behind the act there is an actor whose initiative entitles him to any praise or blame that accrues. I am, and feel, responsible.

ARE MY PREMISES LICENSED BY MY EXPERIENCE?

Thus do I identify and recognise my Self: I am different from you; I have a history and a future; and I will and feel, register and act. The next question is: on what basis do I infer these attributes? At the outset we must remember that my sense of Self is obvious, taken-for granted, second nature: it permeates my entire experience. But we cannot take that at face value. Our beliefs are dissolved in our perceptions; our experience is already theory-laden. If it contains our beliefs, is constructed on the basis of them, then we cannot at the same time accept it as evidence for these beliefs. Having decided that there is a donkey out there we see this limb as a donkey's hind leg: the decision informs the perception. Because I know this to be a cube, I see this line not *as* a line but as an edge — the edge of a cube. So most of what we take as indicating a Self merely indicates a *belief* in a Self, and cannot be considered as referential, as pointing to anything that exists as an entity. We must look a little deeper.

Perhaps there are grounds for believing we exist and persist as *substance*, flesh and blood. We have noted our ambivalence about identifying wholly with the body, but nevertheless it does seem the obvious post to which to hitch our being. Yet science tells us that bodies do not persist: there is no (or very little) constant stuff of which they are made. After a few years the meat that I 'am' today will be gone, to be replaced by an entirely different organism (though it will resemble 'me' somewhat).

And where, if I am to look for my physical boundaries, do

'I' stop? Can I identify my limits in substantial terms? Again the obvious place to look for 'my' edge is the edge of the body. I stop at my skin. But do I? On the one hand I feel identified with objects ('my jewels'), people ('my children') and causes ('a united Ireland') that lie outside my physical walls. If I include such things in the inventory of myself, a threat to them can only be felt as a threat to Me — even though the news had to travel round the world by phone. On the other hand, as we have seen, we are not entirely at home with our substance. 'This blasted leg's playing up again,' someone might say, as if it is not truly a 'member' of my body but a surly tenant who is behaving badly. And in between there is the skin itself: not a barrier between Me and Not-Me at all but a vital trading-station at which the air and nourishment and energy I need are exchanged for CO_2 and waste. If the borders were ever closed, I should die very quickly. My sense of separateness is spurious; I couldn't make it on my own. It is only *because* Not-Me (as air, for example) constantly invades Me that I exist at all.

But surely (a Self will reply) *something* persists. If I may not claim to be the same runner throughout my life, perhaps it is a relay-race: who-I-am being the baton that is passed on, the accumulating detail of my history, my memories. Memory does indeed provide a powerful source of *prima facie* evidence for a persistent Self. If I were not the same person as I was when I was seven, how could I possibly remember my seventh birthday party, when Stephen stole my trumpet and it all ended in tears? Unfortunately cognitive psychology from Bartlett[28] to Loftus[29] has demonstrated beyond a shadow of a doubt that we may not take memory as a reliable reflection of the past. We may believe or wish memory to be a photograph album, a library of records, collected and possessed, but we are in error if we do so. Memory is not a noun but a verb — not remnants of 'then,' but processes 'now,' processes that are subject to current attitudes and interests, to the tendency to regularise, to normalise, to fill in the gaps: to create a present experience, consonant with the story that we tell about our life and times, and to project it back into a hypothetical past. We do not like to think of memory in this way precisely because if it is a conjecture in the present and not an echo or a fragment of a 'real' past, we can no longer use it to support the belief in a persistent Self. If memory is not reliable, I can have no certain knowledge about how I used to be — or even whether I used to be. Bertrand Russell's subversive fantasy that we are all created in this instant, just as we are, complete with comprehensive references to a fictitious past, becomes impossible to reject.

There is much more to say about the mistakes of inference and fact that we make in supporting our commitment to an individual, persisting Self. But I wish here to focus more attention on the way we create and defend the illusory sense of our autonomy; how we dupe ourselves into accepting the myth of personal control. On the fact of it the evidence looks quite good. I have a problem, or an option. I review a list of considerations. I chew things over in a more-or-less rational way. Eventually, having weighed up the pros and cons, I decide what to do, and, when the time is right, I put my decision into action. It is so obvious that 'I' plays an influential role in this process that to go back through the last few sentences putting quotation marks round 'I' and 'my' to suggest that they are problematic seems the height of perversity. Yet that is what our present investigation requires: we must put 'I' on the witness stand, and make it testify in its own defence.

The first thing to note is that of all our conscious experiences it is *thought* with which we identify most closely, and of all thoughts, those that seem to be involved in the selection and control of future action — choosing, deciding, intending, willing — are the most central. My strong sense is that in some crucial respects 'I' am running the show, and that the *way* in which 'I' run it, and exercise control, is through the influence of my thoughts on my actions. Our logic is that for such influence to be demonstrated, an action must follow a thought, and thought and action must agree. What I do must be consequent on, and congruent with, what I *think* I shall do. Though rarely articulated, some such reasoning must under-lie the belief that the existence of Self is corroborated by a demonstrable causal link between thought and action.

Let us examine both the presumed facts and the implicit argument. It is true that sometimes what we do turns out in accord with what we intended. But much more often either there is no antecedent intention or commitment to act in a particular way, or there is, but what actually happens doesn't match it. The whole class of actions we call involuntary, reflex or physiological fall into the first category. I do not decide to circulate my blood or to breathe. (We may say 'I have decided to grow a beard' but we are not thereby claiming responsi-bility for what happens, as we would be if we said 'I have decided to collect stamps.' We are instead claiming the credit for refraining for interfering with what we acknowledge to be a natural, involuntary process. 'My' part is not to do it but to let it happen.) Likewise we do not expect acknowledge-ment for digesting our food, for jerking a hand away from a pinprick, or orienting to a sudden noise.

In addition, I have little investment in many voluntary actions that occur as a matter of routine or habit. I get up, make tea, dress, scratch, sit down, cross my legs, suck my cheeks in, look around the room, sigh, scratch again — even feel bored and wonder what to do — all without any sense of intention or will. Indeed many of my daily choices are made without much, or any, conscious deliberation. Wanting to listen to some music, I flip through the stack of records until one seems to say 'I'm the one' and I put it on. In situations of this sort, thought plays, if we are honest, a very minor role. I might say, in response to the question 'Why did you choose that one?,' that it 'took my fancy,' or 'seemed to fit my mood,' yet the strong suspicion lingers that these are not *causes* of my selection, but justifications or redescriptions of it. 'It took my fancy' says no more than that I chose it. If I chose it, it *must have* taken my fancy, mustn't it? The thought is created to fit in with the action, not *vice versa*. With these three categories of the involuntary, the routine and the unreflective we have covered, at a conservative estimate, a good ninety-nine percent of everything we do – without, we must admit, having any personal sense of authorship or responsibility at all. (When we become 'self-conscious' about them, of course, their status changes.)

So now we are left with the minority of occasions on which action *is* preceded by decision or intention. Of these some thought-action sequences seem to support the hypothesis of Self: that is, they agree. And a sizeable proportion do not. The intention is unfulfilled or forgotten, so that the action to which we are committed does not occur and often something quite different, that we had not bargained for, happens instead. I meant to keep my cool but I just couldn't. I'm supposed not to eat pork but I forgot. I'd decided on an early night but somehow here we are in Piccadilly Circus at four a.m. with silly hats and a bottle of wine.

On the face of it such cases of mismatch are evidence for the *impotence* of Self, for its lack of will or agency, and therefore ought to make us question still further whether this control, in which we seem to have such a stake, is as real as we wish it to be. But they usually do not: because they do not fit our theory, and are consequently uncomfortable, we make them disappear, or reinterpret them in tricky ways. Just like a bad scientist whose investment in his own theory is too strong, we become adept at ignoring, disparaging, or explaining away inconvenient results. Thus we simply do not notice how often we fail to live up to our intentions, or break our word. If we are confronted by someone else about it, we are prone to bluster. 'Really Richard you can be such a *bore* sometimes,' or 'What gives you the right to tell *me* what to do?' – hoping to divert everyone's attention, especially our own, from the uncomfortable awareness of the frailty of our personal theory, and of our panicky and unpleasant attempt to deal with it. If all else fails – and this is a truly audacious sleight of hand – we can reinterpret our failure of control as an actual success! 'I changed my mind,' we say, temporarily withdrawing our identification from the 'mind' that has been 'made up,' and aligning ourselves instead with some higher decision-maker and controller who can 'choose' to override this mind. Somehow or other 'I' manages to emerge from this potentially embarrassing situation, like an astute politician, with its reputation not only intact but enhanced.

It remains to consider those cases where our self control appears to be manifest. I meant to, and I did. I said I wouldn't, and I didn't. However rare such examples are in fact, it is to them, very largely, that our sense of ourselves as being able to stand outside the flow of events and influence them, adheres. Specifically we need to examine I's claim to be rational and causal.

The rationality is certainly in doubt. Suppose we do go through the conscious process of compiling a list of pros and cons, weighing them up, deciding what to do and doing it. This apparent raft of reason is adrift in a sea of irrationality. How did you draw up you list of considerations? Did you 'decide' which ones to look at, or did they occur to you? How long did you take over it? Are you sure that all relevant, and no irrelevant, issues have been considered? Was your 'decision' that certain issues were irrelevant a rational one? Were there not perhaps some semi- or sub-conscious influences on how you framed the question to yourself? How can you be sure? Were the weights that you gave to different arguments rationally decided? Did you not perhaps dismiss some points of view a little prematurely, because you didn't *like* them, or were distrustful of their proponent's motives? Did you decide to trust some authorities and not others? How did you choose when to stop deliberating and come to a conclusion? Were the timing and the manner with which you put your decision into practice carefully thought out? Did you choose to be as enthusiastic as you were, or to stumble over your words at just that point? And so on. It is clear that the neat pattern of our logical thought and executive control unravels and frays at whichever point we tug. The first shock that people experience when they begin to watch their own thought-processes in meditation is just how haphazard, partial, emotional and egocentric this so-called higher faculty is in reality. It is only by selective blindness that we have managed to persuade ourselves of our reasonableness.

And it is only with the aid of this convenient myopia that we can sustain the argument that because a thought precedes a congruent action, it therefore causes or controls it. There are several other equally plausible interpretations. We cannot legitimately infer a causality from a correlation: even when A reliably follows B, it may be that there is no causal connection, but that both A and B issue from some common underlying source. Perhaps what I do, and the thoughts that precede it, spring jointly from a deeper, more organismic, more wholistic, more tacit level of processing about which I have little knowledge and over which, therefore, 'I' can claim no control. Sometimes, for reasons known only to itself, this source issues an action and prints out a thought that match. And sometimes it does not. Were we to identify ourselves with this mysterious source, then whether it ('I') generates congruent or incongruent products might be a matter of interest, but it would never need to be met with either relief or dismay. Only when my identity depends on congruence do I have an investment in it, and only then do I have to wriggle if I find myself doing something different from what I had supposed. Identified with the source, I can be amused by my apparent inconsistency, or lack of control, not threatened by them.

In these terms it makes better sense to see the relationship between thought and action, when it exists, as a hit-and-miss attempt at *prediction* rather than control. My personal theory registers regularities in the world, and these include regularities in my own tendencies and dispositions to respond. Thus it is quite possible, as I get older, to have a sense of what I might do before I do it — a sense that might crystallise, say, into the thought 'I think I'll have a glass of water.' When this is seen purely as a prediction, 'I' refers only to what the *organism* will do. If the anticipated action fails to appear, there is an opportunity to learn about the organism, and to improve my conscious understanding of its reactions — what cognitive psychologists these days call 'metacognition.' But when we confer responsibility on 'I,' then we must read such a thought not as a tentative description of what will happen, but as a prescription about what must. And its failure then becomes a matter of concern.

Likewise we can turn our understanding of deliberation — the 'decision-making process'—on its head, and see it as an attempt to construct a plausible, consistent, self-validating rationale for a course of action whose imminence we have sensed. When the intimation of an impending act is weak, we may not even realise that our reasoning is a reaction to it, so that all we are aware of is the thought-action sequence. In this case it is all the easier for us to misconstrue what is happening, and to misplace the locus of control. The more strongly I believe that my reason is the seat of my control, the more compulsive does this anticipatory story-telling become.

How does a self come about?

If the sense of self is not a biological inevitability (like the development of breasts or body hair at puberty) but an acquired mistake, where does it come from? How is it that we all have one, despite the enormous differences in our up-bringings and our circumstances? There must be some very deep, pervasive influences on the young child that cause us, in almost every case, to go astray.

In approaching these, we must be careful to distinguish between two kinds of influence: those that lead a child towards aspects of Self that are accurate and useful, and those that lead her towards the illusory senses of separateness, identity, per-sistence and control. By the former I mean regularities, consistencies and patterns that relate to our bodies, our preferences, our reactions, our limits and our power. The baby develops a 'body image': she picks up patterns of sensation from within her body that relate to posture and that signal feedback as she moves her head and eyes, hunches her shoulders, reaches out an arm or scrunches up her toes. We develop a (changing) sense of how big we are, so that, like a skilful lorry driver, we can anticipate the gaps we can get through, and avoid getting our wing mirrors dented or our bottoms stuck. We begin to link up different senses, so that we know, when we tell a hand to reach out for a strawberry, what imminent changes in vision, touch and taste to expect. (An infant will assess a coffee-tasting strawberry on its merits: her father is likely to have a fit.) And as we get more sophisticated still, we come to know what effects our actions will have on the world about us, and, through this anticipation, we can seek to bring about the states of affairs that suit us.

Part and parcel of this process is learning what we cannot do, as well as what we can. I can turn off vision by closing my eyes, but I cannot disconnect my skin or ears with such ease. I can reliably control what *my* fingers do, but to control *your* fingers is a much more tricky business. (Even if I get my tone of voice just right; you may not be in the mood to hold and stroke me.) The frustration that children show is a reaction to the discovery of another area of limitation or unpredictability. Although not exclusively so, most of the things over which I have good control constitute my body, and those where my power slackens are 'outside.' (Try as I might, I cannot wiggle my ears. Though I've got my Mum exactly where I want her...) So the pragmatic separation of 'self' from 'other' is a useful one to make, as is the rough division of 'other' into 'things' and 'people.' Things are more predictable: a brick thrown on Monday and Tuesday behaves in much the same way. But my elder sister is a different kettle of fish. I must fine-tune my dealings with her from day to day, and still my predictions are only tentative and my control tenuous. (Note that this use of 'control' requires no Self: all I have to do is store records of what happens, and mesh these appropriately with my shifting sense of what I *want* to happen.)

But overlaid on this developing map of what to do, and

when, and why, and how it feels, come the social influences of language and dissociation. With language comes a lot of judgements about who I am and what I like that other people inform me of. I learn to see myself reflected in the comments and reactions of those around me, which may not connect with, and sometimes cuts across, the shifting, provisional picture of who I thought I was. As Mead said many years ago, 'the original sense of the me is made up largely of the attitudes, words and gestures of others which the child perceives, imitates and responds to. His sense of self is thus a product of other people's behaviour towards him...while he develops a sense of continuity and identity, he never shakes himself free from seeing himself in terms of the roles he plays, that is, in terms of the images other people have of him.'[30] And Luke Rinehart in *The Dice Man*, provides an informal echo. 'What if — at the time it seemed like an original thought — what if the development of a sense or self is normal...but is neither inevitable nor *desirable*? What if the sense of being some*one* represents an evolutionary error as disastrous to the further development of a more complex creature as was the shell for snails or turtles?...(Yet) adults insist on the shell of a consistent self for themselves and their children and appreciate turtles for friends.'[31]

Together with 'who I *am*' come the rules and values about how I *ought* to be — polite, generous, quiet, consistent and the rest. To step outside these bounds is to risk their disapproval, and the quality of service I get deteriorates rapidly when I fail to measure up. So I learn to inhibit my temper, control my need when it threatens to become 'too much,' and divert attention away from what I really feel. Some of who I am gets smothered in a haze of unconsciousness, and as I look down on myself from above, so parts of me are permanently capped with clouds. It seems as if we have the ability to inhibit awareness of dissociation and its signals directly, without putting anything specific in its place.[32] This is the path of repression, in which the thresholds for awareness of feelings are set so high that they cannot, in the normal run of events, break through. As control of behaviour may generalize into a living rigor mortis, so may control of emotional awareness grow into a widespread 'deadening of affect.'

We are now ready to see how the child's sense of himself as being separate from the rest of existence, and possessing reason through which he can make choices, and volition through which he can implement his decisions, comes about. By the time he gets to two years old or so, the child's organism is functioning pretty well. He has detected and registered many of the significant regularities in his world and can intervene in the flow of events to his own advantage with considerable skill. His repertoire of acts is constantly expanding, as is his sense of occasion. Of particular importance, he has discovered the power of language and cracked the code. Now comes the cumulative process of developing the range and delicacy of the messages he can express and understand.

In one corner of this clear sky the clouds of delusion begin to gather. The first is the learnt inattention that we have just discussed. In specific domains the child is becoming not more but less sensitive to his bodily reactions and the circumstances that elicit them. He develops blindspots to some of the events and occurrences that are significant in shaping and calling forth his thoughts and deeds. At the same time, especially if he is a Western child, he is deeply immersed in a language and a culture where to know the causes of one's behaviour is seen as important. Children's fascination with the word 'why' demonstrates their sense of its significance, and simultaneously their puzzlement about it. So our child begins to have a problem. On the one hand he is learning to express what controls or elicits his words and actions, and to value that expression. On the other he is denying to his conscious awareness some of the very triggers – feelings and events – that he is looking for. The answer to what directs and influences me is always some facet of the interaction between organism and environment, the territory of me-in-the-world. Yet often, like a man searching for his hat everywhere but on his head, this is the one place where the child is increasingly inhibited from looking.

At the same time as this is becoming an issue the child is grappling with a particular linguistic problem: to what do the words 'you' and 'I' refer? These common little symbols do not seem very special to begin with: the first sensible hypothesis is that they are addresses, the names of the locations of bodies, rather like 'here' and 'there' but somewhat more restricted. But this turns out not to be good enough. What is the young learner to make of 'I didn't mean to do that,' 'You shouldn't have done that,' 'I will try to be home early'; of the fact that he is allowed to say 'I am drinking my milk,' but not 'I am gurgling my tummy?' 'I' seems to refer to an internal cause of things, or a control that may try or mean to cause things without being successful; but what does the child have inside him with which this strange idea can be identified? Answer: the vacuum, created by his learnt ignorance of the full complexity of events that trigger actions. On the one hand he has, in language, an agent looking for something to do: on the other a gap in his conscious awareness of the antecedents of some of his actions. Clearly the peg without a function and the hole without a peg were made for each other, and the peg happily slips into the hole with very little prompting. The social fiction of the ego engages with the gap in the child's awareness of himself and the illusion clicks into place.

Now he falls prey to the confusion between prediction and control. Up to this point the child has, quite rightly, been developing and using his ability to predict changes in the world and his effect on them. His actions are called forth by fluctuations in the organism-environment field — they are 'caused' we might say, by these fluctuations — and the child has no reason to think otherwise. Until, this is, he is introduced to the game of 'I Did It.' He is like a man, sitting by a stream, idly watching things float past him. After a while he notices a regularity: whenever a cork goes by, a bottle follows. In order to amuse himself the man invents a game in which he pretends not to notice the corks, and every so often calls out 'Let there be a bottle!' Sure enough, whenever he does this, a bottle heaves into view. By ignoring consciously the cue that enables him to predict bottles, he is able to sustain the illusion that he can control or produce the appearance of bottles. Unfortunately the man falls prey to his own magic, and entralled by his new-found 'power,' wanders back into town, where he discovers that the game is all the rage. 'Who did it?' 'I did,' the child learns to say, and I, that label for a vacuum in his own perception, is bestowed, in the child's developing fiction about himself, with the captaincy of the ship. The ship ploughs on, its course set out by the responses of wind and sea, metal and sail to each other, while the captain, through his experience, manages to issue orders that precisely anticipate what was about to happen anyway.

The generalization of 'I' to cover the prediction of perceptions, thoughts, feelings, and, most importantly, the so-called voluntary actions, occurs easily through the child's continuing attempts to understand his parents' language. Not so slowly, and very surely the ideas of his own responsibility, control and agency seep into the core of his understanding of himself. Someone says 'You are a clever boy' when he has produced an action without effort or intent, and again he is led to believe that 'I' must have had a hand in it somewhere. People furrow their brows, look concerned and say 'I tried' when they didn't manage it, and he dutifully learns to do the same, attaching the muscular sense of strain that accompanies physical exertion to quite inappropriate mental activities. And so it goes. His awareness of what is going to happen next becomes more automatic and more immediate until the swiftness of the 'I' deceives the hand completely.

Giving up the ghost

These previous sections have only been sketches: caricatures of subtle, complex issues. But if they have opened up some doubts about the sense of self, that will be enough to allow the possibility that things might be different. If the sense of self is as natural as hands and feet, we are stuck with it. But if it is an idea, a theory, that has been acquired, then we can approach it in quite a different, and less respectful way. We can ask, as we have, impertinent questions of the Self, like 'Do you do a useful job?' and 'How do I know you exist?' And when it begins to bluster (like a President confronted with evidence of his misdeeds), we can rightly suspect that all is not what it had seemed.

But what then could 'I' possibly be? As the enquiry through meditation progresses, so different answers to this arise. The senses of separateness, solidarity and autonomy begin to disperse, as does the mist under the eye of the rising sun. The entity in identity becomes increasingly insubstantial. Instead there seems to be a fountain or a spring inside me out of which this amazing stream of appetites and conversation, notions and emotions, constantly gushes. At one stage of the journey, my sense of identity is invested in the watcher, the witness who sits quietly by, undisturbed by the sound and fury, unattached to the beauty of the cascade. The thoughts and impulses, decisions and mistakes, self-congratulation and self-abuse may continue, at least for a while. But now 'I' watch them happen; I do not 'do' them, and therefore am less caught up and swept away by them. Peace arises, as I see that no possible experience I can have can threaten me, because I have given up taking sides. I need not struggle in my mind with my self-righteous little judgements about all and sundry, nor with the defensiveness and shame that bubbles up when I am caught at it. Who I am is unbesmirched, and I can look at myself with the slightly amused yet compassionate detachment with which parents can react to the tantrums and panics of their children. Inside ourselves there is a vantage point from which we can look out on all those dramas that used to be so important, so meaningful and so personal.

When I am able to be the observer, the weatherman not the

clouds, one thing happens and one thing doesn't. The thing that doesn't happen, but of which people are quite reasonably scared, is that I get worse. A common elaboration of the belief that control is real, and is invested in a part of me that ought to be more moral than the rest, is that 'I' can, and must control 'myself,' and that unless I do, base urges will spill out and I will run amok. Given the premise, the thought of giving up this control must be perceived as really dangerous. As the Chinese proverb puts it, 'He who rides on the back of a tiger dare not dismount.' Luckily the premise is false: I was never split into man and tiger, controller and controlled — though the *sense* of strain and of self-recrimination were real enough. So the dreaded mayhem does not happen. I do not take up wholesale rape and pillage and knocking down old ladies just for fun.

The thing that does happen is the reverse. As I relax into myself I get more and more in touch with my unity, the wholeness and integrity that my *theory* has denied. And much of the uneasiness and tension in my life, that my theory had told me was inevitable and even valuable, begins to disappear. Guilt, shame, embarrassment, self-doubt, self-consciousness, fear of failure and much anxiety ebb away, and as they do so I seem to become, contrary to expectations, a better neighbour. As I can look inwards with more acceptance and compassion, so I can look outwards at others. My needs to dominate and censure, to be wary and manipulative, they melt too. It is truly startling to discover how much of the mischief and misery in the world is attributable to this simple ontological mistake.

Finally, as the examination is pursued, one realises that even the sense of witnessing is itself a point of view, an experience, and is therefore not separate from the play of the fountain but another aspect of it. So I cannot hold on to the witness either, but must eventually let go of *all* positions, and become the source. The body, as Taoism says, becomes a hollow bamboo; experience and action the tunes that are played on this flute. And the player, the breath that draws out these notes, who or what is that? God, Tao, Brahman, Existence, the Ground of Being — these are its names. But how can I say or think anything *about* it when everything I say and think, and even the sense of 'I,' comes *from* it? 'Whereof we cannot speak,' as Wittgenstein[33] advised us, 'thereof it is a jolly good idea to shut up.'

4
Who am I? Changing Models of Reality in Meditation

Susan Blackmore

Susan Blackmore is a visiting Research
Fellow at the Brain and Perception
Laboratory at the University of Bristol. She is
the author of *Beyond the Body* (Paladin, 1983).

I WOULD LIKE to ask what seems a simple question. Why do we feel different when meditating, compared to normal? What, or who, has changed?

And I would like to try to answer it within the framework of Western cognitive psychology.

It is often assumed that the materialistic basis of cognitive psychology precludes any real understanding of the nature of altered states of consciousness and transformations of the self. I think this view is wrong and that these materialistic assumptions are, if pushed far enough, actually quite good at providing insights into a more mystical view of human nature. To explain this I shall take this one question, and give a simple example.

I am sitting one afternoon in my study. I look up from my work. The birds are singing outside, I can hear children playing a long way away and the sounds of a distant radio (I wish they'd be quiet). There is a terrible muddle on my desk (I must clear it up) and the room is full of things. There's an awful lot going on (I must get back to work).

I sit the same afternoon in the same room in meditation. I am still. The birds are singing outside, there are sounds of children playing a long way away, and a distant radio. The muddle on my desk and the room full of things are filled with stillness. There is me sitting. The sounds are full of silence. I hear a woodlouse crawl across the floor.

I am tempted to say that in the first case I am in a 'normal state of consciousness' and in the second I am in an 'altered state of consciousness.' But this tells us next to nothing. It only provokes us to ask the more general question — what is altered in an altered state of consciousness?

There have been many answers given in terms of different psychologies, and different religious contexts. However, western psychology seems to have relatively little to offer by way of an answer. On the one hand, changes in EEG, or heart rate have been found but they do not have much to say about why it *feels* different. At the opposite extreme are occult and religious notions, largely rejected by psychology.[34] Tart's systems approach to consciousness is probably the best attempt to reconcile the two, but he also has to resort to paranormal concepts to account for the origin of transcendent experiences.[35]

I would like to try to answer my question without taking such a step: staying within the assumptions of cognitive psychology. I shall put forward a few simple proposals about the nature of consciousness and altered states of consciousness. I shall then show how these can provide insight into some of the changes in consciousness which take place during meditation, or during some kinds of mystical experience.

All these proposals start from the assumption so important to cognitive psychology, that the cognitive system is essentially a model builder. We assume that perception is a process of constructing representations of the world based on sensory input. We assume that thinking and remembering are likewise constructive processes in which representations or models are built up from information in either input or memory. We take it for granted that the self is a construct — a complex model consisting of body image, self image, and everything we can remember about what has happened to them. Underlying all this is the assumption, which I shall also make, that there is nothing more than this (and extensions and implications of it): that human nature is entirely dependent upon the cognitive system which constructs it; that 'we' are entirely dependent upon the physical organism. Cognitive psychology admits of no soul, spirit or astral body to provide a 'vehicle for consciousness' or to leave the body and have experiences without it. It is therefore a challenge for it to account for experiences like that of seeming to leave the body,[36] or seeming to trancend its limitations. Even if the proposals I make have severe shortcomings, they will at least provide a way of exploring that challenge.

The proposals are as follows.

Firstly, all mental representations or models (like those constructed by brains) are conscious.

Secondly any model is self-conscious to the extent to which it includes a stable representation of the system which created it.

Thirdly, 'normal' human consciousness is typified by having one over-riding 'me-now' model which co-ordinates behaviour and self-representation. This is our usual 'model of reality.'

Fourthly, altered states of consciousness (ASCs) can best be understood in terms of changes to the model rather than to the modelling system. In extreme altered states different 'models of reality' are used.

Fifthly, meditation involves strategies which deliberately change the model of reality. Some mystical, out-of-body and other experiences involve spontaneous changes in the model of reality.

I shall discuss each of these in turn.

The suggestion that it is models which are conscious may seem to be just playing with words. It may even seem nonsensical. However, I think it is an idea worth exploring. I am suggesting that as soon as something represents something else, that is, there is a level at which it constructs and models attributes of something else, then there is consciousness of those attributes.

Try asking the question so often asked when young — 'what is it like to be a stone?' The most reasonable answer seems to be 'Not much.' It seems likely that stones do not experience much. As far as we know they process virtually no information, do not respond to events, and have no knowledge of their own shape, size or anything else. On the other hand if we ask 'what is it like to be a representation of a stone?' we may imagine that it might be like being rounded, smooth, rolling or whatever. The very act of representation of those attributes makes it possible to imagine what it would be like to have them. In this sense I am tempted to say 'being conscious is what it is like being a mental model.'

Now of course it rather depends who or what is doing the modelling. The stone does not model itself (as far as we know) and is therefore not conscious. A painting of a stone only represents a stone if someone is looking at it and interprets it that way — that is, builds another model of it. The painting constructs no model and is therefore not conscious. But an ant crawling over the stone may construct a very simple representation of this obstacle and to that extent there will be consciousness of it. Finally a person may, in thinking, perceiving or remembering, construct a representation of a stone. If that representation is fleeting, not related to anything else, then any consciousness it implies will be likewise fleeting and isolated. By contrast, if the image of a stone is complex, stable and related to other representations, for example of the person herself, then it takes on quite a powerful quality. In this way I suggest that all mental representations can be considered as conscious, even though their consciousness may be very limited.

So if we ask what is it like to be human, we cannot answer in terms of what it is like to be a lump of flesh and blood, but we can answer in terms of the models which that lump constructs. We may ask what it is like to be a model or representation of something.

First we should ask what kind of models humans do construct, and this is largely what cognitive psychology is all about. We know a great deal about it in some respects. We know that humans are very complex information processing systems and construct representations at many interrelated levels. Now, if all representations are conscious (as I am suggesting) then this implies that such a model-building system must be sustaining innumerable separate 'consciousnesses.' Does this make sense?

First we have to be clear about what is meant by models or representations at different levels. A simple analogy is to think of reading a book. One may pore over the spots of ink at one level. At another level one can read letters, and at yet another level words. At another level the words form a story, and at another level the book may be an attack on some prized theory. We naturally tend to think of these as successively 'higher' levels. The fact that the ordering of levels and the distinctions between them may be partly arbitrary, or may interact, does not detract from the usefulness of the notion of levels of representation.

In human information processing there are innumerable levels. For example, in the visual system, there are retinal representations of input. These are fleeting and unstable and are used to build more integrated models further on in the system. They contribute to the eventual construction of an image of what is 'out there.' We may view this system at the level of the neurons which are firing, the interactions between neurons, the algorithms the system is using, the problems it is trying to solve, or the hypotheses it is constructing.[37]

I am interested here, not in the ways in which we (as observers) may dissect this system into levels, but in the kinds of models constructed, especially those at the highest levels which represent complex attributes of the world. Of course, these depend on lower level models and at every level there are new representations. Does it help to say these are all conscious? And if they are, why aren't 'I' aware of them? It does help, I suggest, when it comes to thinking about the kind of consciousness which the higher levels throw out. This is best explained by reference to the next two proposals.

Secondly, I suggested that models are self-conscious if they include a stable representation of the system which constructed them. This implies a model at a higher level, representing a lower level of the system. For example, my model of self includes a representation of my arms and legs and head, and even of my brain. It is this fact which makes me self-aware or self-conscious. 'I' am a mental model. I am self-conscious because that mental model includes a representation of a body, behaviour, actions, and so on, which it labels as self. Interestingly that kind of representation of lower levels of the system is largely absent in dreams, but more of that in a moment.

An implication of this view is that any system which constructs a representation of itself will be self-conscious. So, for example, most computers do not represent themselves. The higher level modelling going on does not include any modelling of the hardware itself. They are not, in these terms, self-conscious. On the other hand some robots, because they need to move about, do represent their own shape, position and so on. They will therefore have some kind of self-awareness. Dogs, cats and other creatures obviously need such self-representations, and construct them according to their capacity for information-processing and model-building. The quality of these models will, I suggest, determine the quality of self-consciousness experienced.

We can never experience another's consciousness. My cat's model of itself is forever entirely separate from my own model of self. Nevertheless I may achieve some insight into what it is like being my cat, by imagining the kind of model of self which her brain constructs. That is, which 'she' is.

You may note the importance of distinguishing two things which we normally confuse; that is the information-processing system and the models which it constructs. When I refer to 'him' I may mean either or both. In this discussion I wish to distinguish clearly between the whole system, as an observer might see it (I shall call that him − without quotes), and the model of self which that system builds. I shall call this 'him.' 'He' is self conscious. 'He' has experiences. 'He' is a model of himself.

I asked, but did not answer, the question, why am 'I' not

aware of all those other models going on in the system — even though they are all conscious too. This is best answered by referring to the third proposal, which was that 'normal' human consciousness is typified by having one over-riding 'me-now' model which co-ordinates behaviour and self-representation. This is our usual 'model of reality.'

Imagine again, the complex model building system of the brain. The reason for all this modelling is to coordinate and plan behaviour. To do that it needs a very good model of self in the world. This model consists of self-image, body-image, motives, intentions, and indeed everything concerning what 'I' am doing. It includes the entire structure built out of perception — what 'I' am perceiving. If you like it is a 'me-now' model. It is my 'model of reality.' This model is enormously stable. It has similarities day after day, even though sleep intervenes. It keeps track of changing events, and responds to them.

So I would say that our 'normal' state of consciousness is characterised by being entirely dominated by this stable, complex model of self. That is normally what 'I' am. Its persistence, at least during waking, and its continuous reference to a self-image, provide the illusion that it is in sole charge of that body. It is a useful — even necessary — illusion. But illusion it is, in an important sense. If it gives the impression that 'I' am something separate from my body it is a false impression. 'I' am a construction of that body; a high level representation. Mystics have long told us that it is an illusion. We can now see how this illusion comes about and why it is so convincing.

Now if we ask what it is like to be such a model, I would answer, it is just what it is like to be 'me.' We are coming closer to answering the question 'what is it like to be a human?'

But if 'I' am such a model, why aren't 'I' aware of all the other models which are built by the same brain as 'I' am? The answer is now quite simple. If any model is entirely separate from the 'me-now' model of reality, then it does not form part

of it and is not available to it. That is, it is not available to 'me.'
Since 'I' am one model, at one level in the system, 'I' can only
be aware of others if they become linked up to 'me' or make
sense to 'me.' Such linking up requires further processing, or
thinking. It may be possible to access all sorts of other models
in the system. We have no idea at present how far this
possibility extends, but I think it is safe to say that models at
some levels will forever be inaccessible to models at other
much higher or lower levels of representation.

Am 'I' the highest level? I shall not attempt to answer that
question but only suggest that the answer is not obvious.

We now have a new way of understanding the old analogy
of the torch-light of attention flickering around the dusty
attics of the mind. Rather than being static objects in the roof
space, these contents are innumerable changing mental
constructs or models. Only if they are linked up to, and can
make sense to, the 'me-now' model can they 'enter consciousness.' Of course from their own point of view they may well
have been conscious all along. 'They' may (if they are
complex enough) think that 'we' have just entered *their*
consciousness.

This provides an interesting insight into some rather odd
conditions, for example that of multiple personality. I have
suggested that 'we' are normally characterised by having one
stable and apparently continuous self-model. But it is possible to imagine systems which have more than one high-
level model vying for connection to 'reality': to the world
perceived 'out there.' Only one can do this at once, but both,
or all, have some kind of continuing consciousness so long as
the appropriate model is being constructed.

I would now like to turn to the fourth proposal and try to
answer the question 'What is altered in an altered state of
consciousness?' My answer is that it is the model of reality
which is altered. And since 'I' am such a model 'I' am altered.
This explains why it feels to 'me' as though 'I' have changed.
'I' have. Thus we can tackle any ASC by asking about the
changes which have taken place in the model of reality the

person is using. Of course anything which affects cognitive processing will affect that model and hence the state of consciousness. Mildly altered states may involve only slight changes. For example alcohol affects cognitive processing and induces a slight sense of an altered state. But perhaps more interesting are the 'discrete ASCs,'[38] in which the world and the self are perceived in quite different ways. Among these are dreams, lucid dreams, near death experiences and out-of-the-body experiences. I have previously used this approach to build a theory of out-of-the-body experiences.[39] This has even provided some testable predictions which have been confirmed.[40] Here I shall say a little about dreams, and then see how far we have come towards understanding the changes in meditation which I illustrated at the beginning.

Going to sleep is a very odd experience — even though we are quite used to it. We shut our eyes, relax and very soon stop experiencing things. In deep, or dreamless, sleep we have virtually no experience at all. In a sense 'we' cease to exist. Whereas in dreaming sleep we experience all manner of bizarre events. The odd thing is that we do not seem to question them, or at least if we do, we usually come to come equally bizarre conclusion about them. We very rarely conclude, during the dream, that we are dreaming. But occasionally this does happen, and it is known as lucid dreaming.[41] It is dreaming while being aware of being in a dream. It has an odd and very special quality. Often the dream seems more real, more controllable and in some way closer to waking life. When we wake from ordinary dreams we usually accept the bizarre events as being just dreams. We dismiss them. Interestingly the lucid dreams seem less easily dismissed; more a part of our own experience.

Do these obvious facts about the experience of dreaming make sense? Very little of modern research on the psychology of sleep and dreams even mentions what it feels like to be asleep. But that is precisely what we want to know if we are interested in sleep as an altered state of consciousness. I suggest we start by asking what models of reality are constructed during sleep and dreaming. I think the answers make good sense of the experience. In deep sleep rather little modelling is going on. There is too little arousal. Since there is no adequate model of self, 'I' do not experience anything. In dreaming sleep, arousal is much higher and model building (presumably) is much better. However, the models are very unstable because of the lack of sensory input, and there is still no integrated model of self. We typically cannot remember our name, the day of the week, or even construct an adequate body image. The main model (if indeed there is one over-riding model) is very different from the normal 'me.' So who is experiencing the dream? Any models which are constructed are, *ex hypothesi,* conscious. But am 'I' conscious of them? Only in as much as 'I' (my model of self) is part of them. In normal dreams it is very little so. Hence I find them hard to remember and they do not seem part of normal life. They are experiences of a 'dream self' — a different model of self.

In lucid dreams the model of self is much better (by waking standards). Some people can even say their own name during lucid dreams, and 'see' themselves lying in bed. The model of self is much closer to that in waking life and hence the experience is almost 'mine' and there is more continuity with waking life. The experiencer of those dreams was more a part of 'me.' 'I' was more conscious in that lucid dream. Out-of-body experiences involve even better models of self and the world (just from a different perspective) and therefore seem very real — very much part of 'my' experience.

Where there is continuity of a model or representation of self, then there is continuity of experience. Normal waking life is of course the best in this respect. A very good model of self keeps on being constructed all the time. From that same model 'we' can remember previous experiences. 'We' seem to be a continuous self.

In this way, I suggest, progress is made by asking about the models of reality which are constructed during dreaming and other ASCs. So can we now answer the question with which I began? Why do I feel different during meditation as compared with other times?

The simplest answer is that my model of self in the world is different. Indeed, since 'I' am a model of self, 'I' am changed. That is why 'I' feel different. More specifically we may ask what kinds of changes have taken place in the model of reality. Let us take the example I gave. In the first case I was sitting at my desk. My model of reality consisted of self and the world — well divided from each other. 'I' consisted of a stable body image with arms and legs, a model of myself as someone working, a lot of modelling of the substance of what I was writing. 'I' had plans for future actions (I must tidy up) and wishes that things were different (I wish I could concentrate harder) as well as thoughts about previous actions done wrongly (why didn't I finish this yesterday?).

The world around consisted of the room, the sounds outside; the birds (Oh there are some birds singing. Don't they sound nice? I wonder what sort of birds they are. I saw a woodpecker on the lawn last week); the children (I wish they'd be quiet), the radio (I hate the noise). There is no capacity left over for the humble woodlouse. But even if there were, she would just become 'Oh, there's a woodlouse crawling across the floor. I wonder where she came from? I must clean the carpet.' My model of self in the world, my model of reality, 'I,' is a vast, intricate construction, forever trying to model everything; and forever at the mercy of changes in input.

Now let us take the second example, where I am sitting in meditation. Let us suppose I have sat with eyes open and let trains of thought go their way into stillness. What sort of model of self in the world do I have? What am 'I?' In some cases 'I' may be very simple: just sitting. When I hear the sounds of birds I hear the sounds of birds. I do not respond. I do not elaborate. I do not even begin 'Oh, there are some birds . . .' I am quite uncritical of the music or the children. Whatever the input, I accept it without comment.

In this different way of constructing reality, the usual 'I' may cease to exist. 'I' now am as much the sounds as the hearer of the sounds *because I have not constructed the model which distinguishes them.* If there is an 'I' at all it is a new 'I.' It is simple and still. It is not at the mercy of the changes in input. By becoming one with them it is free of them. In a different meditative state I may not even hear the sounds of birds, or at least not label them birds, or even sounds, though I do not block them out either. The early processing in the system may be just the same, but never leads to a complex high level model. At that level there may be nothing. I have elaborated no model of self and so 'I' do not exist.

I have taken just two kinds of meditative state, and I do not mean to imply that all others are the same. However, I do suggest that the same approach can be used to understand all sorts of changes in states of consciousness. To understand why it feels different to be in some altered state, we should ask 'What model of self in the world has this person constructed?' or 'What am "I"?'. If all our experience of the world is a constructed reality, we may, given the skills, entirely change the kind of construction we build; that is, entirely change 'ourselves.'

This brings me to one last point. You may note that it is I, the whole system, which has those skills. 'I' may not have them, in the sense that 'I' am not consciously aware of how I do it. This shows again the importance of keeping clear the distinction between 'I' the model, and I the whole system. I know many things which 'I' do not know I know! The skills of meditation, or of changing states of consciousness may be among these. It sounds paradoxical to say that in meditation I let myself go, or I dismantle myself. It is not paradoxical to say that I have let 'I' go: the whole system has ceased to construct the usual model of a self. If we accept ourselves as just the construction of a modelling system, some of the effects of meditation make more sense. I would even hazard the suggestion that, with this acceptance, meditation itself may become easier.

By taking this simple example, I hope I have made the principle clear. I believe that the thoroughly materialistic, information-processing assumptions of cognitive psychology form a very good basis for thinking about meditation. By accepting that 'we' are nothing but models, constructed by an information-processing machine, we may lose our clinging to one 'self.' If we take it far enough, and accept it thoroughly enough, we may find that our western psychology leads us to much the same place as the spiritual traditions have been leading others for thousands of years.

5
Selfhood and Self-consciousness in Social Psychology: The Views of G.H. Mead and Zen

Martin Skinner

Martin Skinner is a Lecturer in Psychology at the University of Warwick. His research focuses on social psychological accounts of self-consciousness and selfhood and their parallels with traditional spiritual accounts.

THIS CHAPTER SETS out to emphasize the importance of an appreciation of self-consciousness and selfhood in Social Psychology. It attempts to show how those concepts are given a scientific grounding in the social psychology of G.H. Mead. It points to the parallels in this treatment of self-consciousness and selfhood with that given them by Zen Buddhism, and explores some aspects which this observation highlights.

The point of observing the parallels between Mead's views and those of Zen, seems to be two-fold. Firstly it means that the two accounts not only validate each other, but that each aids in the understanding of the other, so that the individual who understands anything of one, can more easily understand the other. Secondly, some of the features of self-consciousness and selfhood can profitably be discussed in terms of both approaches. This chapter looks particularly at the concept of self-control, where both Zen Buddhism and Mead would seem to provide the means of accounting for the phenomenon without postulating an homunculus sitting behind the scenes.

In being about self-consciousness this chapter addresses an aspect of consciousness. Consciousness is considered here to be the same as awareness, to be a function of sensory systems and the defining characteristic of sentient beings. When such sensory function can represent the organism which entertains it as a whole, there is consciousness of self or self-consciousness as the preceding chapter has argued.

Self-consciousness in the everyday sense of embarrassment could be considered a consequence and specific instance of self-consciousness in the broader meaning here employed. Self and selfhood refer to the organism which manifests this process and to the quality of such existence respectively. But despite having made a somewhat rarified and exact delineation of the term self-consciousness, I should add that the concept is supposed to refer to the most obvious, immediate, and inescapable experience which we all have of being someone. It refers to the feeling of being a unique and apparently isolated centre of experience.

Social psychology has not shown a great interest to self-consciousness or selfhood. As a branch of psychology it has followed the major paradigm shifts which have characterised the parent discipline ever since the possibility of an empirically based science of human mental life was opened up by Wilhelm Wundt[42] in the latter part of the nineteenth century. Thereafter an interest grew in conscious experience using the doomed technique of introspection to look at the structure of experience. (Doomed because, to anticipate a later section of this chapter, such a method creates a false distinction between the process and the products of thinking.) During this period the study of consciousness was given shape and impetus by William James' classic *The Principles of Psychology.*[43]

This period was brought to a close by the advent of behaviourism which cut through the confusion of conscious experience by ruling it out of court for a science. Behaviourism would, instead, restrict psychology to that which could be counted, weighed, measured or timed. Any construct not definable in terms of operations which could be subjected to such scrutiny could not be part of a science.[44] Behaviourism chose to segment the flow of human activity into units of stimulus and response, and to formulate rules whereby the latter were functions of the former.

The outcome of this paradigm, although it has developed

to allow hypothetical constructs to intervene between stimulus and response, has been to set psychology and hence social psychology on a course which has not had much to do with selfhood and self-consciousness. In the past fifteen years, though, a body of criticism has grown from within social psychology which has drawn attention to and criticised the discipline's legacy from this dominant paradigm, mainly in the form of the assumptions it makes about its subject matter: its so called 'model of man.' Harré and Secord[45] identify what they see as the dominant paradigm with a number of central features, all of which, they argue, are inappropriate for the explanation of human social behaviour. social psychology has, in their view, tried to explain human social behaviour in mechanistic terms, using the terminology of cause and effect appropriate to Newtonian physics. This is linked to a philosophy which construes the universe as constant facts, existing independently of human scientific efforts, waiting to be discovered. They propose that a better model would be one which treats people as self-conscious followers of rules, who monitor their own performances as agents and act in terms of meanings. A fundamental principle here is that one can only understand the activity of human beings on social occasions by looking at what that activity is part of rather than what its parts are.

Another account which has criticised psychological explanation of social behaviour for similar reasons is that of Gauld and Shotter.[46] They, too, argue that social psychology's inheritance from its behaviourist roots has immersed it in a fundamentally mechanistic model of man which is inadequate for the explanation of human powers. Their case is for a psychology which sets out to elucidate meanings underlying human social behaviour rather than to discover laws which underlie mechanisms.

What such critiques share is an agreement on the centrality of self-consciousness and selfhood as the starting point for anyone who would set out to explain human social behaviour. It is both the absence of the concepts from social psychology and their importance according to these critiques which makes any account of these elusive concepts in material, behavioural, scientific terms all the more important.

The account exists in the work of G.H. Mead and school of social psychology developed from his work known as Symbolic Interactionism. Symbolic Interactionism was the name given to Mead's approach by one of his students to encompass its central claim that human social interaction is effected through the exchange of symbols.[47] Although Mead produced no overall account of his views on self-consciousness and selfhood, one exists in C. Morris's edited collection of lecture notes from Mead's Social Psychology course entitled *Mind, Self and Society*.[48]

Mead set out to explain the essential reflexiveness of human consciousness: the fact that human beings seem to be able to represent themselves as a whole entity. At the simplest level he says that to be able to represent oneself as an object in one's own thoughts one needs to be able to take the standpoint of other people because one already is an object in their thoughts. Mead provides an account of how this is achieved which works as an explanation at both phylogenetic and ontogenetic levels.[49] But how does one take the standpoint of another person? The answer is to be found in the significant symbol, principally in the form of language, possession of which provides access to the internal states of other people, and presents the platform from which one can grasp oneself reflexively.

There are three important concepts to be grasped in Mead's discussion of self-consciousness: the significant symbol and its genesis; social objects; and social acts. They are all so interdependent that it is impossible adequately to discuss one without assuming an understanding of the others.

The Significant Symbol is, for Mead, an action or event with a shared meaning so that it produces a similar conventional response in the organism producing it and the onlooker. His account of its genesis begins with what he calls the 'conversation of gestures'[50]: a mindless act-react behaviour based on reflexes, which he sees even in a pair of dogs fighting. Gestures emerge from the flow of behaviour in such interactions. When an organism can associate the initial segment of an event with the completed event, the segment which it responds to is considered by Mead to be a gesture. For example the behaviour involved in preparing to land a blow could become the gesture which represents the completed act. Once the gesture produces the same response in both sender and receiver it is a significant gesture. It is quite likely that much of animal communication, alarm calls for example, involve significant gestures. When, by convention, the gesture ceases to possess any of the characteristics of the act of which it was once part and which it now signifies, it becomes a significant *symbol*.

To understand Mead's discussion of social objects, one must first see that as a pragmatist philosopher he had a particular view of objects in general. From such a philosophical outlook objects emerge from the interaction of organism and environment, and their meaning can only be understood in terms of that interaction. The ways in which organisms create objects vary from processes built in to the neural structure (in simple organisms) to abstract symbolic processes employed by language users.[51] The common feature, though, is that both types of organism create the objects as a function of their behaviour. This view does not deny any reality beyond sensory experience, but states that *objects* of experience are created out of interaction between organism and environment.

When organisms employ symbols they enter a new realm in the creation of objects. Just as human beings can act towards physical objects, so they can, with the use of symbols, create objects by consensus and act towards them in a certain way, thereby bestowing meaning upon them. In this way an entire objective reality of social objects which cannot be wished away can be created.[52]

Social acts are themselves social objects. They are the type of social object which can be made from human behaviour.

As Harré and Secord[53] state, behaviour can be viewed as actions which combine to form an act. Behaviour acquires its meaning through reference to the act which is created by performing it. Thus the meaning of actions cannot be determined by discovering what they are made up of in terms of behaviour, but arises from the social object, or act, that is created by their performance.[54] This connection between objects, social objects and acts will turn out to be of importance in the understanding of social control discussed later in the chapter.

In Mead's discussion of selfhood, being a self implies that one acts towards oneself as an object: one knows oneself, one praises and blames oneself. Of all the significant symbols in use among a community of people, the ones which the other members use to signify the object which 'you' represent to them will have special significance. Just as one internalizes the meanings of other significant objects, so one internalizes those pertaining to oneself. Signification of an object gives it an experiential existence beyond that directly sensed. Thus the signification of one's material being allows it to be experienced in its entirety: not merely as experienced through the senses. The self then is made an object in the same way as other objects are: through the definitions of others.

Clearly social objects are not created in a vacuum, bearing no relationship to the physical world. There is an interaction between the physical world and the world of social objects created out of it. Obviously human beings are constrained by the fact that life is a physical process and certain conditions must be satisfied for its continuation.[55] The discussion of the relationship between human life as a biological process and the social objectification of that process forms an important part of Mead's account. Mead sees the maintenance of selfhood as involving two analytically separable but experientially inseparable phases. One phase embodies whatever is spontaneous or biologically propelled.[56] This Mead terms the 'I,' or 'self as subject.' The other arises whenever this activity is signified, defined and regarded from the standpoint of another: it becomes in Mead's terms 'Me,' or the 'self as object.' Indeed the 'Me' is the social object created from spontaneous conduct. The relationship between the 'I' and 'Me' is best described as a dialectical relationship because the 'I' is continually recognised in social terms, making it the 'Me' which instantly becomes the ground state for the next phase of 'I' and so on. Thus the 'I' can never be self-consciously experienced as such for in that moment it has already become 'Me.'

The process of self-consciously acting towards oneself with significant symbols, as if from another's point of view, is what Mead considers Mind to be. It can be described as an internal conversation between the individual and another person, and is indeed an outcome of real interpersonal conversations which have become internalized.[57]

To sum up Mead's position, human beings become self-conscious when they can represent as social objects the social acts in which they are implicated. The process has been summarised by Meltzer:

> 'It is through language (significant symbols) that the child acquires the meanings and definitions of those around him. By learning the symbols of his groups he comes to internalize their definitions of events on things, including their definitions of his own conduct.[58]

But now consider the following quotation:

> ...the power of thought enables us to construct symbols of things apart from the things themselves. This includes the ability to make a symbol, an idea of ourselves apart from ourselves. Because the idea is so much more comprehensible than the reality, the symbol so much more stable than the fact, we learn to identify ourselves with our idea of ourselves. Hence the subjective feeling of a 'self' which has a mind, of an inwardly isolated subject to whom experiences involuntarily happen.[59]

The agreement between these two quotations is not very noteworthy until one realises that the former is from an academic social psychologist writing about Symbolic Interactionism, while the latter is taken from Alan Watts' *The Way of Zen*. The question which the rest of this paper addresses is: how far does this similarity, between apparently very different modes of thought, actually extend.

Zen Buddhism is the result of the fusion of Buddhist teachings with Taoism in China during the fifth Century AD. But by this time Buddhism was 900 years old and Taoism possibily twice that. What emerges from this fusion is something which, like all forms of Buddhism, is neither religion nor philosophy in the senses that these words are used in the western world. It has been described as a 'way of liberation,' and such a description seems apt in the context of this chapter because that from which it promises liberation is precisely the state of affairs which Mead describes: the identification of one's existence with the social object signified by the linguistic community in which one lives.

It is, then, the implication of symbols in the construction of self-consciousness which creates the link between Symbolic Interactionism and Zen in its doctrine of *Maya*. As we find in the former that symbols create objects, so we find in the latter that words create objects and grammatical conventions determine which aspects of experience are to be considered processes (verbs) and which are to be considered objects (nouns).

In its teaching on *maya*, Zen points to all knowledge as conventional. It urges us not to confuse the world as it is with our symbols for it; in other words our consensual, conventional knowledge of it. Facts and events are terms of measurement rather than realities of nature. Zen points to a confusion between measures and the world so measured, the most important example of which from a social psychological point of view and the purposes of this chapter is the confusion between self and the organism so signified. This essentially relational view of truth is implicit in Symbolic Interactionism, explicit in Zen, and contradicts the positivist view of science which assumes a world of facts existing independently of our dealings with them.

When Zen is turned towards the concept of mind we are told that the separation of thinker from thought, knower from known is once again conventional. This view that thoughts are thinking, at odds as it is with the assumptions which normally we implicitly make, is in close agreement with Symbolic Interactionism where mind and self are seen as a process, the process of creating social objects out of one's conduct by employing significant symbols. For Mead, when this process is going on, mind is present.

Zen further suggests that if we cease identifying our organismic, physical existence with our idea of ourselves the relationship between knower and known, subject and object in the organism will change. The experience and the experiencer become one and the same. In Alan Watts' words 'I breathe' may equally well be thought of as 'it breathes me.' Enlightenment, or liberation, comes when, in the terminology of Symbolic Interactionism, one ceases identifying oneself with any significant symbols, when the self ceases to be experienced in terms of the objects created by the surrounding linguistic community. To say, as one finds in Zen writing, that we should experience the world with a mind that is not thinking, is to say in the language of Symbolic Interactionism that we should experience the world without acting towards that experience with an exchange of significant symbols, construing it in terms of social objects.

This analysis of self-consciousness, with the importance it attaches to understanding the nature of social objects and social acts, is perhaps of greatest value in enabling us to think about self-control without involving the concepts of 'free-will' or 'will-power.' Self-control is an important concept; it is closely related to the concept of agency, concern with which plays an important part in the critiques of social psychology mentioned earlier.

It is difficult to discuss self-control without getting into an infinite regress. We are prepared to consider an action the outcome of self-control rather than of spontaneity if it was preceded by a decision on our part to perform it. This, however, only shifts the problem 'back' a stage and we have to ask whether or not self-control was exercised in the decision to perform the action. Common sense descriptions of such activity, and some psychological ones, rely on an homunculus which sits somewhere in the head overseeing behaviour.

The Zen conclusion in matters of self-control seems to be that *everything* is spontaneous and that we consider we have exercised will-power if that which happened is what we wanted to happen. Watts makes this point by suggesting that we can in fact neither forget nor remember an object at will.[61] In meditation one can neither be mindful nor mindless at will: one does one's best to let it happen. (And again Zen would ask 'who' is doing 'whose' best?)

Such a view is similar to the account of freewill given within Symbolic Interactionism, an account for which an understanding of acts as objects becomes once again important. Mead's account starts with behaviour; it proposes that the flow of behaviour contains impulses, disturbances to equilibrium, which are the initial stages of acts. These initial stages signify the act to follow. Thus one becomes aware of one's own behaviour in the sense that one experiences the acts that one is on the point of initiating. One grasps the completed act and one's performance in it, which in turn is an object known to stand in some sort of relationship to one's self. On the basis of this relationship the impulse may or may not be inhibited. If it is inhibited no-one else will have access to these events internal to the organism, which will appear to be and indeed is exerting self-control. There is though no self *doing* the inhibition, and the 'regress' does not become infinite. The impulse is spontaneous; the consequences inevitable; the outcome fixed though socially conditioned.

This discussion of self-control is really no more than an elaboration of the 'I'/'Me' dialogue in Mead's account of mind and self. It does however point to the essential spontaneity of human behaviour which is the only alternative to the infinite regress: a regress not satisfactorily avoided in some contemporary social psychological accounts of self-consciousness. The Zen programme or indeed any Buddhist programme is directed towards making these experiential discoveries about selfhood and self-control. The Symbolic Interactionism of G.H. Mead can lead us intellectually, through a scientific mode of discourse, to the same conclusions.

This understanding of one's self is enlightening and enriching. It can be achieved through Buddhist practice, and it can, in my opinion, be achieved in a different way with a different type of knowledge of the same truth in Symbolic Interactionism. The experience of one type of knowledge assists and reinforces the experience of the other. To move from one to the other is to experience the complementary relationship of mystical and scientific understanding.

6
The Spiritual Psychology of Rudolf Steiner

Fraser N. Watts

Fraser Watts is a clinical psychologist on the scientific staff of the Medical Research Council Applied Psychology Unit in Cambridge. He is a past Chairman of the British Psychological Society Division of Clinical Psychology and the editor of *New Developments in Clinical Psychology* (British Psychological Society, 1985).

Rudolf Steiner is a challenging, but enigmatic figure. He describes a path of spiritual development and awareness which he claims to have followed himself and encourages others to follow too, a path which yields direct knowledge of 'higher' or 'supersensible' worlds. Much of his writings and lectures contain the results of his investigations of this world, an enterprise that he calls 'spiritual science.' The contents of these investigations are very varied. Some describe human phenomena which are open to verification by other methods. Others describe phenomena that are so far removed from ordinary experience that there seems no possibility of verifying them by other methods (and, unless one has the powers of discernment of the spiritual worlds that Steiner claimed to have, no way of verifying them at all). Some are closely related to perennial esoteric wisdom (especially the teachings of Theosophy, with which Steiner was associated for a few years as General Secretary of the German Section); others are original, including much that is directly human and practical.

Steiner was clearly aware of the problem of how to evaluate the results of his spiritual science, and his lectures are peppered with remarks that can be paraphrased as follows: 'I know that this may all sound very puzzling and difficult, but I have taken great care in investigating these matters and I can assure you that what I say is true. It may be difficult to integrate what I say with what is commonly believed, but this is because contemporary knowledge gets everything so jumbled up. Though my claims may be puzzling, I certainly don't want you to accept them as true just on my authority. If you follow the path of spiritual science that I have described, you will be able to verify these things for yourselves.'

What is one to make of a person who reports some apparently outlandish results of his spiritual investigations (along with some eminently sensible ones) and claims this kind of authority in doing so? Colin Wilson has recently addressed this issue in a neutral, responsible way,[62] and I agree with his broad conclusions. Steiner was not a charlatan. Neither was he mad. The story of his life and work[63] contains too much evidence of his intelligence, scholarship, integrity, conscientiousness and deep seriousness of purpose for such dismissive hypotheses to be entertained. It also seems clear that he had unusual and highly developed psychic powers of some kind. However, there is no reason to regard him as infallible. Colin Wilson suggests that his method of investigation was quite good, for example, at discerning the history of a place (such as Tintagel Castle, that he visited in the last year of his life), but less good at arriving at exact historical dates. This seems plausible, and there may be many other similar points to be made about where he is more or less reliable. This leads to the conclusion that he should be read with discrimination and this, as I understand it, is what he wished. His view was that human development had now reached a stage at which a 'guru' was inappropriate. He thought that a modern seer should make his teachings freely and publicly available, and that pupils should be entirely free to select and use whatever was appropriate to their own path and stage of spiritual development.

His psychology presents fewer problems than some areas of his teachings, because it is a field in which it is fairly straight-forward for people to check claims against their own experience. Indeed, some of his psychological ideas are open to verification by conventional scientific methods, though there has been little attempt to do so. What Steiner has to say on psychology is best taken as the hints and indications of an exceptionally gifted person, who used unusual methods, and took a spiritual vantage point for the study of human nature. They deserve to be taken seriously as of potential importance but not accepted uncritically.

Another claim that Steiner makes for his teachings is a pragmatic one. It has become commonplace for academic theologians to make such claims of value for religious teachings. Usually the suggestion is that religious assertions should be taken, not as making factual claims, but as having helpful effects on believers. Steiner, in contrast, wishes to claim both factual truth *and* pragmatic value. Furthermore he sees the pragmatic value of his teachings as going beyond providing an inspiration to lead a good ethical life, though he makes it clear that any progress on the path of knowledge that he describes must be accompanied by moral progress. His major pragmatic claim is that the act of entertaining the wisdom teachings he provides will begin to have an effect on psychic functioning. 'Think these thoughts,' he seems to say, 'and it will begin to transform your capacity for thinking and expand the scope of your consciousness.'

Why is his contribution of potential importance? The answer to this is two-fold, of which part is the shared assumption of the various chapters in this book that contemporary academic psychology has too restricted horizons and can learn from spiritual psychologies which concern themselves with a wider range of phenomena and approach them from a broader perspective. However, among the seers of the world who have given us a family of spiritual psychologies, he may have particular importance. Steiner had a strong sense of time and place. He was, deliberately and self-consciously, a seer of the West and of this modern age. He saw oriental and occidental humans as having quite different relationships to the spiritual world. There was no question of favouring one rather than another. He saw them each as having their own part to play, though his own role as a Westerner was concerned with the Western path. Some of his thoughts on this are captured in his *West-East Aphorisms*,[64] of which the following is an extract:

> In the ancient East the poet felt that spiritual powers were speaking through him...The cosmic word sounded down from the gods to humanity. In the West it has become the human word. It has to find the way up to the spiritual powers. Man must bring a poetry into being which may be heard by the spirit...Then the East will say: The divine word, which once streamed down to us from heaven to earth — this now finds the way from human hearts back into spiritual worlds. (p.20)

Steiner saw it as a central task to find a *language* for spiritual matters. This concern to articulate truth is a characteristically Western interest. Buddhism, in contrast, is keenly aware of the value of stilling unnecessary thought and talk. Steiner saw it as his task to approach the spiritual world in a spirit of enquiry, to struggle to find words for the supersensible realities he had glimpsed, and to describe them accurately. However, he emphasises that this enterprise should not be approached in a spirit of idle curiosity; there has to be a noble purpose to these attempts at description of supersensible realities. There was probably some personal cost for him to seeking to translate his experiences into words, as they could lose some of their personal immediacy in the process of description. There was also the enormous risk of being grossly misunderstood. Whatever Steiner's reasons for seeking to articulate supersensible awareness, the result is a body of spiritual wisdom that can be mapped on to contemporary science more readily than any other wisdom literature I know of. This chapter will be concerned with his psychology, but there are parallel contributions to physics, physiology, medicine and many other disciplines.[65]

Steiner was an Austrian who lived from 1861 – 1925, and there are certainly enormous differences between the German academic style at the beginning of this century, and the contemporary Anglo-Saxon one. Nevertheless Steiner's is probably the best available attempt by a seer to translate spiritual wisdom into the categories and concerns of contemporary science. So far as psychology is concerned he saw Brentano as the most promising psychologist of his time, and much of his contribution can usefully be seen in that context. Brentano's influence on contemporary psychology has been considerable, and much humanistic psychology can be traced back to him. So the psychological tradition in which Steiner placed himself is far from obsolete.

THE FRAMEWORK OF STEINER'S IDEAS

Steiner also had a strong sense of human history or, more specifically, what he called the 'evolution of consciousness,' a topic that is now coming into fashion.[66] In outline, but not in detail, his views are similar to the theosophists. Steiner sees the development of human beings as proceeding through nine successive stages: Physical body, Etheric (or life) body, Astral (or sentient) body, Sentient psyche (*Gumutsseele*), Consciousness psyche (*Bewusstseinsseele*), Spirit Self (*Manas*), Life-Spirit (*Budhi*) and Spirit Man (*Atma*)[67]. The full scope of this development need not concern us here. However, his sense of how far the evolution of consciousness had reached, and what further developments were now required, is closely intertwined with his psychology. We are now, according to this scheme, living in the age of the consciousness psyche (and have been since around 1450). Charles Davy has offered the helpful alternative name of the age of the 'onlooker consciousness.'[68]

Whether or not one accepts Steiner's esoteric scheme in total, there is little doubt that his account of the age of the onlooker consciousness fits well with what can be observed about the last 500 years. It has been an age of enormous advance in scientific knowledge, based on the adoption of experimental method and a detached, manipulative approach of man to nature. It has also been a period of increasing self-consciousness, increasing concern of humans to understand themselves, but in which their thirst for self-knowledge seems not to have been adequately met. On the contrary, a sense of alienation and meaninglessness have become commonplace. The existentialist movement (which, of course, largely post-dates Steiner) captures well this mixture of self-concern and alienation which has accompanied the scientific age. These are all central aspects of Steiner's account of the age of the 'onlooker consciousness.'

His diagnosis is that the onlooker consciousness has lost the capacity to relate the world of nature to the world of spirit. As Steiner saw it, the traditional wisdom of the East is based on immediate access to the world of spirit, but regards the natural world as illusion. In contrast, the West accepts the reality of the natural world, but regards the spiritual world as a matter of ideology rather than experience. Steiner grew up at home in both the worlds of spirit and of nature. He seems to have been a natural clairvoyant who as a boy effortlessly experienced aspects of the supersensible world, as well as being at home in the natural, material world. His childhood problem, which he grew to see as a reflection of the general problem of the age, was how to relate the spiritual and natural worlds to each other.

Though Steiner saw the age of the onlooker consciousness as the one that has least idea of how to relate the spiritual and the natural, he did not see the remedy for this as being simply a return to archaic modes of consciousness that humans had largely left behind. On the contrary, he believed that if a sense of the connection between the natural and spiritual worlds is to be recovered, it will be achieved in the future in a new way. In brief, in the past humans tended to see spiritual beings as living in nature (that is, animism); in the future the spiritual world will be experienced, if at all, inwardly. The old animistic consciousness was universal and effortless, the new spiritual consciousness will depend on an effortful development of individual powers of spiritual discernment. The old consciousness saw social order as emanating from external authority; if social order is to be maintained in the future it can only be built on individual will. (This theme is reflected in the Judaic-Christian tradition as a contrast between the 'law' of the Old Testament era and the 'spirit' of the New Testament era, a theme that Paul developed in the Epistle to the Romans.) Language has also reflected this shift in consciousness. The history of language can be traced back to root metaphors where the same words applied to both natural and spiritual realities. (The Hebrew word *'ruach,'* meaning both wind and spirit, is a classic example.) Over time these natural metaphors have been dissolved into more literal language. Metaphor is now an act of human creation, not a natural way of naming things in a reality in which spiritual and natural were seen as intertwined.[69] This is a grand theory of human history that Steiner elaborated in much detail over many different domains.

In terms of Steiner's nine stages of the development of human beings, the present age of the onlooker consciousness will complete their *psychological* development. The transition that is now required, if the sense of alienation of the onlooker consciousness is not to increase, is the gradual spiritualisation of their psychological faculties. Though Steiner see the full-flowering of this transition as a long way off, he was much concerned with how the seeds of a strengthening or spiritualisation of psychological faculties could take place now. There is thus a continual interplay between his psychology and his spiritual concerns.

DEVELOPMENT OF 'HIGHER' KNOWLEDGE

It is in keeping with Steiner's general position about the interrelationship of psychological and spiritual faculties that the path to supersensible knowledge that he describes begins with exercises that appear to have no esoteric aspect at all. At least, they are very similar to methods used in many other traditions, including modern cognitive therapy.[70] However, Steiner is insistent that preliminary work at the psychological level is indispensable if any spiritual progress is to be made. The six 'accessory exercises' that he describes in several places'[71] are a good exemplification of this level of work. The first is the control of thought, learning to grasp thoughts of our choice rather than allowing consciousness to be dominated by chance associations and intrusions. Next is the control of action, learning to execute decisions that have been made, however trivial they may appear. The third is control of feelings, which Davy[72] describes as 'learning to live poised within them, neither estranged nor engulfed by our emotions, but in balance (p.266)'. These three exercises correspond, of course, to the traditional Aristotelian categories of cognition, emotion and will that Steiner adopted and made his own. The fourth exercise is positivity, the capacity to see what is beautiful and noble in all circumstances. Steiner emphasises that this is not to be confused with lack of discrimination. Next is open-minded receptivity, overcoming the reluctance to engage with what is unfamiliar. The sixth exercise involves the integration of the other five. These are described, not to suggest that they are highly original, but rather so it can be seen how closely what Steiner recommends at this level corresponds to what is found in other traditions.

Next we come to the development of three higher faculties (higher in the sense of extending beyond external sense perception), which Steiner calls imagination, inspiration and intuition. It is the development of the faculty of imagination that he sees as one of man's central tasks in the age of onlooker consciousness. Imagination is a 'strengthened,' 'living' form of thinking, capable of directly perceiving living processes, not just discrete objects.

It will be helpful in explaining what Steiner meant by imagination to begin with the related method of 'exact sensorial fantasy' developed by Goethe.[73] Steiner was much influenced by Goethe,[74] and he spent a number of years in Weimar in the early part of his life working on a complete edition of Goethe's scientific writings. Goethe's approach to the observation of plants provided Steiner with an early scientific application of the kind of method of expanded awareness that he was developing. Central to Goethe's method was careful observation, so that parts of the plant form could be retained very clearly in consciousness. For example, he observed leaves at various stages of development, retaining each sufficiently clearly that he could pass from one to the next in his 'mind's eye' and actually *see* the process of metamorphosis by which the first form of a leaf was transformed to the final form (rather like seeing movement rather than a series of still shots in a cine film, except that here the trick is achieved by the development of cognitive capacities rather than machinery). With this basic cognitive skill, Goethe made important observations about the principles of metamorphosis in plants, how one part of a plant is related to another, and how ultimately all plants are variants on the single archetypal plant form. There is a classic meeting between Schiller and Goethe,[75] in which Schiller said of the archetypal plan 'That is no experience, that is an idea,' but Goethe replied 'I am glad to have ideas without knowing it, and to see them with my very eyes' (p.104). Goethe had taught himself to actually see nature not 'divided and in pieces' but 'working and alive, striving out of the whole into parts.' His method demands both a hightened attentiveness to nature, but also restraint in introducing unrelated ideas not derived from what is being observed.

This Goethean method can be set beside one of Steiner's many accounts of the development of similar cognitive capacities.[76] He begins by describing a mood of 'surrender' to experience, based on a sense of wonder, reverent devotion to reality, and knowing oneself to be in harmony with the world. Now, says Steiner, when for example you look at the world in this spirit of 'surrender,' you will feel a sense of inner movement and balance, and discern in the outer world either 'coming into existence' or 'passing away.' You will both feel within yourself and perceive in the outer world, the 'etheric' domain (for which the world of 'formative forces' is perhaps the best paraphrase). 'Surrender' characterises the mood that is necessary for the perception of formative forces.

In more purely cognitive terms, a capacity for the formation of vivid, but sense-independent mental representations is required. Goethe's exercise required the formation of representations of the leaf at difference stages of development, that were very vivid, but achieved without the leaf being physically present. The importance of the capacity for vivid, but sense-independent thought recurs throughout Steiner's writings. He talks, for example[77] about developing a capacity of day-time imagination which is as vivid and sense-independent as dreaming, but is unlike dreaming in being under voluntary control, and not liable to be mistaken for external reality. The paradox, as Steiner loved to point out, is that the power of seeing spiritual realities is developed by the conscious and deliberate presentation to consciousness of what is outwardly unreal.

One of the many consequences of developing this faculty that he claims is the capacity for voluntary 'screen' memories, that is, the experience of the whole of life stretched out in a panorama and perceived instantaneously. These are similar to involuntary experiences often reported by people in imminent danger of death, but Steiner claims that they can be achieved voluntarily. Seeing one's life in this way, one can grasp the continuity in one experiences in somewhat the same way as Goethe taught himself to perceive the metamorphosis of a leaf by passing between mental representations of leaves at different stages of development. A new sense of self-identity results.

'Inspiration' and 'intuition' are further stages of knowledge beyond imagination, (but, because he is much briefer about them, I will be briefer too). Inspiration involves a development of *feeling* and can be prepared for by developing strong emotional responses to truth and falsehood. Here, we experience in consciousness what we normally experience only in sleep. It leads to perception of a world of spirit beings. At this level, one discovers one's higher-self. (Steiner's distinction between the ego and the higher-self is very similar to Jung's between the ego and the self.) Intuition in contrast, is developed from a hightening of *will*, and involves not merely knowledge of this spirit beings, but the possibility of a direct relationship with them.

SYSTEMATIC PSYCHOLOGY

Steiner thus maps his three 'higher' faculties of imagination, inspiration and intuition on to the traditional Aristotelian psychological categories of thinking, feeling and willing. This is characteristic of how he sees the spiritual and psychological worlds as interweaving.

Let us now consider Steiner's treatment of thinking, feeling and willing in more detail. He sees a polarity between thinking and willing. Within the psyche he describes two main forces, desires which arise from will, and judging which results in the mental representations which are the content of thought. There is some discrepancy between sources as to where negative feelings should be located in this scheme. In the 'Psychosophy' lectures[78] both positive and negative feelings arise from desire. In the 'Study of Man,'[79] only sympathy arises from desire, and antipathy has a role in the formation of mental representations. So far, this is a variant on a theme that was current from the psychology of Brentano.

One of the more unusual aspects of Steiner's scheme comes in its use of time, and this is one of many points where we can discern the scholar and the occultist in Steiner finding a meeting point. Representations are seen as arising in a stream that flows from the past into the future, whereas feelings arise from a stream flowing from the future back into the past. At one level, this is not too difficult to grasp. Memories which are the main content of thoughts come from the past, whereas feelings are often anticipatory and arise from expected future events. However, Steiner largely has in mind streams of time that extend before birth and after death. Desire (or sympathy) arises from what flows back towards us from life after death. Representations arise from what flows forward from pre-birth experience.

Steiner says that though we have waking consciousness in relation to thinking, we have a sleep consciousness in relation to willing. Again, there is some common-sense plausibility in this. We are indeed often unaware both of making decisions, and of our reasons for them. Decisions are often made tacitly, and motives are often confused and poorly understood. (The efforts of psychoanalysis to unravel them testifies to their opacity.) However, Steiner's important point is that willing is something of which we potentially *could* be conscious. Further, willing is the carrier of our destiny and of the most direct kind of knowledge of the spiritual world. Spiritual 'intuition' depends on becoming conscious of, and hightening, willing. Steiner is again partly doing straight-forward (though old-fashioned sounding) psychology, and partly linking it up with radical claims which are central to his spiritual view-point.

There is perhaps something characteristically Western about the high seriousness with which Steiner treats the will. It is one of the points that distinguishes his contribution from the spiritual psychologies of the East. Taoist philosophy, for example, would have a very different attitude to the will. Steiner sees the will as potentially man's highest spiritual faculty. 'Striving' is a word that Steiner frequently uses with approval, albeit in a sense of noble non-egotistical striving. For Steiner, it is when humans learns to permeate their thinking with will that they becomes free (in the sense of being able to choose what to think). Similarly, Steiner saw it as important in spiritual development for actions to become deliberately willed, rather than done semiautomatically.

Duty is another related concept of which Steiner spoke with warm approval, though he sought an approach to duty which glowed with fervent love[80] and was much more than a mere carrying of responsibilities.

Contemporary psychology has so little grasp of volition that any plausible offerings are welcome. It is one of Steiner's justified complaints about Brentano that he does not deal with will, and it would still be a reasonable complaint about psychology today. It may therefore be of interest to develop Steiner's treatment of will a little further. He offers us[81] seven levels of will phenomena that correspond to the stages of the evolution of man. (1) Firstly there is *instinct*, which is at the level of the physical body, and is no different to what is found in animals (for example, a beaver building a dam). (2) Next, associated with the etheric or life body, there is *drive* (*trieb*), which though more 'inward' than instinct, is like it in operating constantly through life. (3) Thirdly, associated with the astral or sentient body, there is *desire*. Unlike the previous two, this is episodic in character, but still found in animals as well as humans. (4) Next, at the psychic level, there is *motive*. (5) The remaining three levels are at the spirit level. Accompanying motive like an undertone, Steiner says, is a *wish* to do something better. He is clear that he is not talking about repentance, which is retrospective and often egoistic. This wish to do better he associates with the Spirit-Self (*Manas*). (6) When this becomes a specific picture of how to do a thing better, that is, *intention*, it is associated with the Life-Spirit (*Budhi*) level. (7) Finally, at the level at which the psyche is freed from the body, at the Spirit Man (*Atma*) level, the intention becomes *resolution*. These last two levels should probably be taken as referring to will phenomena that Steiner saw occurring between death and re-birth. Steiner offers this scheme only briefly as part of a single lecture, and there has been little attempt to develop it or probe its usefulness. It is typical of his material in its systematic approach and its attention to the whole man. He does not confine himself to dealing with spiritual aspects. Perhaps the most interesting element is the *wish* to do something better, a 'soft undertone' of which we can become increasingly conscious of, and which belongs to the higher man. This is contrasted with a neurotic sense of inadequacy.

Feeling has an intermediary role between thinking and willing. Steiner acutely observes how the relationship between the three tends to change during the life-span.[82] In children, feeling is most closely associated with willing, while thinking is relatively independent. By old age, feeling has become more closely associated with thinking, and will has become relatively independent. There is thus a developmental task of freeing feeling from willing, and associating it with thinking. Steiner's comments on feelings of anger provide a good illustration of the way he sees psychological and spiritual phenomena as intertwined.[83] He firmly rejects 'superficial theosophy' which states simply that people must conquer their passions. Steiner, in contrast, sees anger as having a role in one's spiritual development, and looks towards its metamorphosis rather than its suppression. The mission of anger is twofold. In part it enables one to develop a sense of separateness and autonomous individuality. It can also be a way of responding instinctively to what is right and wrong, and thus, provided it does not give way to rage, functioning as an educator of the ego.

It would be possible to continue this survey of the intertwining of the spiritual and the psychological across many fields of psychology such as child development,[84] individual differences[85] and physiological psychology.[86] However, a consideration of one more field will suffice, at least to illustrate Steiner's way of approaching these topics. This is the senses, and their classification.[87]

Not surprisingly, Steiner's treatment of the senses involves a number of non-material senses. He proposes a list of twelve, which are arranged on a spectrum from 'inner' to 'outer' senses: touch, life (that is, well-being), movement, balance, smell, taste, sight, warmth, hearing, word (that is, speech), thought, and ego (that is, another person's ego).

Though the terminology is unfamiliar, there is nothing problematic here. For example, the distinction between a word sense and a thought sense is implicit in much recent research on depth of processing that distinguishes between acoustic and semantic processing of language.[88] There are two main components to Steiner's 'inner-outer' distinction. With the inner senses the world impinges on us; with the outer senses we reach out to the external world. Also, the outer senses are more subjective in that what we perceive is more dependent on our psychological state. This is quite close to Schachtel's distinction between allocentric and auto-centric senses.[89] Both Steiner and Schachtel see the application to one sensory mode of a style that belongs to a different sensory mode (for example, reacting to thoughts with the kind of pleasure or displeasure that is more appropriate to tastes) as being a kind of pathology of the senses.

There is nothing puritanical in Steiner's account of sense perception. Neither is there any sympathy with the view of some religions that the world that the senses reveal is illusory. He would see detachment from sense experience as just as unhealthy as addiction to particular sensory experiences. Rather than disparaging the senses, Steiner characteristically draws connections between them and the three higher faculties of imagination, inspiration and intuition. These higher faculties are a kind of extension of the spectrum of increasingly outer-directed senses, in that they press beyond sense experience, and are much more dependent on the state of development of the individual. He draws parallels between imagination and sight, inspiration and hearing, and intuition and the thought sense.

IMPLICATIONS FOR THERAPY

Steiner had a very practical mind, and saw no opposition between his sustained interest in supersensible realities, and a detailed concern with practical affairs.[90] On the contrary, he believed that both required a new kind of imaginative thinking that would enable people to grasp living realities more directly. It is a reflection of his practical concerns that one of his most systematic treatments of psychology was given as a lecture course to the teachers of a new school of which he had been asked to be educational director. Despite his wide range of practical interests,[91] Steiner said little directly about psychological therapy. Had he been living today, he would probably have said more. He was aware of the development of psychoanalysis, but was unimpressed by the strong tendency he discerned in early psychodynamic theorising to explain higher psychic phenomena in terms of low-level impulses.[92] However, it is possible to draw from his work an approach to therapy.

There is clearly much similarity between the kind of exercises undertaken as preliminaries to the spiritual path and the kind of therapeutic methods developed to alleviate psychological distress.[93] In a sense, therefore, the meditational exercises he describes[94] can themselves be taken as a contribution to therapy. However, Steiner emphasised that the spiritual path he described was not suitable for the psychologically disturbed. In particular he believed that you needed to be very sane indeed if you were to distinguish between truth and illusion in the supersensible world. Also, he spoke with feeling on many occasions about how people who follow a spiritual path perceive the more ugly parts of their personalities with a new clarity and directness. Not everyone is ready to cope with this, and so the spiritual path is often unsuitable for the psychologically disturbed, (an issue explored by Guy Claxton in his concluding chapter to this book).

However, psychological experiences which have a basis in spiritual realities may not be the preserve of those who *choose* to follow a spiritual path. Steiner believed that humankind would shortly begin to cross a 'threshold' into direct experience of spiritual realities, and that this would be a general process that would overtake people who were unprepared for it. The confrontation with the Lord of Death that he describes as being entailed in crossing this threshold can be experienced as a force of darkness and destruction. John Davy,[95] applying this line of Steiner's thought, has suggested that the experience of depression may in part follow the impact of these spiritual realities. (He also suggests that the widespread sense of the impending annihilation of the planet may also be a misreading of a basically spiritual experience.) It seems clear that Steiner would not see all psychological distress as something to be removed as efficiently as possible. His remarks, already referred to, on the constructive 'mission' of anger, have counterparts for other emotions. Depression may also have a spiritual mission to perform. Davy points out that the Lord of Death has a constructive role, 'to destroy old life to make way for new, and to free the spirit from matter' (p.264). It is interesting in this connection that some people who become depressed appear to have a sense that integrity prevents them from seeing reality as other than bleak; their depression seems to be linked to a moral commitment to truthfulness. Clearly, it is very difficult to distinguish spiritual aspects of psychological disorders from other aspects, but an attempt to do so must be part of an approach to therapy based on Steiner's contribution.

However, it also needs to be emphasised that Steiner was not opposed to biological approaches to psychological disturbance. He took a holistic approach to human beings from which the biological level was certainly not excluded. Disturbances and imbalances can develop at a variety of different levels and need to be treated in appropriate ways. This is clear, for example, from a case of depression described in 'Fundamentals of Therapy.'[96] The underlying formulation of the patient (pp.120−122) is in terms of a 'sentient' body that is sluggish, and is also insufficiently connected with the 'physical' and 'life' bodies. The treatment included the prescription of a variety of substances, such as arsenic in the form of a mineral water to strengthen the sentient body.

Steiner's general concern with the development of a living,

imaginative kind of thinking can be applied to psychological phenomena as part of an approach to therapy. This is perhaps most appropriate in people who find life empty and mean- ingless, or who have lost a sense of direction in their lives. It will be recalled that he saw a sense of alienation and meaninglessness as one of the general problems of the age of the onlooker consciousness, and the development of imag- ination as central to remedying it. Autobiographical material can be used as the basis for exercises in the development of imaginative thinking, and a style of counselling has been developed on this basis. Steiner offers a relatively rich theory of life-span development that provides a theoretical basis for such work.[97] There is much in Steiner's systematic psycho- logy that can be applied to the formulation of psychological problems, such as the pathologies of the senses already referred to, though its application has not been worked out systematically.

There is one particular theme in Steiner's work which I believe has the potential to provide a useful general model for personal growth and therapy. This is his theory of evil. He believed that there were two different forces for evil, forces which were opposed to each other in many ways, though with a tendency to form an alliance.[98] One, which he as- sociated with Lucifer, represents grandiosity, arrogance and self-indulgence. The other, associated with Ahriman, is manipulative and acquisitive, but ultimately sterile. They are associated with different forms of thinking: Lucifer with a tendency to hazy mysticsm, and Ahriman with analytic definitions and formulae. Steiner characteristically asserts that even these evil forces also have a necessary and con- structive role. We owe art to Lucifer, and technology to Ahriman. They have bcth played a crucial role at different stages of the evolution of consciousness in enabling human beings to find a path of development towards love, wisdom and freedom. Thus, for Steiner,[99] 'the task of evil is to promote the ascent of man' (p.74). Because in this scheme there are two forces of evil, not just one, good is not seen as being opposed to evil. The forces of good, associated with Christ, are seen as balancing, redeeming and healing the two evil forces. Steiner's principal application of this schema is to the development of humanity, but it can also be applied to individual human development. Similarities with psychoanalytic schemata are not difficult to discern. Lucifer and Ahriman somewhat resemble the id and superego of Freud. There are also similarities to the ego-self axis in Jungian thought.[100] Lucifer corresponds to a premature identification of the ego with the self, Ahriman to the alienation of the ego from the self. These similarities are sufficient to indicate the applicability of Steiner's scheme to therapeutic work. However, it has some interesting novelties, such as the ideas that Lucifer and Ahriman tend to form an alliance against spiritual development, and that they each have constructive effects at one stage of development but a damaging impact at another. Some may be put off by the names of the spirit-beings by which Steiner refers to these forces, though of course they can readily be detached from the remainder of the schema. However, there may be psychological value, as James Hillman has argued,[101] in this kind of 'personifying.' It puts matters in a form in which they can more readily be taken to heart, as well as being an aid to discrimination.

Finally, there is the issue of the relationship between the patient and the therapist. Steiner was concerned with 'karmic' aspects of relationships, that is with the significance of an encounter between two people in terms of the development of the repeated earth-lives of the two souls concerned. Most people will be unable to discern what is the karmic significance of a relationship, and many will be sceptical about repeated earth lives. However, even to *raise* such questions about a relationship leads to a new attitude to it in which integrity and moral seriousness are prominent. This atmosphere will colour therapeutic relationships that are influenced by Steiner's work. A therapist influenced by Steiner would try to be alert to karmic aspects of the therapeutic relationship in the same way as a Freudian would try to be alert to transference aspects.

CONCLUSION

Steiner's significance lies in his having striven to incarnate spiritual wisdom in a form that could integrate into contemporary, Western, scientific culture and lead to that culture's renewal. Psychology is only one of many arenas in which he attempted this, though he is almost alone among seers in having devoted so much attention to developing a framework for understanding psychological phenomena *per se*. He endeavoured not only to chart a path of personal development that others could follow, but to describe psychological phenomena and their interrelationship with the spiritual in terms that the scientific community could begin to comprehend. It is not an achievement that should be seen as standing unchanged for all time, but it provides signposts that others can use in embarking on a parallel task, from their own point of spiritual development and in the context of the scientific culture of their own day.

7

Buddhist Psychology: A Paradigm for the Psychology of Enlightenment

Joy Manné-Lewis

Joy Manné-Lewis has been studying the psychology of the Pali texts, and teaching Pali, at the University of London School of Oriental and African Studies, and is currently studying these texts further at the Kern Institute, Leiden, Holland.

It is a present problem in psychology how to understand the Buddha and Buddhism. This problem becomes ever more pressing and urgent on account of the contemporary increase both of personal interest in, and also of scientific research into, the methods for psychological development described in Buddhist literature.[102] In order to solve this problem I think we can adopt no more powerful method than that advocated by Popper[103] and try to see what problem the Buddha was trying to solve. There is a very clear statement of this in a sutta[104] called the *Quest for the Enlightened*.[105] This sutta also suggests that the Buddha's method of approach to his problem was no different from that of any modern scientist; that is to say, the Buddha's approach was to identify a problem, formulate a hypothesis, test it, modify it in the light of experience, and to proceed once again with his research by testing the reformulated hypothesis.

In this sutta, which is purportedly autobiographical, the Buddha gives an account of a 'peak experience' during which he perceived that he had been aiming at the wrong goal: that he had been after those very things — such as a wife, children, servants, domestic animals and status animals — which, like himself, were all subject to birth, old age, illness, death, grief, and moral impurity. A horror of old age, illness and death seem to have been a powerful factor in the Buddha's own

personality in the initial phase of his quest for Enlightenment. The realisation that his ambitions had been mistaken
opened up to him the concept of a different kind of goal, some
state of being that was 'not born, free of old age, illness, death
and grief; free of defilements; the highest freedom from
bondage; *Nibbana*.'[106] From the outset of his search it was
axiomatic for the Buddha that such a state existed and was
attainable.

Knowledge acquired while mastering the teaching of his
first teacher led the Buddha to reformulate his problem, and
to redefine it as the problem of finding a practice (*dhamma*)
that would lead to 'disgust with worldly life, absence of
passion, cessation, tranquillity, higher knowledge, Enlightenment, *Nibbana*.' Once the Buddha had solved his problem, he attributed to the method or practice that he had
discovered the qualities of 'being Enlightened, bringing
about insight, bringing about knowledge; and leading to tranquillity, higher knowledge, Enlightenment, *Nibbana*.'

The problem the Buddha set himself to solve, and succeeded in solving, was that of finding a suitable method
through whose practice Enlightenment could be attained.
The method which he discovered and taught includes both
theoretical and practical aspects.

An examination of the literature shows that this Psychology of Enlightenment comprises five most important constructs, each of which can be shown to have been both
axiomatic for the Buddha prior to his attainment of Enlightenment, and also to have become fundamental to his developed psychology. I shall therefore refer to these as the
Axioms of the Psychology of Enlightenment. They are:

1. There exists a state of Enlightenment.
2. Enlightenment is attainable by a person.
3. There is a method for the attainment of Enlighten-
    ment.
4. There are discrete, ordered stages leading to En-
    lightenment.

5.   Enlightenment is both a cognitive and an affective state.

1.   There exists a state of enlightenment

This is the fundamental axiom of the Psychology of Enlightenment.

For the Buddha the very nature of human existence implied a state of Enlightenment. He said, 'There is the not born, the not manifest, the not made, non-conditioned; if there were not that not born, not manifest, not made, non-conditioned, [one] could not come to know freedom from the born, the manifest, the made, the conditioned.'[107]

The Buddha defined the State of Enlightenment, which he called *Nibbana*, as 'unconditioned'; the end of craving and passion; free from influences; Reality; beyond the cycle of transmigration; subtle; very difficult to perceive; free from weakness; permanent; free from decay; invisible to eye or consciousness; without the mental diffuseness that is brought about through craving, conceit and wrong view; calm; free from death; excellent; fortunate; safe; without craving; wonderful; marvellous; healthy; benevolent; free of passion; pure; release; without attachment; a refuge.[108]

This conceptualization of *Nibbana* becomes clear when it is related to 'Buddhist Behaviourism.'

According to Buddhist Psychology, the whole of existence is interdependent and conditioned. Nothing mental or physical can arise unconditioned by the law of cause and effect. All psychological states, including the highest Altered State of Consciousness, were regarded by the Buddha as conditioned. Only *Nibbana* is outside of this rule. It is beyond conceptualization and description, and can only be known experientially. That is why the second postulate is so important.

2.   ENLIGHTENMENT IS ATTAINABLE BY A PERSON

The empirical and scientific nature of the contents of the Buddhist literature deserve emphasis. If the Buddha had defined Enlightenment as a hypothetical state which could only be attained after physical death by some unspecified sort of entity who was, therefore, unable to provide evidence, explanation, or description of it, he would not have produced a scientific Psychology of Enlightenment. Instead, the Buddha described Enlightenment as a mental state with defined features. Furthermore, the existence of this state has been regularly confirmed throughout the history of Buddhism. Indeed, the Buddha emphasised that his method was available to all beings so long as they were participating in a human reincarnation.

It is a feature of the early literature and tradition that it emphasises the very humanness of the Buddha. It contains the history of his birth, of various formative incidents in his childhood and youth, and of the experiences that led him to seek Enlightenment and to decide to teach his method to others. It attests to his success as a teacher in its numerous histories of disciples who succeeded in attaining Enlightenment. It attests that the Buddha was subject to all the physical vicissitudes of old age, including aches and pain and physical debility. In the *Mahaparinibbanasutta*,[109] the Buddha compares his body to an old cart, held together by leather thongs, and says that he is only able to endure its discomforts through having attained concentration of mind.[110]

The really interesting question to psychologists is: what is meant in the Buddha's Psychology by 'humanness,' or 'being a person.'

In the texts, the Buddha describes two aspects of personhood: the everyday (*sammuti*), general, conversational, casual designation of the self as 'one's self,' 'myself'; and the particular scientific definition of a person which is part of the theory of the Psychology of Enlightenment. The model of the person in the Buddha's Psychology of Enlightenment is a process model. No permanent self is postulated, but instead there are processes, or functions, which succeed each other without interval.

The Buddha recognised six internal sense organs, each with its own external object. These are: the eye and the material world; the ear and sound; the nose and smell; the tongue and taste; the body and tactile objects; and the mind and mental processes. When a connection is established between an internal organ and its external object, the result is the commencement of a process. Processes are classified into five groupings (*khandha*):[111]

The first group or category of processes is the Classificatory Grouping *rupa*, which can be understood as body, or form, or the material element. According to Walpola Rahula,[112] *rupa* includes 'our five material sense organs, that is, the faculties of eye, ear, nose, tongue, and body, and their corresponding objects in the external world, that is, visible form, sound, odour, taste, and tangible things, and also some thoughts or ideas or conceptions which are in the sphere of mind objects.' It has been suggested[113] that the thoughts, ideas and conceptions that are included in this category in the sphere of mind objects include such mental representations of the outside world as imagination.

Second is the Classificatory Grouping *vedana*, which includes all affective or emotional life whether consisting of pleasant, unpleasant or neutral sensations.

Third is the Classificatory Grouping *sanna*, which is defined as that function which recognises, and the example that is given in the texts is the recognition of colour. A preliminary comparative analysis of this term in the Sanskrit literature suggests that it is the function of recognising and naming.

Fourth is the Classificatory Grouping *sankhara*, which includes all volitional activities and therefore directs the enactment of both moral and immoral actions, through body, speech and mind. A Western psychological theory that is useful in relationship to Buddhist Psychology is G.A. Kelly's Personal Construct Theory.[114] In Kelly's view, all humans operate in the world as scientists, formulating, testing, and then reformulating hypotheses. Applying Kelly's model of 'Man the Scientist,' *sanna* and *sankhara* can be understood as follows: *sanna* may be the process of forming elementary and basic constructs and hypotheses; *sankhara* that of putting these together, concretising them, in Kelly's terminology, into testable predictions. The commentaries take the view that *sanna* is the recognition of basic worldly phenomena. They give as an example of *sanna* colour recognition. An example that would fit this theory could be the recognition of something as blue, as a *sanna*, and then the theory or prediction that it may be water, and the ensuing intention to drink it or to bathe or go fishing or drown your enemy in it, acting upon which would then test the theory, as *sankhara*. That is to say, *sanna* includes both having a construct, and being able to recognise its appearance in reality; *sankhara* is both a prediction and a test. The view that *sankhara* is the formation and testing of theories is supported by the literal and etymological meaning of *sankhara* which is 'put together' or 'composed.' Perhaps as contemporary psychologists the way we can understand these two processes is to conceive of *sanna* as the process of recognising what we know: that is of matching and comparing the basic physical, sensory and mental data that we have with what we are observing at any one time; and to conceive of *sankhara* as what we then decide to do.

Fifth is the Classificatory Grouping, *vinnana*, which is conventionally translated 'consciousness,' but which may perhaps more precisely be regarded as 'apperception.' It is a function that arises through contact between a sense organ and its object, that is, visual consciousness arises through contact between the eye and an external object; auditory consciousness through contact between the ear and sound, etc.

Vinnana is made up of a rapid succession of discrete units called thought moments, each of which comprises a mental state of either emotion, *vedana*, or recognition, *sanna*, or one of fifty defined mental states of intention or volition, *sankhara*. It is also frequently compared to a flowing stream.

Where, on the conventional level, it is the person who attains Enlightenment, technically, Enlightenment means the absolute discontinuation of these processes and therefore the abandonment of 'personhood.'

3. THERE IS A METHOD FOR THE ATTAINMENT OF ENLIGHTENMENT

The Buddha was an experimental scientist. His system for the discovery of a genuine method for the attainment of Enlightenment was to test upon himself the various available methods purported to achieve this goal. He would find a good teacher, research his methods and test them by practising them to their limits, that is, until he had become the equal of the teacher.[115] At this point he would critically compare where he was at, so to speak, with his intended goal, and as we are told in the texts, he invariably found the available methods unsatisfactory and rejected them. Once he had discovered a method that satisfied him, that is, a method through which he succeeded in attaining a state of Enlightenment, he then made it available to others on the same terms. His disciples were not asked to believe him, but to test his method through practising it themselves. The success of his method is attested not only in the Buddhist literature, but also in its ever increasing practice among those in search of Enlightenment all over the world at the present time.

Very briefly, the Buddha's method for the attainment of Enlightenment is the equal development in every aspect of the Eightfold Enlightenment Path (*ariya atthangika magga*). This comprises:

> i.   Right Understanding (*sammaditthi*), which is the complete understanding of the Four Enlightenment Truths (*ariyasaccani*), that is, the Enlightenment Truth of Suffering (*dukkha*),

the Enlightenment Truth of the Arising of Suffering (*dukkhasamudaya*), the Enlightenment Truth of the Cessation of Suffering (*dukkhanirodha*), and the Enlightenment Truth of the Path to the Cessation of Suffering (*dukkhanirodhagamini patipada*).

ii. Right Intention (*sammasankappa*), which is specified with reference to renunciation of worldly life, harmfulness and ill-will.

iii. Right Speech (*sammavaca*), which means abstention from lying, back-biting, harsh speech and gossip.

iv. Right Conduct, (*sammakammanta*), which means abstention from taking life, from stealing, and from all sensual misconduct.

v. Right Livelihood (*samma-ajiva*), which means abstaining from all methods of earning a living that involve the taking of life.

vi. Right Effort (*sammavayama*), which means making the effort to discard the evil that one has already in oneself, and to prevent the arising of any further evil; and also to develop the good that has not yet arisen in oneself, and to enhance the good that already exists there.

vii. Right Mindfulness or Recollection (*sammasati*), which is the development and practice of *Vipassana*, or Insight Meditation. The results of this method of meditation are frequently comparable to the insights achieved through some psychotherapies, in that the focus of insight includes the practitioner's own behaviour patterns.

viii. Right Concentration (*sammasamadhi*), which is the development of the jhanic states through the practice of concentration.[116] The jhanic states are a series of Altered States of Con-

sciousness. These are attained in a prescribed
order through the practice of this form of
meditation.

This is a most technical and abstract statement of the method
for the attainment of Enlightenment. In fact the Buddha's
methods are very comprehensive, very flexible, and very
diverse. Within each aspect of the Eightfold Enlightenment
Path are a variety of methods and sub-methods which range
from the application of a commonsense recommendation, to
the application of sophisticated techniques. Included in the
method is the diagnosis of hindrances and of problems, and
the prescription of particular conditions and practices for
their eradication. Furthermore the literature abounds in case
histories which illustrate how particular problems were
successfully dealt with, and solved.

4. THERE ARE DISCRETE, ORDERED STAGES LEADING TO
ENLIGHTENMENT

The Buddha described three stages leading to Enlightenment:
the pre-Enlightenment stage which is exemplified by the
Ordinary Person (*puthujjana*), the trainee stage (*sekha*), and
the adept, who is called an *Arahant*. The trainee stage is
further divided into three levels: the Stream-enterer (*sotapanna*), the Once-returner (*sakadagamin*), and the Non-returner
(*anagamin*). A scientific criterion for the categorisation into
stages is provided. This is the presence or absence of ten
specified 'fetters' (*samyojana*). These are

i. The view that a permanent self or soul exists
    (*sakkayaditthi*).
ii. Certain specified doubts (*vicikiccha*): includ-
    ing doubts about the Buddha, the Teaching,
    the Order, the disciplinary rules, the past or
    the future or both of these; and about the
    Buddha's theory of Dependent Origination

(*paticca samuppada*). This theory states that nothing exists without a cause.

iii.   Adherence to rites and ceremonies (*sīlabbata-paramasa*) as if Enlightenment were attainable through their practice.

iv.   Sense-desires (*kamaraga*).

v.   Ill-will (*byapada*).

vi.   Attachment to the Realms of Form, that is, attachment to those Altered States of Consciousness associated with the four lower *jhanas* (*ruparaga*).

vii.   tachment to the Formless Realms, that is, attachment to those Altered States of Consciousness associated with the four higher *jhanas* (*aruparaga*);

viii.   Pride (*mano*).

ix.   Restlessness (*uddhacca*) and

x.   Ignorance (*avijja*).

There are additional criteria for discriminating the stage attained. One of these is the presence or absence of the 'influences' (*asavas*). These are the influence of sense desires (*kamasava*), the influence of wishing for rebirth (*bhavsava*), the influence of speculative views (*ditthasava*), and the influence of ignorance (*avijjasava*). Another criterion is provided by the assessment of the strength of the psychological drives of passion (*raga*), hatred (*dosa*) and delusion (*moda*).

As the higher levels are attained, trainees reduces their liability to rebirth until finally, at the stage of *Arahant*, they are completely free from the cycle of becoming. This is the meaning of the ultimate stage of Enlightenment.

5.   ENLIGHTENMENT IS BOTH A COGNITIVE AND AN AFFECTIVE STATE

From the point of view of the unenlightened observer there appear to be two aspects to the state of Enlightenment. One is the non-behavioural undescribable mental state of the meditating *Arahant* 'experiencing' *Nibbana*. The other is the observable result of that experience, that is, the social and public behaviour of the non-meditating *Arahant*. This has both cognitive and affective aspects.

The essence of the cognitive aspect of the state of Enlightenment is the attainment of Right Understanding. This means the complete understanding of the Four Enlightenment. Truths.

Understanding the First Truth, Suffering, means perceiving that birth, old age, illness, death, grief, lamentation, suffering, dejection, unsettled conditions, not obtaining one's desires, and the Five Classificatory Groupings, are all suffering.[117]

Understanding the Second Truth means perceiving that the Arising of Suffering is Craving (*tanha*). Craving appears to be the equivalent in this Psychology of Freud's pleasure principle. It is described as having as its characteristics the search for pleasure and passion, and the capacity for indiscriminate enjoyment. Craving leads to continual rebirth. It is described as threefold: craving for sense pleasure (*kamatanha*), craving for existence (*bhavatanha*), and craving for non-existence (*vibhavatanha*).[118]

Understanding the Third Truth means knowing the total abolition and abandonment of craving.[119]

Understanding the Fourth Truth means knowing and practising the method for the attainment of Enlightenment: the Eightfold Enlightenment Path.[120] Part of this Right Understanding is the perception that the nature of existence is impermanent (*anicca*), unsatisfactory (*dukkha*), and without a permanent self or soul (*anatta*). These, then, are the contents of the cognitive aspect of the state of Enlightenment.

The Buddha's Psychology of Enlightenment specifies not only the nature and content of the knowledge necessary for the attainment of Enlightenment; it also defines the sort of knowledge that is irrelevant for the attainment of Enlightenment. Included in this category are speculations concerning what happens to the Buddha after his physical death; whether the universe is finite or infinite; whether the soul and the body are the same or different; and speculations concerning one's past or future existences, and the nature of the self. Such speculations are defined as characteristic of the pre-Enlightenment stage, that is, of the stage of the Ordinary Person (*puthujjana*).[121]

Once again Kelly's Personal Construct Theory is useful. It enables us to say that, whereas the Ordinary Person characteristically formulates unrealistic and speculative theories about the nature of existence, in the *Arahant*, who has completely developed Right Understanding, and who has become entirely free from conditioning and influences, the situation is quite different. In the Enlightened state of consciousness all personal constructs have been eradicated, and there is a perfect correspondence between the mind of the perceiver and the phenomena perceived.[122]

What about the affective state that comprises Enlightenment?

Progress through the lower stages is achieved through the annihilation of such affective motivating drives as sensual desires, ill-will, attachment, passion, hatred, craving, and so forth. These gradually lose their impulsive energy during the trainee stages, until, at the highest level, in the *Arahant*, they are quite powerless as motivating forces. Instead of being impelled by such drives as desire, or turbulent emotional states, the psychological drives of the *Arahant* are Friendliness (*metta*), Compassion (*karuna*), Kindliness (*mudita*), and Equanimity (*upekkha*).

Friendliness technically means 'the desire to bring to others that which is good and conducive to their welfare';[123] Compassion: 'the desire to remove suffering and what goes against their welfare from others'; and Kindliness: 'the desire that others should not be dissociated from what is good and beneficial.' Sometimes these three are thought of as 'active love,' 'preventive love,' and 'disinterested love.'[124] It is, however, profoundly difficult to explain Equanimity in psychological terms. It can possibly be conceived of as the ability to observe, and to see things as they really are, without becoming involved, that is, as a sort of wise impartiality.

I began with the problem of how contemporary psychology was to understand the Buddha and Buddhism. It seems rather that the Buddha has understood it! His Psychology of Enlightenment, and indeed the very concept of a Psychology of Enlightenment, is extremely relevant to modern psychology and indeed has important practical and theoretical implications for it.

Practically, the definition of the goal of this Psychology of Enlightenment, its concept of the person, the methods it offers, and its concept of developmental stages, all provide a challenge to psychological theories concerned with personal change.

With regard to the theory of psychology, this Psychology of Enlightenment provides a challenging new model of human beings, an Enlightenment model. At the moment the psychological model is largely mechanical, based on the computer; we are all machines carrying out programmes. The Buddha, too, observed that people are somewhat mechanical − his technical term for this is 'conditioned' (*samkhata*) − and he provided a method through whose practice it was possible to become unconditioned (*asamkhata*). Just as the the widespread adoption of the mechanical model has affected the way people conceive of and behave towards each other, so too the Enlightenment model has important general implications. A machine cannot feel hurt and is not responsible for its actions, but it must surely be the case that the more aware one is of one's own potential for becoming Enlightened, the more aware one will become of the conditions contingent upon it. ·Such persons, for example, would not risk putting their Enlightenment in danger by harming another living being.

Further, each of the axioms − definitions of the goal, the person, the methods, the stages, and of the cognitive and affective contents − which are developed to the extreme in

Buddhist psychology, is present in a weak or strong form in every psychotherapy. Moreover, each of these postulates, and therefore the paradigm itself, is completely doctrinally neutral. This paradigm therefore provides a theory within whose framework the amorphous collection of modern psychotherapies can be understood and evaluated.[125]

8
The Three Facets of Buddha-mind

Andrew Rawlinson

Andrew Rawlinson is a Lecturer in Buddhism at the Department of Religious Studies at the University of Lancaster. His main research fields are early Mahayana Buddhism and the new religious movements. He is currently writing a book on Western gurus and enlightened masters.

THE MAHAYANA HAS a great range of technical terms that can be rather daunting to people who come across them for the first time. But in fact the central teaching of the Mahayana is very simple: right here and now there is available to us a constant stream of warmth and light. It is like liquid gold — pure, flowing, clear. We may temporarily obscure it, but no action and no thought, however self-obsessed, can completely prevent this spontaneous welling up of delight. It is a gift that is always offered and in the end we will accept it. And when we do, life will be simultaneously still and vibrant, magical and completely ordinary.

The Mahayana brings together three terms in order to express this idea, and fuses them into one. They are: Buddha, mind (*citta*) and emptiness (*sunyata*). 'Buddha' does not (just) mean the historical Gautama — it refers to the state of enlightenment (*bodhi*). The term enlightenment-mind (*bodhicitta*) is common in Mahayana texts. According to one *sutra*, the enlightenment-mind is brightly shining (*prabhasvara*). Another says: 'There is no other mind apart from the reality-mind (*dharmatacitta*) which is brightly shining.' Saraha, one of the Eighty-four Siddhas, says: 'Mind is the universal seed; both *samsara* and *nirvana* spring forth from it.'

Yet, as the *Lankavatara Sutra* makes clear, this mind (*citta*) is empty (*sunya*) — that is, it is not full of itself but open, unrestricted, immeasurable. According to Tilopa, another of the Eighty-four Siddhas and the teacher of Naropa, although mind is empty, it contains all things. In fact, we could say that *because* it is empty, it contains all things. Why? Because it is open to all things and rejects nothing. It is present everywhere — a living presence.

Naturally, this mind cannot be grasped; it is empty, therefore there is nothing that we can get hold of and make our own. Emptiness (*sunyata*) is identical with no-self (*anatman*). It is that which the Buddha realized but it cannot be restricted to him as an individual. The Buddha's realization is his acceptance of the gift, universally offered. This mind is Buddha-mind — empty, open and free.

On this central pivot of Buddha-mind, the Mahayana balances its three fundamental moves. These are the three facets of Buddha-mind which comprise all forms of experience. In fact, the Mahayana has two sets of three terms which both do the same job. One is concerned with the nature of consciousness and the other with ways of being in *samsara*. (In other words, one's inner condition is reflected in one's behaviour towards others.)

THE NATURE OF CONSCIOUSNESS	WAYS OF BEING IN SAMSARA
sila (morality)	*karuna* (compassion)
samadhi (concentration)	*upaya-kausalya* (skill-in-means)
prajna (wisdom)	*prajna* (wisdom)

They intertwine with each other to form an inseparable unity and can be discussed in any order.

It is of very little help to translate *sila* by 'morality' (though this is its literal meaning). It is certainly an ethical concept but not one that is dependent on convention. Rather, it is the response to excellence. The three terms that sum it up best are generosity, purity and love. That is, we are free of their opposites: greed, impurity and selfishness. It is therefore easy to see the good in others and to appreciate their qualities. We are generous because we are not seeking anything for ourselves (which is the essence of love). But this generosity can only be if we are pure — which simply means that we do not harbour negative emotions and project them onto others. In short, we have an essential trust. And this trust is what allows compassion. Not in the sense that we are alright and wish graciously to help others who are not. Quite the opposite, in fact. We are all in the same boat and our compassion is of the form 'Yes, I know what it's like,' not 'I'm sure it's terrible; it certainly looks it.'

The consequence of this purity and trust is that life becomes very light and joyful, like a warm summer's day. We are constantly giving without calculating what the value of our gift is or how much it costs us. It is a child-like quality and it stems from the same source as the trust that a child has: we are also being given that warmth and light. We are looked after. *Sila* is the activity of an open heart.

The word *samadhi* is often translated as 'concentration' but in the context of the Mahayana this is very misleading. What it really means is that the universal Buddha-mind is infinitely flexible. There are two sides to this idea, both of which are included in the teaching of skill-in-means (*upaya-kausalya*). Cosmologically, it means that all the forms of the universe have their source in mind — that is, reality-mind (*dharma-tacitta*). So things are not separate at all, as they appear to be to one who is closed (and therefore himself separate). Everything is in the embrace of the one Buddha-mind. As the T'ien T'ai school of China put it: 'Every colour and every fragrance is none other than the middle way [= truth = reality-mind = Buddha-mind].' Psychologically — that is, in terms of experience of the world — what is implied by the notion of skill-in-means is that every situation without exception is a means of transformation. And the best words to sum up the *samadhi* facet of Buddha-mind are transformation, communication, workability. Naturally, the cosmological and psychological aspects of skill-in-means are connected. Those who know that the universe is like a vast ocean containing waves, ripples and spray, also know that there is nothing that can restrict them. Traditional Buddhism had taught that everything is impermanent; the Mahayana sees the other side to this assertion — that everything is flowing. Every situation contains its own solution or resolution. There is always room for action; we are never pinned down. And because the universe is always flowing, we can say that it is always communicating. And because it is the nature of Buddhamind to communicate, to constantly transform, we always benefit. Every situation is workable — that is, there is always space to move. It is only when we are afflicted with the opposite attributes to *samadhi* — namely, rigidity and coagulation — that we believe otherwise.

The quality of life that we experience as a result of *samadhi* is that of magic and energy — like a spring morning. Thus the lightness and joy of *sila* are complemented by the inexhaustible flow of transformation that *samadhi* reveals. (And it *is* a revelation because Buddha-mind communicates and therefore reveals; the opposite of shutting off is revealing.) Anything is possible because awareness (= Buddha-mind) is free. So the world is magical — which is to say, transformable. And unlimited energy is available to us to bring about this transformation. It is as much a gift as the lightness and joy of *sila*. And because it is associated with action and energy, it has the quality of being in one's prime, that glorification in physical expression that is the acme of a human being's bodily existence. If the image of *sila* is a child's smile, then the image of *samadhi* is the strength of the father. To provide energy is to receive it. It is the activity of an open hand.

Wisdom (*prajna*) complements *sila* and *samadhi*. It is the insight that comes from letting go, the realization that nothing can be possessed. It is therefore entirely effortless, for one who has this realization has nothing to prove. Like a wise old man who has seen everything, wisdom has an open mind. (This does not mean, of course, being liberal in one's opinions; an open mind is one that contains everything because it does not judge and therefore does not exclude.) Its qualities are instantaneousness and clarity. It is easy to see that these are closely related to the corresponding qualities of *sila* (lightness and joy) and *samadhi* (magic and energy). Similarly, the insight of wisdom is simply another facet of the communication of skill-in-means and the love of compassion. On a clear day, you can see forever.

These three patterns of Buddha-mind and their opposites (see diagrams) provide a rich vocabulary of experience — and one that is linked to the seminal terms of Mahayana Buddhism. The principles on which they are constructed are simple but the ramifications are subtle. For example, *ayoniso manasikara* is translated as 'weak attention' but since it is the opposite of *samadhi* which has the sense of flexible/strong/energetic mind, its proper meaning is 'inflexible mind.' This, of course, goes well with rigidity and fixedness. And it also neatly connects with *dvesa* or hatred, which is not limited to the emotion of hatred but refers to a refusal to change. In other words, *dvesa* is a compulsion to say 'No,' a rejection, a turning away from the possibility of transformation. And we know from our own experience that we often practise this form of negativity — but without connecting it with the emotional violence of hatred. Yet the two are indissolubly linked; rejection always underlies hatred. Similarly, flatness and boredom are also versions of *dvesa* (because weak attention has no energy). They are a kind of desperate self-protection which precludes all risk because of an overwhelming fear of failure. They give rise to the strategies of over-carefulness and the over-exact — the consciousness of the closed hand. Or we could say: not diving into the stream for fear of getting wet (let alone the fear of drowning). But the flexible mind enjoys the water and is exhilarated by the flow. Besides, we cannot drown — we are always carried along.

Just as there is a psychology of *dvesa*, so there is a psychology of *raga* or passion. The opposite of compassion is self-indulgence, an attempt to devour the world. *Raga* is the compulsion of the overdose which must always consume and can never truly share. This is why it leads to heaviness and despair — for despair is the movement of the heart that can find no peace because it cannot trust. *Raga* is terrified of gaps in experience, which is why it seeks to fill every gap to overflowing. But this strategy can never succeed. The gaps are part of reality-mind and out of them shines the pure light of joy. But *raga* cannot just let this light shine; it demands a substitute because it cannot bear to wait. But the substitute never satisfies. Indeed, *raga is* dissatisfaction (because it is the inevitable consequence of greed). And what is the solution? To give up one's demand. And this giving up is not a calculation; it is not giving up in order to receive. It is very simple and pure (as all aspects of *sila* are). It is giving up our demand because there is no need for it. The warmth and light of Buddha-mind are an inexhaustible treasure — and in the face of it, there can be no demanding, no hoarding, no meanness. This is the generosity of an open heart.

The psychology of *moha* (delusion) is, if anything, even more complex. This is because *moha* is the compulsion to complicate everything. It is associated with all clumsiness, prevarication and muddle. Its essential quality is self-deception, which is the root of all ignorance (*avidya*). This self-deception is a wilfulness not to see clearly — for if we do see clearly, we have to accept responsibility for ourselves and everything and everybody we are involved with. To avoid this terrifying consequence, we put off resolving anything — just so that we can become lost in the struggle to find a solution. For as long as we are lost, we can avoid responsibility. So we carry our burden, bemoaning its weight and inconvenience, but holding on to it all the time. If we put it down, then who would we be?

We would be Buddha. We would be empty. We would be free.

It sounds too good to be true — but an open heart has the supreme confidence that it is so. It sounds like too great a task to accomplish — but an open hand is ready to try anything. It sounds too simple to be convincing — but the wisdom of an open mind knows that one day it will happen.

Quietly, without fuss, with great love and inexhaustible energy, in every colour and fragrance, however dark or turbulent our lives — Buddha-mind keeps on giving. It is a presence that never leaves us. This is what the Mahayana teaches.

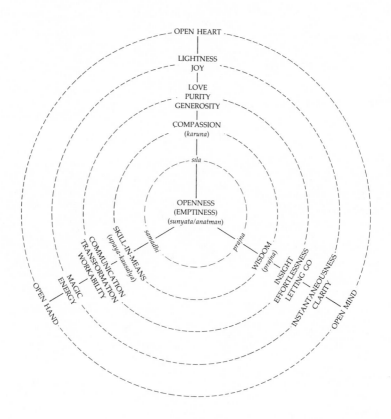

The three facets of Buddha-mind...

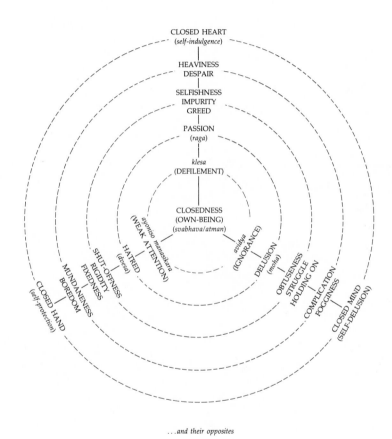

CLOSED HEART
(*self-indulgence*)

HEAVINESS
DESPAIR

SELFISHNESS
IMPURITY
GREED

PASSION
(*raga*)

klesa
(DEFILEMENT)

CLOSEDNESS
(OWN-BEING)
(*svabhava/atman*)

ayoniso manaskara
(WEAK ATTENTION)

avidya
(IGNORANCE)

HATRED
(*dvesa*)

DELUSION
(*moha*)

SHUT-OFFNESS
RIGIDITY
FIXEDNESS

OBTUSENESS
STRUGGLE
HOLDING ON

MUNDANENESS
BOREDOM

COMPLICATION
FOGGINESS

CLOSED HAND
(*self-protection*)

CLOSED MIND
(SELF-DELUSION)

...and their opposites

Part Two
Applications

9
Buddhism and Psychotherapy: A Buddhist Perspective

Ian Wray (Advayacitta)

Ian Wray (Advayacitta) is currently Senior Clinical Psychologist at St. Andrew's Hospital, Norwich, with a special interest in schizophrenia and in psychological problems associated with criminal offending. He is also a member of the Western Buddhist Order, regularly teaching meditation to beginners.

BUDDHISM HAS FOR over a century been of great interest to Westerners, its combination of intellectually sophisticated doctrines, down-to-earth practicalities and spiritual profundities being especially fascinating. Along with this interest there has been a real difficulty in understanding precisely what Buddhism actually is. It has been considered to be a religion, a philosophy, a system of ethics and even a form of protocommunism. Each of these views has neglected some aspect of Buddhism which did not really fit in with it.

Nowadays Buddhism's parallels with psychotherapy are being noted, and it is being studied from a psychological perspective. Thus another body of opinion is growing up that Buddhism is more like a form of psychotherapy, with perhaps the same goals as Jungian analysis, or psychoanalysis, or behaviour therapy. This is part of a general trend of looking at Eastern traditions as forms of psychotherapy, or at least seeing the parallels between them.[126] This is arguably a considerable improvement over the other views, in that it recognises that Buddhism is concerned with helping people change and with helping them overcome emotional suffering, as are the various psychotherapies. It also recognises Buddhism's psychological sophistication and its practical and theoretical concern with human character and mental states. Comparing Buddhism with psychotherapy is very valuable, but there is a danger. To understand the unknown the first step is that of assimilation — of trying to fit it into existing categories of thought — but there is the further step of accommodation, the extension of those categories so that they take account of what is new in the unknown. If the process of accommodation does not occur there is a danger of distortion, in this case of seeing Buddhism as merely a form of psychotherapy and nothing more.

Parallels there certainly are, and very interesting ones; they are many and varied. One could, for example, study the story of the Buddha's Enlightenment and find clear examples of Jungian 'archetypes' in it. Or one could look at the Buddha's sophisticated understanding of psychological 'defences' from a psychoanalytic point of view. Alternatively one could note the similarities between the Buddhist doctrine of '*anatta*' and the psychological analyses of the *Abhidharma* on the one hand, and behavioural psychology on the other (see Chapter 12).

However the divergences must also be recognised — the spiritual distinguished from the psychological. The above examples do not imply that the Buddhist path to Enlightenment is the same thing as the process which Jung termed 'individuation,' or that Buddhism is essentially the same as psychoanalysis or behaviour therapy. The different aims of Buddhism and psychotherapy, and their different bases, need to be clearly recognised. Psychotherapy aims to establish emotional health, with the overcoming of psychological problems and the cure of neurosis, whilst Buddhism aims to go much further than this, with the attainment of emotional health being but the first stage in its path of human development. Psychotherapy is based upon the intellectual traditions of the West, whilst Buddhism claims to be based upon a Wisdom which transcends the intellect.

THE PSYCHOTHERAPIES

Psychology and the psychotherapies are relatively recent

developments within Western culture, and their basis is very much that of mainstream Western thought − particularly 'science' − although some schools of psychotherapy would dispute this. Academic psychology grew up in the nineteenth century as a deliberate attempt to study the mind from a 'scientific' perspective − William James called psychology 'the science of mental life.' Psychoanalysis started in similar fashion, and nowadays the mainstream of clinical psychology follows the 'scientific' direction of academic psychology, especially of behaviourism and cognitive psychology.

Let us look first of all at the scientific basis of psychology. From the time of Wilhelm Wundt in the nineteenth century academic psychology has self-consciously attempted to be a science. Such a view is still dominant. Typically the term 'science' is used with 'materialist' connotations − employing the latter term in its philosophical sense − that is, that the universe consists of nothing but physical matter. Thus 'science' is assumed to be exemplified by the study of physical matter. Physics is true science, so the argument goes, and other subjects, including psychology, to be truly scientific must be ultimately reducible to the study of matter, with their theories and methodology modelled upon those of physics. To allow that there might be more to the universe than physical matter is to be superstitious, subjective and unscientific − or so this particular philosophy of science would have us believe.[127]

Thus in the West we are in the curious situation of believing that our ideas are only legitimate if they are in accord with 'science,' a situation which extends into the religious sphere with the result that those who are not fundamentalists adhering rigidly to a set of scriptures feel the need to justify their ideas as being acceptably scientific. This has many consequences. Since the materialist philosophy associated with this common idea of what is scientific is actually in conflict with religious or spiritual thought, then anyone who uncritically accepts 'science' and what it is supposed to have proven, and who has a religious or spiritual aspiration, is in a very difficult position. His religion is likely to amount to a form of humanism, without any spiritual or transcendental content. There is also a further consequence: religions (and for the moment I include Buddhism under this heading) are *studied* from such a 'scientific' perspective, with their non-materialist claims disbelieved a priori, or 'bracketed' as certain sociologists put it.[128]

So a curious development has happened. In the Western world the study of human beings is modelled upon the study of physical matter, and this is seen as appropriate. There is a further curiosity — therapies to help people overcome their emotional problems are apparently legitimated by, or derived from, such materialistic psychology. Freud, for example, began as a neurologist, and based his thinking upon assumptions derived from nineteenth century physics. Psychiatry is based upon physical models of mental illness. Behaviour therapy, which dominates clinical psychology, stems theoretically from behaviourism, a radically materialist form of academic psychology which reduced 'the science of mental life' to the study of behaviour, the observable physical changes and actions of an organism.

Of course human beings are rarely without their contradictions, and this is true of psychologists and therapists as well. Freudians, behaviourists, and other therapists all go beyond their materialist theories in actual practice. Moreover, they also derive ideas from other sources outside of science, whether explicitly or not, and as such are influenced by other factors within Western culture, including Christianity, and also what I would call the 'liberal humanist' tradition. There are other influences too, from existentialism and from the more heterodox Western religions, as in Jungian Analysis.[129] So the theories behind psychological therapies are composite, consisting of ideas derived explicity from 'scientific' tradition and those derived from other sources within Western culture, with a different mix of ideas depending on the type of psychotherapy.

A more indirect influence on psychotherapy than science,

and perhaps more obvious to the 'outsider' such as a Buddhist, is that of Christianity. This has imposed structures upon Western thought which science and other modern disciplines have not necessarily overcome, embedding certain assumptions within Western thought, or leaving certain gaps, which may only become explicit when one encounters a non-Western tradition which does not have them. The first such assumption stems from the Christian conception of the basis of ethics, the importance of which will become clear when I discuss the Buddhist conception of the relationship of ethics to mental states.

Now the predominant trend in Christianity is to think of ethics in legalistic terms as stemming from an external person who has authority and power, that is, God. This is very clear in the Old Testament, with its 'ten commandments,' in which ethics 'is conformity of human activity to the will of God' and the question 'what ought I to do? receives the answer 'obey God.'[130] It is also evident in the Gospels, in which even the Sermon on the Mount can be taken as representing 'the absolute will of God' and Jesus' ethical teaching summarized as a 'twofold commandment' of loving God and one's neighbour.[131]

There are of course other strands to Christian ethical thinking. Obeying God is not necessarily perceived as obeying the commands of an arbitrary or contingent power, since God is believed to be intrinsically good. Associated with this there is a conception of natural ethics and natural conscience, although this is vague. So for the Christian, following one's conscience and what seems naturally right or good is in reality to obey God's will. However, no matter how ethics are conceived by Christians, their ultimate justification is believed to stem from God, either as ultimate authority or as creator of what is natural. In either case they are seen in terms of moral *law*.

The rise of science has seen the denial of the existence of God, with the subsequent breakdown in the belief in the existence of ethics, since these are still seen implicitly in legalistic terms. If there is no ultimate authority and power to legislate ethics how can they exist or be important? Almost inevitably ethics have come to be seen as matters of convenience, rules by which social groups function harmoniously — and as different groups have different rules, which conflict, there can be no objectively existing, natural ethical principles, or so it seems to many a modern person. Thus the dilemma seems to be: either God and ethics, or neither. The only possible alternative seems to be that ethics involve the pursuit of happiness, where happiness is frequently taken to be synonymous with economic prosperity. That ethics might be intimately connected with a person's mental state is a possibility that seems not to have been seen.

The other aspect of Christianity which I wish to discuss here is what I would term its traditional lack of a therapeutics, by which I mean the lack of any real body of ideas and practices to help people change. The theologian Tillich argues that Christianity has been primarily concerned with the problem of 'justification' rather than that of 'sanctification,' that is, in being saved through the grace of God by believing in him, not so much with improving oneself morally and otherwise through one's own efforts (although this is perhaps more a Protestant view). This emphasis is reflected in the lack of Christian practices aimed at practical self-improvement (especially in comparison with Eastern traditions.) Christianity emphasises being saved through the grace of God, whether this be through a once and for all rite such as baptism, through the mediating actions of priests, or through on-going activities such as prayer and 'meditation' upon scripture or doctrine. Spiritual exercises tend to follow a pattern of prayer and meditation, though these are very different from Buddhist 'meditation' (which is more appropriately termed 'cultivation'). Even the spiritual exercises of Christian 'mystics' follow this pattern, of dwelling intellectually upon the dogma of Christianity and praying to God to help one change (and thus even sanctification is seen not so much due to one's own efforts but to God's grace). Of course there is also 'contemplation,' a higher form a prayer which bears closer resemblance to Buddhist 'meditation,' or at least some types of it, and the descriptions by some Christian 'mystics' of their experiences during contemplative prayer seem to bear a resemblance to *dhyana*, an important outcome of Buddhist 'meditation.' Nevertheless such experiences are still seen as gifts of God's grace, neither essential for salvation nor accessible to any but a fortunate few, and contemplation has not traditionally been seen as a method of self-development for all.[132]

It is against the background of this lack of a Christian therapeutics that the rise of modern psychotherapy must be seen, for the near total absence of practical aids to human psychological and spiritual growth within Christianity left a vacuum which psychotherapy had to fill, based upon principles which it had to discover for itself. Let us turn now to took more closely at these principles.

Literally hundreds of different therapies have been developed, based ostensibly upon very different principles. In a chapter as short as this it would be impossible to discuss any of them in depth, but let us look briefly at the different types of therapeutic school. These are usually divided into three categories — psychodynamic, behavioural, and experiential/existential.[133]

Psychodynamic therapy stems principally from Freud, although there are important schools which differ widely from the Freudian, such as the Jungian (to which I shall return). Such therapy is based upon the notion of neurosis being due to internal, unconscious conflicts within the psyche, conflicts which almost inevitably arise during the early years of life due to the frustrations which the reality of living with other human beings imposes upon the child's attempts to gratify primitive instincts. Therapy is aimed at making the patient consciously aware of those unconscious conflicts which underly his neurosis. Thus 'insight' into those conflicts is seen as the crucial aspect of change, although 'catharsis' — the re-experiencing of repressed emotion — is also seen as important. Such conflicts are deliberately brought into the open by the therapist taking an emotionally cool approach so that 'transference' occurs, that is, the patient experiences emotional reactions to the therapist which are in effect his earlier emotional reactions as a child to significant adults, 'projected' inappropriately onto the therapist. Later schools emphasised a warmer therapeutic relationship, and also stressed the social-psychological aspects of neurosis, in comparison to Freud's emphasis on neurosis being the result of biological instincts.

Behaviour therapy, on the other hand, stems from behaviourist learning theory, and emphasises that psychological problems are in some way 'learned' and that the patient can 'learn' to overcome them, providing techniques and exercises by which the patient can do this. Behaviourism is a school of psychology which, philosophically, is materialist, and as such emphasises that only overt behaviour is open to objective study, thoughts and emotions always being matters of conjecture, if they exist at all. In practice behaviour therapists are not so extreme in their philosophy, and readily take into account more than a person's overt behaviour — as a therapist must of necessity. These days cognitive-behaviour therapy is growing in importance. It is a development from behaviourism and cognitive psychology which in effect contradicts the basic tenets of behaviourism as it emphasises the influence of thoughts upon behaviour and emotions. Behaviour therapy and cognitive behaviour therapy have been fruitful sources of effective therapeutic techniques, due to their optimistic emphasis on learning, their concern with demonstrating practical efficacy, and the humane therapeutic relationships which behaviour therapists build up with their clients (and which contradict the mechanistic and occasionally authoritarian language in which the theories of behaviourism is often couched).

Experiential schools, sometimes referred to as humanist-existential, stem from other sources. Existential therapies, Rogerian 'client centred therapy,' and Gestalt therapy are perhaps the three most important types. They explicitly emphasise individual human growth, and can recognise a higher spiritual element to this, concerning themselves with 'the whole man' and the meaningfulness of life. Therapeutically they emphasise the positive, encouraging the autonomy and self-responsibility of the patient or client, usually focussing on 'the here and now' — especially the clear communication of one's true feelings unhindered by neurotic obstacles. Existential therapists especially recognise the importance of 'meaning' in a person's life, and hence that neurosis can result from a 'meaningless' life. Rogerian 'client-centred therapy,' or 'counselling,' emphasises the 'warmth, genuineness, and empathy' of the therapist, the need to be 'nondirective,' and the encouragement of the client's positive self image and sense of worth. Gestalt therapy has a practical concern with techniques to encourage genuine emotional expression unhindered by neurotic blocks.

This threefold division of therapies is perhaps an oversimplification, as there are schools which do not fit into it very easily. Therapists whose ideas and practices stem from the work of Milton Erickson or Gregory Bateson would be important exceptions. Jungian analysis can justifiably be seen as rather different to psychoanalysis, especially as it is not based upon ideas derived from nineteenth century physics and recognises the validity of religious life. Jung's theories concerning 'archetypes' and 'individuation' are of course playing an increasing role in the psychological approach to religion, and are an important bridge over which people can cross from a 'scientific' to a religious or spiritual view of life.

So the schools of psychotherapy have different starting points and perspectives. They also discover different things about therapy and about human beings. Nevertheless there are many things which they have in common, especially when therapists are less dogmatic about theory and concern themselves with the practicalities of helping people change. Many would in fact call themselves 'eclectic,' implying that they are open to ideas and practices from different schools.

Indeed I believe that in recent years therapists of different persuasions have been discovering which practices really do work, with the result that the different schools of therapy are drawing closer together. As just one example of this one could compare cognitive-behaviour therapy and 'strategic therapy,' the latter emphasising practical techniques and 'task setting' as much as the former, without any adherence to behavioural learning theory. As well as drawing closer together, and associated with this process, therapists have been building up a specialised body of knowledge of great practical benefit. There are many aspects to this: how to construct a graded series of tasks so that a patient overcomes a phobia; how to challenge someone's ideas so that they no longer 'think themselves' into depression; how to get the parents of a schizophrenic to talk to him in a manner which will not cause a relapse; how to use precisely the right wording to overcome a person's resistance to a particular aspect of therapy; how to get him to express himself honestly without anxiety — and there are many, many more examples which could be cited.

So the psychotherapies have grown up to overcome human psychological problems. They use a great variety of techniques to bring about psychological health, and although they are divisible into different types there seem to be important similarities, especially where effective techniques are concerned — a point to which I shall return later. How then do they compare with Buddhism?

THE BASIS OF BUDDHISM

At first sight the many schools of Buddhism might seem as disparate as the varieties of psychotherapy. However they are united by a common basis which appears to be uniquely Buddhist. That basis is *prajna*, or 'transcendental wisdom.' Buddhist ideas and practices ultimately stem from the experience of *prajna*, or the experience of the world from the standpoint of an individual who has cultivated *prajna*. This experience, or vision of the world, is expressed on the intellectual level in such doctrines as *'anatta,' 'sunyata'* and *'pratitya samutpada,'* which are unique to Buddhism, and it is the practical aim of committed Buddhists to develop *prajna* so that they see the truth of these doctrines for themselves. It must be emphasised that *prajna* is not merely an intellectual quality (nor even mundane wisdom), and that its cultivation requires the preliminary development of both ethical conduct and a positive mental state to very high levels indeed. *Prajna* is as much Compassion as Wisdom, and requires loving kindness as a prerequisite. Hence the intellectual study of these doctrines, although at times important, is insufficient, the corollary of this being that any parallels between non-Buddhist ideas and these intellectual expressions of *prajna* are likely to be deceptive. The terms *'anatta,' 'sunyata'* and *'pratitya samutpada'* are usually translated as 'no self,' 'emptiness' and 'conditioned co-production' respectively, translations which give few clues to their meaning and which can easily lead one astray. The original terms are best learned, even on an intellectual level, in context — through the thorough study and practice of Buddhism. Some glimpse of their meaning can perhaps be gained by studying a few of their implications, for example what Buddhism has to say about human development, and about psychotherapy and the theories upon which it is based.

I have already alluded briefly to the Buddhist conception of human development in mentioning the cultivation of *prajna* and the preliminary development of ethical conduct and a positive mental state. These together form the three-fold path of *'sila, samadhi* and *prajna'* — the cultivation of increasingly ethical conduct, of a concentrated, tranquil but vibrantly energetic and joyful state of mind, and of the subsequent Transcendental Wisdom and Compassion arising like a flower on a healthy plant. Buddhism is essentially about such human development — the intrinsic purpose of the *Dharma* is human growth. Indeed, the doctrines of *anatta* and *pratitya samutpada* imply that there is no fixed personality and that given the appropriate conditions development will occur. Let us look more closely at this process of development.

First there is the question of 'ethical conduct' to consider. Earlier I discussed the question of ethics in Christianity and the West, and made the point that ethics were seen in terms of 'law.' The Buddhist conception of ethics is very different, although this is not often appreciated. Buddhism does not talk in terms of 'right' and 'wrong' but uses the different concepts of 'skilfulness' and 'unskilfulness' (which are very definitely not synonymous with the former concepts.) Skilfulness is an ethico-psychological concept: actions are seen as skilful if they are the expression of, or conducive to, skilful mental states, that is, mental states characterised by compassion, tranquillity, joyfulness and clarity. They are unskilful if they are expressive of greed, hatred and delusion. Skilful actions are those which are conducive to human development, and particularly to the development of *samadhi* and *prajna*. It is axiomatic in Buddhism that skilfulness is beneficial to both self and other, whilst unskilfulness brings suffering eventually to both.

Secondly, one of the most frequent terms one can come across in Buddhist texts is *'dhyana'* (Pali: *jhana*), a word for which there is no adequate translation. It refers to various states of mind characterised by concentration, tranquillity and positive emotion; *dhyana* can become more and more intense, and traditionally is divided into different levels. (*Dhyana* is synonymous with *'samadhi'* in the sense in which I have used the latter term above.)[134] Perhaps 'states of mind' is not quite correct — 'levels of personality integration' would perhaps be a better term. The attainment of *dhyana* is a very important prerequisite for the cultivation of *prajna*, and much of Buddhist meditation, or *'bhavana,'* is aimed at the development of *dhyana*. The state of mind, or level of personality integration, in which one has to be in order to begin the cultivation of *dhyana* is in itself representative of a high level of psychological health. Thus higher spiritual development is dependent upon prior psychological health, or, putting it another way, the first task of the average neurotic Westerner intent on spiritual development is to overcome his or her neuroses. Thus the concerns of spiritual life overlap in the beginning with the concerns of psychotherapy, although spiritual development eventually goes far beyond psychological development as conceived by psychotherapists.

Now 'neurosis' is not a Buddhist concept, and traditional Buddhism does not concern itself with the cure of neurosis as such. But it does concern itself with overcoming the various obstacles to *dhyana*, and these are worth looking at from a psychotherapeutic point of view. First there are the inner 'hindrances' to *dhyana* — worry, hatred, doubt, sensuous craving, sloth — that seem to comprise in themselves a catalogue of neurotic mental states. Here 'hatred' includes self-hatred, and 'doubt' self-doubt; 'sensuous craving' can be a straightforward desire for sense gratification strong enough to divert one's mind from its meditation, but also can be a form of craving for sensuous experience to make up for a feeling of inner emptiness. I think that psychotherapists will recognise the ubiquity of the hindrances in neurosis fairly readily. One of the hindrances is worry, which also includes anxiety and fear, and is recognised as often being the result of unskilfulness, that is, of actions rooted in mental states of greed, hatred and delusion. This subject is too vast to go into in detail, but one point worth noting is that Buddhist theory implies that we can be to a certain extent responsible for causing our own neuroses, by acting unskilfully in the first place. As I mentioned above, skilful actions (including speech and thought) are important in bringing about a healthy mental state: in other words ethical behaviour is a prerequisite for mental health. So our thoughts can affect our mental state, as the cognitive therapist knows well.

Buddhism also recognises that external conditions can also influence our mental state, as many people who have been meditating 'on retreat' discover. They find that the enjoyable and more concentrated mental state they have developed on retreat is rapidly dissipated by outside influences, a phenomenon which bears thinking about, for if many meditators discover that their mental state is affected by their environment, what effect is that environment having on other people? There are various aspects of the external environment which are of importance: physical surroundings, social relationships and friendships, intellectual and emotional influences. Thus a simple yet beautiful physical environment, emotionally enriching friendships, and exposure to emotionally positive ideas clearly expressed are of great importance to the development of *dhyana*. Their opposites are recipes for neurosis. Perhaps I should stress the importance which ideas have in their effects on mental state. Ideas, and systematised ideas such as philosophies, religions, and political theories can be unskilful, in that they may be expressions of unskilful mental states and can encourage the development of such states in people who are exposed to them. The Buddhist must then consider any system of ideas in the light of how 'skilful' it might be — and this includes psychotherapy.

What of Buddhist practices such as meditation? Can these be of use to the person suffering from neurosis, even if he is a long way from attaining *dhyana*? The straightforward answer is that they can, in that neurotic people (and even psychotic people) have gained great benefit from meditation without first attaining *dhyana*. Through the practice of the meditation called the 'mindfulness of breathing,' for example, people can become more tranquil and relaxed than they were previously; they can release more emotional energy to cope with the demands of life; and they can actually clear up their neurotic conflicts as their awareness of their own minds deepens through the practice of the meditation. They see through their neuroses and what is maintaining them. The 'mindfulness of breathing' is a meditation which is intended for the cultivation of 'mindfulness,' a crucial faculty according to Buddhism, which one can perhaps paraphrase as 'awareness.' The meditation itself, apart from cultivating awareness, is also effective in bringing tranquillity and clarity to the mind, and increasing a person's energy. Of course not everyone finds it easy to do the meditation, or get immediate results, and I do not know how to predict which beginners will obtain immediate effect and which will not. Perhaps the differences might be explained by looking at the balance between the different effects of the meditation: some people might begin by experiencing the tranquillising effects first, whilst others will be thrown into an immediate awareness of the very problems which they are trying to escape without as yet having the resources to deal with such an awareness.

This brings in another practice of importance, the '*metta bhavana*,' a peculiarly difficult meditation for Westerners. The term means something like 'the cultivation of loving kindness' or 'the development of friendliness.' Loving kindness and friendliness, especially directed towards oneself, are of crucial importance in spiritual growth, their existence enabling one to progress when the going is difficult. The difficulty of the meditation underscores the general isolation and lack of deep friendships in the West; nevertheless it is still a potent meditation, especially when it can be put into effect in an environment where people are intent upon developing deep friendships, as in the 'spiritual community.' This latter point raises the issue of the relative limitations of doing spiritual practices outside of a spiritual community. If one is living or working in an environment where people are not being skilful then it is that much more difficult to practice and to change. This point should be remembered when using spiritual 'techniques' on a psychological basis only — although even psychotherapeutic practices can be much more effective if the environment is helpful rather than a hindrance, of course: hence the development of 'group' and 'family' therapies. Nevertheless, Buddhism, although it is concerned with human development to a much higher level than ordinary psychological health, has practices which are beneficial in overcoming neurosis.

THE BUDDHIST VIEW OF PSYCHOTHERAPY

Is psychotherapy conducive to skilful mental states? Hopefully it is, as it is trying to overcome neuroses and I have implied that this means the development of skilful mental states, but we need to look at this more closely. Earlier I looked briefly at the ideas and theories underlying psychotherapy. What about the 'scientific' approach to psychology or psychotherapy, for example? Well, insofar as this carries with it the philosophy of materialism it must be regarded as unskilful. From the Buddhist point of view materialism is a species of 'nihilism' in that it denies consciousness, ethics and the possibility of spiritual development. Then there are more specific ideas which are current, at least among some psychotherapists, such as the notion that one should express one's emotions rather than suppress them, no matter that they might be hurtful to someone else − catharsis at whatever cost. Whilst at times it *might* be less unskilful to honestly express one's hatred or craving than to fearfully keep it suppressed (and hence expressed in other ways instead), a Buddhist could hardly commend the practice generally, as unskilful actions lead to suffering.

However I do not wish to dwell upon unskilful elements in psychotherapeutic theory and practice, but upon the skilful. Now I mentioned above that psychotherapists, of different schools, are building up a real practical understanding of neurosis and of effective means to overcome it. I would venture to predict that where therapy is effective it is skilful in the Buddhist sense, and that the similarities between therapies are due to their independent discoveries, albeit unwittingly, of the practical necessity of skilfulness for helping people change. This practical necessity is twofold, involving the skilfulness of the therapist on the one hand, and the efficacy of therapy in developing skilfulness in the patient, on the other (the two being, of course, related).

Skilfulness in the therapist involves both emotional and

intellectual requirements: warmth, friendliness and kind-ness accompanied by clarity of mind. Therapists' positive emotions need to extend towards themselves and thus in-volve a kindly and loving self-regard, and self-confidence. Clarity of mind allows them to see what is important in a given case and to draw upon any relevant specialist know-ledge or experience that they have; it also allows them to communicate clearly with their patients so that the latter have the best chance of learning what is being taught and acting upon it; further, it enables them to structure therapy into a manageable sequence of tasks (for both therapist and patient).

There are various other aspects of the therapist's 'skill' the ability to listen carefully, the ability to 'speak patients' language,' the ability to give the patients confidence and a positive self-regard, and the ability to motivate them towards change. There are many more aspects as well.

These are of course general aspects of therapy. One could also look at specific techniques in this way, but this is a vast subject, for which I have no space here. Instead I will simply accept that many such techniques are skilful. This does not mean to say that Buddhists have necessarily thought of them, which brings me to another point, that psychotherapeutic practices (and ideas) can be useful to the person in the first stage of their spiritual life, in which they are trying to achieve a state of psychological health instead of neurosis. (Implicit in my assertion is that such practices which are of use are skilful.) Whether they are necessary to the Buddhist, or whether traditional Buddhist practices are sufficient to over-come neurosis is another matter, and one which I am not in the position to decide upon. Perhaps the specialised know-ledge of psychotherapy is necessary for some of the ills of the modern West, or maybe the traditional *Buddhadharma* is quite adequate. And perhaps, as they are practised at present, they both have deficiencies which dialogue between them will be very fruitful in overcoming, so that they complement each other in the treatment of neurosis.

CONCLUSION

The Buddhist understanding of spiritual development needs to be contrasted with psychological development as understood in the West by psychologists and psychotherapists, before specific parallels are made between particular psychotherapies and particular schools or aspects of Buddhism. However, psychological development can be seen as the first stage of spiritual development, with the overcoming of neurosis and the establishment of psychological health the first task of spiritual life. The concerns of psychotherapy overlap with those of Buddhism in this stage, and dialogue between Buddhism and psychotherapy could be very fruitful for the development of better methods for overcoming neurosis. The Buddhist approach to psychotherapy and psychology is essentially a practical one, to see what help these disciplines can give during this stage of spiritual life; it is also one which must take account of the skilfulness of the psychotherapies. A Buddhist would predict that psychotherapies work insofar as they are skilful, and would take issue with any theories and practices which do not seem skilful, whilst being warmly appreciative of any practical help and specialist understanding psychotherapy can give in the establishment of psychological health. At the same time he would recognise that psychotherapy, no matter how important and useful it may become in overcoming neurosis (and important and perhaps invaluable in the beginning of many people's spiritual lives) is still limited if it does not recognise any higher development beyond psychological health.

10
Beyond Illusion in the Psychotherapeutic Enterprise

Stephen J. Parry and Richard G.A. Jones

Stephen Parry is Principal Clinical Psychologist at Syon House, Angmering, a residential psychotherapeutic centre for religious and clergy. He received an M. Psychol. in Clinical Psychology from Liverpool University and has worked in a Special Hospital and the National Health Service.

Richard Jones is a Senior Clinical Psychologist based at the Wessex Unit for Children and Parents in Portsmouth. He is interested in the application of Systems Thinking to problems in human relations.

SELF-KNOWLEDGE IS possible only when the identification of subject and object takes place; that is, when scientific studies come to an end, and lay down all their gadgets of experimentation, and confess that they cannot continue their researches any further unless they can transcend themselves by performing a miraculous leap over into a realm of absolute subjectivity. D.T. Suzuki[135]

INTRODUCTION

To the Western mind the concept of *anatta* or 'no-Self' is initially both puzzling and threatening; puzzling because it is hard for the Self to consider its existence as being anything other than that which involves a distinction between Self and Other, and threatening because it consequently seems to undermine our very existence and understanding of the world. Western thought is built upon the notion of an individual Self/Soul/Ego, that is separate from, but interacts with, the world and other selves; Man's separation is depicted in the Book of Genesis, where the developing egocentricity of Adam and Eve leads to separation from God and expulsion from Eden; and much of Western philosophy can be seen to descend from Plato (with his preoccupation with the existence of souls) and Descartes (with his philosophy predicated on 'Cogito ergo sum').

Today, Western psychology is largely predicated on evolutionary theory and humans are no longer seen to be at the centre of the universe. Yet acceptance of the continuity of species and of our relative position in the universe has done little to affect our egocentricity, with our concern for self-image and self-esteem. Psychoanalytic thinking has contributed to the notion of a separate Self through Freud's tripartite conceptual apparatus, where the conscious ego strives to obtain a balance between the demands of external reality, the libidinal forces of the id and the restraining forces of the super-ego, the latter two both operating to some degree at an unconscious level. Thus there is an implicit dichotomy between this 'psychodynamic' balance and external reality.

One reaction against psychodynamic thinking was the development in the 1960s of learning theory and behaviour therapy, where the idea of Self was absorbed into the over-inclusive term 'organism,' and the Self-Other dichotomy continued under the guise of organism-stimuli. However, both the psychoanalytic and behavioural camps have led to various off-shoots, the former having spawned client centred therapy, gestalt therapy, group analysis, as well as various refinements of psychoanalytic theory, including theories that address the concept of Self centrally, while the latter has itself developed in sophistication and given rise to more cognitively based therapies. (Of course not all the developments and off-shoots now fit neatly into one camp or the other, and some schools of thought may have only tenuous links with either.)

So there is now a vast variety of therapeutic approaches available to the psychotherapist, yet in nearly all there is an implicit acceptance of the reality, in whatever disguised form, of a Self, separate from but interacting with other selves. It is this notion that this chapter wishes to address; it is not our intention to review the burgeoning literature on the Self, nor to provide a critical analysis of different theoretical approaches. Rather we shall attempt to suggest that the Buddhist concept *anatta* can enrich apparently diverse theoretical frameworks while acting as a point of contact between them. It will be argued that belief in the reality of a separate Self, rather than enhancing psychological well-being, actually leads to suffering. It follows that therapies that themselves accept uncritically the notion of Self are clinging to the suffering they aim to alleviate.

'ANATTA' – THE BUDDHIST DOCTRINE OF 'NO-SELF'

The preceding section used the terms Self/Soul/Ego somewhat interchangeably, to refer to that human 'duality' which is separate and distinct from other aspects of the world. *Anatta* is the Buddhist doctrine of 'No-Self' or 'No-Soul.' It is not to be regarded as referring to that which is not Self, but rather to a *disconfirmation* of Self. We cannot seriously deny that we think and are aware, and use of terms such as 'we' and 'I' point to a distinction. But in Buddhism this distinction is illusory, a delusion that we cling to and which, like all attachments, gives rise to suffering. The practice of Zen Buddhism has as one of its aims the dismantling of this construct of a separate Self and all the constraints that go with it.

> When we practice zazen our mind always follows our breathing. When we inhale, the air comes into the inner world. When we exhale, the air goes out to the outer world. The inner world is limitless, and the outerworld is also limitless. We say 'inner world' or 'outer world,' but actually there is just one whole world. In this limitless world, our throat is like a swinging door. The air comes in and goes out like someone passing through a swinging door. If you think, 'I breathe,' the 'I' is extra. There is no you to say 'I.' What we call 'I' is just a swinging door which moves when we inhale and when we exhale. It just moves; that is all. When your mind is pure and calm enough to follow this movement, there is nothing:

> no 'I,' no world, no mind nor body; just a swinging door.[136]

It is this 'limitlessness' that begins to emerge as the constraints of 'Self' are relinquished. (In Zen Buddhist meditation halls there often can be found a statue of 'Monju on the Beast' — Monju is the personification of our earnest and vigilant training in Buddhism, who sits on the 'Beast of Self' who never sleeps and whose eyes are always open!)

SELF IN RELATION TO PSYCHOTHERAPY

Psychoanalysis

There has been much discussion as to whether 'ego,' 'super-ego,' and 'id' are to be taken as a convenient conceptual scheme, as a structure that has a neurological referential basis, or as terms that translate readily into behavioural terminology.[137] 'Ego' is itself used in various ways, though in general it describes a persons's ability to cope with the demands of day-to-day reality in the light of past experiences. Clients who are deemed able to withstand the rigours of psychoanalysis or psychoanalytical psychotherapy without, for example, undergoing a psychotic disintegration, are described as having sufficient 'ego-strength' for psychotherapy. The 'healthier' one's ego, the more one is able to cope with the demands of daily life.

According to contemporary psychoanalytic theory, an individual's 'sense of Self' goes through various developmental stages: from early identification with mother to gradual separation and the developing awareness of one's own boundaries. It generally is held that the nature of one's experiences during the early stages of separation will affect subsequent development of self-image and 'ego-functioning.' Some of these experiences may contribute to later 'pathological' behaviour that serves to maintain a 'strong' sense of Self.[138] Hence 'strength' of self-concept does not readily correspond with psychological well-being.[139] Psychoanalysis specifically aims to bring about more adaptive ego functioning by working through unconscious conflict. Changes in the nature of 'ego-defences' during therapy lead to greater accessibility of unconscious material. Thus, the unconscious is made conscious. Parallel to this development in ego function is a re-organised 'sense of Self.' But despite the often long and intensive nature of psychoanalytically based therapies, the goal does not reach beyond that of healthy/adaptive ego functioning and it is generally accepted that there will remain a sizeable residue of unconscious material.

However, this restrictive view has been challenged by a small number of psychoanalysts, most notably Jung and Fromm. Fromm[140] in particular has attempted to relate psychoanalysis to Zen Buddhism, seeing the former as attempting to uncover a limited aspect of unconscious functioning, whereas the latter strives for the 'total experience' of the unconscious. He sees the ability to achieve this as being due in part to the regular practice of meditation. Meditation stimulates 'primary process' thinking[141] thereby allowing direct experience of unconscious material:

> Where analysis aims to illuminate the unconscious with the clear light of reason,...Zen strives to eliminate the intellect, as a noxious interference, from the otherwise free flow of the unconscious. Analysis heightens awareness of self; Zen ideally eliminates self-awareness. [142]

Various authors have advocated the use of meditation as an integral part of psychodynamic therapy.[143] Kutz,[144] for example, sees meditation as a 'cognitive therapeutic technique' whereby one sits as a detached observer of a process where thoughts and images enter the mind and disappear, feelings and sensations come and go, in a constant flow.

> Eventually, the meditator not only becomes aware of the content of thoughts and images, but also begins

to recognise patterns and habits that dictate thought
formation and dissolution[145]

Like Fromm, Kutz sees this 'cognitive' technique as leading
to a shift towards more predominant primary process thinking, a mode of thinking that is largely 'intuitive,' unbound by
logical and formal rules, and essential for the cohesive
integration of a sense of Self.

Unfortunately, Kutz does not pursue meditation or Buddhist practice beyond the stage of inducing a 'sense of Self'
that is 'ineffable and experienced as feelings of inner trust
and serenity.' He sees meditation rather as a 'primer' for
psychotherapy. Kutz is rightly critical of the limited aims of
conventional psychoanalytic thinking, but he himself stops
short of S. Suzuki's 'limitlessness' by clinging to a notion of a
Self: one that is an 'observer' during the process of meditation.

Cognitive Therapy

Over recent years there has been increasing attention paid
towards therapies that focus specifically on the way our
thinking affects emotion and behaviour, therapies that primarily have developed from the theories of Beck,[146] Ellis,[147]
and Kelly.[148] However, Ponce[149] traces the origins of the view
that psychological suffering is a result of our 'construction' of
reality, to the ancient Greek civilization in the West, and the
historical Buddha in the East; in support of the latter assertion he quotes from the opening passage of the *Dhammapada*:

> We are what we think.
> All that we are arises with our thoughts.
> With our thoughts, we make the world.
> Speak or act with an impure mind
> And trouble will follow you.

and he cites Ellis, Frank, Kelly, Bateson and Branden as
modern exponents of some variant of this view. Cognitive
therapy, then, aims to influence the manner in which a client
construes reality. It challenges assumptions and beliefs and

aims to achieve what Ponce, borrowing from Kuhn,[150] terms a 'paradigm shift' in our way of perceiving the world. He goes on to argue that there are three areas of major concern to cognitive therapists: the individual's core assumptions about the nature of the *world*; the individual's core assumptions about how one ought to relate to the world; and the individual's core assumptions about the nature of the *Self*. The premise is that what brings the client into psychotherapy is some maladaptive relationship between the core assumptions and life's experience. He points out that cognitive therapists focus almost exclusively on the first two classes of assumption while taking the notion of Self as given.

Buddhism, however, offers a radical challenge to these assumptions. In particular it teaches that: (1) The world is interconnected and constantly changing (*anicca*). (2) Therefore, the only viable relationship with the world is one of non-attachment, for attachment to that which is constantly changing is doomed to frustration. (3) Therefore, attachment to a construct of Self that is separate and unchanging likewise is doomed to frustration.

Despite the claims of cognitive therapists to alter a individuals' deep assumptions concerning themselves and the world, it is doubtful whether the methods employed lead to changes sufficient to merit the description 'paradigm shift.' Indeed, Ponce[151] joins others mentioned above in advocating Zen Buddhist methods as an integral part of therapy: '... meditation is a skilful device ... to facilitate the necessary transformation of the person's world views.' He further adds that:

> Meditation very quickly demonstrates to the meditator (1) The autonomy of, and therefore the futility of controlling, his/her internal processes like thoughts, images, sensations, percepts. They seem to have a will of their own, and come and go in consciousness of their own accord; (2) The Self (I, Ego, Me, Willpower) is discovered not only to be impotent as a

controlling agent of these processes, but turns out to be merely one of the numerous thought forms that flits in and out of consciousness; (3) At some point in the meditative experience the knower (subject), the known (object) and the knowing (process), become a single flowing process, obliterating separation and fragmentation. All that remains is the sound, the image, the breath, the mosquito bite. It is at this level that the world is perceived as interconnected.

In Tibetan Buddhism there is a painting known as 'The Wheel of Life,' copies and versions of which are used often to portray the world view of Buddhism. Of particular relevance to the present discussion is the manner in which conscious thought is portrayed. It is represented graphically by a 'chattering monkey': as monkeys leap from branch to branch, so do our thoughts leap from one subject to another. It is this 'monkey mind' that deals in the world of categories, labels, and polarized constructs and prevents us from seeing the world 'as it is,' for 'when the opposites arise, the Buddha-mind is lost.'[152] When we categories we set boundaries and limits, and so we do with our idea of Self. We tell ourselves what we are or are not able to do, what we can or cannot stand, and then we react violently, even psychotically when we have reached our 'limit.' Through Buddhist training we begin to realise that there are no limits, that the constraints are of our own construction.

Applied Behaviour Analysis

This is the application of the radical behaviourism of B.F. Skinner to the solution of practical problems, and is included here because of the undoubted importance of Skinner in psychology,[153] because he eschews cognitive psychology,[154] and because his position represents a radical departure from conventional notions of the Self. Skinner is also a writer who is often critised but, we suspect, read less often. He has addressed himself regularly to subjects such as the 'Self,' 'awareness,' 'consciousness,' and 'private events.' In particular he has been especially critical of 'ghost in the machine' theorizing that postulates any interior entity that, for example, 'thinks,' 'remembers,' 'plans,' or 'solves problems.'

> I have found it necessary from time to time to attack traditional concepts which assign spontaneous control to the special inner self called the speaker. Only in this way could I make room for the alternative explanation of action which it is the business of a science of verbal behaviour to construct.[155]

Skinner draws a clear distinction between 'mental' and 'private.' Statements about the mind either refer to a fictional explanatory construct or turn out on translation to be statements about actual behaviour. Whereas sentences about private events refer to events taking place at a covert level (toothaches, feelings, dreams, images, etc.) and that are accessible solely to the person concerned. These events, he holds, share the same status as overt behaviour and hence are subject to the same laws and principles as overt behaviour. The skin is viewed as an arbitrary boundary: feelings, emotions, and thoughts are subject to the same variables that influence any other behaviour. Consciousness, thoughts, dreams, do not occupy a special world of their own, nor do they have any special casual role. They are simply more examples of ways of behaving that are amenable to explanation. The Self is, at worst, an explanatory fiction and, at best, 'a repertoire of behaviour' that has developed as a result of our interaction with our environment.

> It is often said that a science of behaviour studies the human organism but neglects the person or self. What it neglects is a vestige of animism, a doctrine which in its crudest form held that the body was moved by one or more indwelling spirits . . . Traces of the doctrine survive when we speak of a *personality*, of an ego in ego psychology, of an *I* who says he

knows what he is going to do and uses his body to do it... A person is not an originating agent; he is a locus, a point at which many genetic and environmental conditions come together in a joint effect.[156]

Our 'sense of Self,' then, is inferred from our behaviour (as are, according to Skinner, the various 'cognitive processes' that are then studied erroneously by cognitive psychologists). And in this picture any personal growth or self-development will result from advantageous interaction with the environment.

> Measures taken to change feelings — as in 'developing the ego' or 'building a vital sense of self' — work by constructing contingencies of reinforcement, by advising a patient where favourable contigencies are to be found, or by supplying rules which generate behaviour likely to be reinforced in his daily life.[157]

More recently, a disciple of Skinner's, Willard Day,[158] has addressed the concept of Self specifically in terms of what it means to talk of personal growth, ego defences, a strong sense of Self, and so on. Day suggests that in self-development we are looking for a cluster of behaviours that might include: greater honesty, less anxiety, appropriate assertion, self-confidence in novel situations, ease with others, and so on. His argument is that self-development is so difficult because of '...the almost universally destructive social environment in which the self-developing person has to live.' Self-development is therefore regarded as a process of learning to cope with, and adapt to, the difficulties of the world, a process that he concludes is not worth the effort:

> There is, of course, another alternative to the course described above, of struggling to modify people... This is to think seriously, as Skinner persistently urges, about changing the general characteristics of our social *environment*...

Skinner has presented us with a philosophy to which it is impossible to do justice in such a brief discussion. Nevertheless, it is not clear from radical behaviourist writings what the implications are for the individual of giving up the illusion of the Self to which Skinner refers, or indeed to what extent one should do so. Furthermore, it would seem that radical behaviourists create their own limits by bowing so deferentially to the authority of the environment. And by operating strictly within a scientific framework they '...can never expect to reach the Self, however much they desire to. They can no doubt talk a great deal *about* it, and that is all they can do.'[159]

Systems approaches to change

The development of a systemic view of the problems faced by individuals, families, and networks of people has reflected moves in other disciplines, for example contemporary physics[160] in seeking descriptions of reality which highlight complexity and organisation as distinct from matter and energy. The origins of this shift in interest can be traced back to the paradigm shift in the physical sciences which occurred at the beginning of this century, although in the social sciences the change has been rather slower to find expression. Bateson[161] offers the following comment in the context of a discussion on the usefulness of focusing on metaphors which seek to describe form as opposed to substance:

> ...the conservative laws for energy and matter concern substance rather than form. But mental process, ideas, communication, organisation, differentiation, pattern and so on, are matters of form rather than substance.

The most widely known application of these ideas in the clinical context has been in the area of Family Therapy, which had its origins in the late 1940s and early 1950s in the United States in the work of, for example, Nathan Akerman and Murray Bowen, and more specifically in the developments spear-headed by Gregory Bateson, Jay Haley, John Weakland, Don Jackson and Milton Erikson. This work has been pursued by these and others including Salvador Minuchin, Mara Selvini Palazzoli and Paul Watzlawick.[162]

The systemic approach to therapy and in particular the Milan approach offers a perspective which echoes the no-Self understanding described in Buddhist thought. Palazzoli and others[163] orient the reader to their understanding in the following passages:

> ...we must abandon the casual-mechanistic view of phenomena, which has dominated the sciences until recent times, and adopt a systemic orientation. With this new orientation, the therapist would be able to see the members of the family as elements in a circuit of interaction.

and

> Since in a systemic circuit each element interacts with totality, dichotomies, such as body-mind or conscious unconscious, lose their meaning.

With this perspective, therapists come to know that they are profoundly part of the system that they attempt to understand, and that in the process of this contact there is no injunction to distinguish between themselves and the family. Palazzoli and the Milan group, recognising this, stress the importance of live consultation and the use of a therapeutic team. This method of working maintains some difference in the family/ therapist system, where difference (following Bateson) is viewed as information, and new information results in systems change, and hence behaviour change. The family's problems are those of the therapist and vice versa. The therapist becomes part of the informational flow which constitutes the family's reality.

However the paradox of no-Self is that it appears in the context of Self. How should the therapist therefore under-stand and explain to himself the way in which he is *not* part of the family? Salvador Minuchin[164] offers the following explanation in discussing the complementarity between Self and no-Self:

> If this . . . is carried to family therapy, the self is seen as both whole and a part of a whole — 'both a particle and a wave.' Which aspects it shows depend on the situation. In individual experience, the focus is on the individual as a whole. But when the complementary aspects of the self become parts of a whole, the other parts of the whole, which also are discrete entities, are seen as affecting the behaviour and experience of all parts. Beyond the parts, there appears a new entity; an organism multibodied and purposeful, whose parts are regulated by the rules of the whole.

The systemic perspective has subtlely altered the way of understanding the individual in the therapeutic context, so that history has a different meaning, and need not be differentiated from the present in the patient's report. When using a systemic framework, memories are more clearly understood to be related to the totality of the person's experience, and not contained separately and distinctly. To be unaware of the past is the same as being unaware in the present. To be more aware of the present is to be more aware of the past.

Concluding, Minuchin offers a pithy view of how it is that the family unit is a useful system with which to work:

> Sociologists remain too distant from the specific reality of the individual, addressing themselves only to the homogenized reality of the institution; individual theorists get stuck in the tremendous idiosyncratic complexities with which an individual transacts in context. And both approaches may lose the rhythm of the dance.[165]

No-self and the therapist

> To dedicate oneself to the salvation of others with the conviction that there exist others who need

saving is as much a source of bondage as to devote
oneself to the task of one's own liberation under the
impression that one has a real self to be liberated.[166]

A glance at any psychology text will reveal that a considerable
effort has been expended on defining the concept of Self. In
the process of producing a more and more refined view,
however, the possibility that Self is merely a hypothetical
construct has been obscured. The unquestioning acceptance
of this construct is misleading in that it leads to the construction of intervening variables between life/ existence 'as it is'
and the awareness of that experience. There is a certain irony
about the way in which we attempt to develop models which
are increasingly flexible and elegant constructions of what is,
but by their very existence stand in the path of direct
experience. Yet there is a further paradox, and that is that it
appears that in order to communicate this, it is first necessary
to have a model to reject.

What do 'I' mean by this concept of Self, and how should 'I'
be located and understood in the context of therapy and
social intercourse? In the social context of information exchange with a fellow human being, it is possible to identify
two organisms, and in so far as Self refers to and is coter-
minous with the biological organism, the Self cannot not
exist. However, in the process of information exchange, it is
not things which are exchanged, but ideas,[167] and for this
reason it is not necessary to make a distinction between two
people. The two individuals constitute a system in which
information is in circuit.

It is possible to examine the circuit at any point, for
example by focussing on the mind of one of the participants.
However in any open system there is a continuous process of
modification, although there will be some difference in the
extent to which this enters the conscious awareness of the
two people. Unless 'I' am aware of how each verbal and
nonverbal cue alters my perception 'I' am not in a position to
know how 'I' am being influenced, and because it may be

impossible to be aware of all this information it becomes necessary to accept that the work of analysis and comprehension is 'being done for me' in the processes that constitute thinking, feeling, knowing, and doing in a relationship with another. 'I' must always remain on the map, and never in the territory.

Thus in the context of an exchange between two people, two 'Is,' the concept of no-Self arises through the punctuation of the act of communication by the participator/ observer. It lies in the recognition that in a totally open exchange there is no attempt to preserve a particular position, other than the position that it is more useful to communicate information freely. In order to have an open exchange, therapists must be open to new information: it is important that they do not feel trapped into defending a particular viewpoint. They communicate with the other person in an immediate fashion. They trust that they will make the only response that they can in the circumstances. This is not meant to imply that they have no obligation to learn, but that they should accept that they will not always be able to account for the words that they are about to speak, the action they are about to do. And the urge to explain itself constitutes an attempt to reify a self-concept.

Therapists should be prepared to act into the unknown and wait to see what the consequence of that action is. As soon as they have some notion of what to expect, then they have begun to build a concept of Self, because the act of making a distinction in the world in the hope of rendering it predictable, means that 'I' begin to operate on the basis of what 'I' *assume* to be rather than what *is*. Therapists should strive to 'remember' that in solving any problem, in interacting with the world, they know the best answer without recourse to a distinct and separate decision-making process. This issue is crucial in the client/therapist relationship. Whilst the therapist strives for predictability based on the hypothetical construct of Self, 'I' impose my meaning on the client's behaviour. Where the therapist operates as no-Self then, paradoxically, 'I' validate every behaviour of the client because there is no 'I' to intervene and interpret.

How can no-Self be operationalized in therapy? What would the observer notice about someone operating according to these principles? In the client-centred therapy of Carl Rogers,[168] something of this sort appears to be indicated when he writes 'But when this same client has come to accept deeply the fact that 'I am what I am,' then she can be spontaneous and can lose her self-consciousness.' In a client-centred approach one of the key concepts used to describe the relationship is 'unconditional acceptance,' and this may relate in part to what is here described as operating with no-Self. However it is not clear how the client-centred therapist reaches this position, nor exactly how to describe the therapist's position. The reason for this may be that what is going on in therapy is still construed in terms of the two individuals: the therapist and the client. Thus while this view is one description or punctuation, it restricts itself to an 'either/or' understanding: either the client or the therapist. Where the no-Self understanding operates there is room for both 'both/ and' and 'either/or' descriptions of relationships.[169] It is not necessary to identify a client and a therapist.

The process of therapy is redefined so that there are no experts, only people exchanging information and partaking in a mutual sharing and learning activity. Until therapists are clear that there is no mission to save the client, they will strive to rescue the 'sick' person and, from the point of view of systemic thinking, become one of the elements in the connecting pattern which maintains the problem. This problem remains whilst we continue to work as therapists, and there is no easy answer to the question of how we redefine our role so that we can be seen to be doing something different from attempting to 'cure sick people.'

COPING WITHOUT SELF

The majority of psychotherapies act, directly or indirectly, to improve clients' self-image, and to strengthen their concept of Self rather than eliminate it. Indeed, it may be thought that this can only be so, for how else could one cope with daily life without some distinction between Self and Other? May[170] points out that the development of self-image is generally regarded by personality theorists to be one of the most important processes in childhood, especially in the West where the strength of this self-image is highly regarded.

Writing from a predominantly Christian perspective, May observes that it is frequently later in life that some form of 'spiritual awakening' occurs, and that it is as if the whole process is repeated in reverse: 'Now what is needed is not heroic mastery but the simplicity of becoming as a little child; not self-determination but self-surrender; not self-assertion but dying to self.' This second process is made more difficult by the first, so is it necessary to develop a sense of Self? Are those with 'weak ego strength' more aware spiritually? Is the psychotic closer to experiencing 'that which is?' The answer is that it is necessary to develop a healthy ego before one can relinquish it; it is necessary to develop a strong sense of Self (or more specifically, a strong *positive* sense of Self) before surrender to Self. It is necessary to learn how to cope with living in the world before we can become 'experts in living.'[171]

The writings of Buddhists, in particular Zen Buddhists, are often dramatic, having an almost magical feel to them, but what is emphasized less often is that the process of Zen training is never ending and often arduous. Most of us will spend much of our lives striving to achieve a healthy ego, a strong sense of Self, with perhaps occasional moments of real understanding. Krynicki puts it thus: 'those experiences of oneness. . . tend to wax and wane, and become balanced by some sense of separateness. Zen practitioners tend to have a 'double orientation.' That is, they are oriented not only to the experiential world of union (which has been most emphasized in writings on Zen) but also to the experiential world of separateness. They are not stuck in a chaotic world of self/object blurring, as is the psychotic.'[172] The process is not dichotomous: as we continue in our training we become less egocentric, and increasingly more attuned to the feelings and needs of others. And it is this that is perhaps of most importance to the psychotherapist — to be able to see our clients more 'as they are' and less through the blinkers of our own theories and preconceptions.

Concluding remarks

Theories can serve a valuable function for the psychotherapist. They can act as a means with which to organise and make sense of the information we receive from and about our clients. Their function is to guide and to serve as a useful tool. Furthermore, it is important to develop as cohesive a theory as possible: swinging, monkey-like, from one theoretical tree to another will produce muddled thinking. But theories can outgrow their importance, so that we start to see only that which will fit into our theoretical framework, or we too eagerly set out to translate everything into our own theoretical data-language. Then theories act to constrain rather than facilitate, to distort our perception and appreciation of that which is. And so it is with a sense of Self. It is a useful construct, one that acts as a helpful tool in the daily business of living. But it too can outgrow its importance, and then we become constrained by the boundaries of this 'theoretical construct' and the information we receive from the world is distorted to fit the theory. It is liberation from this contraint that is of no little concern to client and psychotherapist alike.

11
Applications of Buddhism in Mental Health Care

Malcolm R. Walley

Malcolm Walley is Head of Studies in Psychology at Nene College of Higher Education, Northampton. Over the past seven years he has run workshops and weekend courses on applications of Buddhism and the relationship between Buddhist and Western psychology.

An increasing number of psychologists and members of related professions such as psychiatry and nursing are becoming interested in the potential Buddhism might have for both the practitioner and the recipient in the caring process. It is the intention of the present discussion to explore those aspects of Buddhist theory and practice which may prove valuable to those who work directly in the care and welfare of others. This theme will form the first part of the chapter. Whilst the focus will be mainly upon mental health care, many of the points raised are appropriate to other helping professions also, for example general nursing, social work and education. In the second part two pilot projects, one in the area of mental health care and the other on the training of helping professionals will be described.

THE BUDDHIST APPROACH TO MENTAL HEALTH

To begin with it is worth restating that the task of Buddhism is first to understand the nature of suffering in its various forms and then to apply methods which step by step alleviate and eventually completely eliminate all suffering and states of dissatisfaction. Such a panoramic view of human potential

lies somewhat beyond the scope of Western views of personality and therapy. However, within this panorama Buddhism
does touch modern approaches towards the care of others
directly and it is to these issues that we shall now turn.

A position central to Buddhist psychology is the view that
the root causes of human unhappiness and dissatisfaction lie
within individuals' firmly held attitudes and beliefs about
themselves. For convenience these self-cognitions may be
referred to as the self-image[173] and in Buddhist terms a
person's well-being is directly bound to the fluctuating for-
tunes of this sense of 'self' or 'I.' Buddhist theory would
propose that individuals will become psychologically vulnerable to the extent to which they identify with their self-image
and to the extent to which the self-image serves to overshadow
the full range of personal experience.

The implication here is crucial to the contribution of
Buddhist psychology to the helping professions. According
to the Buddhist view our self-image is distinguishable from
what has been described as our natural state of mind and
qualities of this natural state are warmth, openness and
intelligence.[174] Mind is regarded as essentially pure and has
been defined in Tibetan Buddhism as 'clear, formless cog-
nizing.' Given the appropriate methods the mind is potentially purifiable and the conventional mind, clouded by the
processes of self-grasping, ignorance and the self-cherishing
attitude, is merely in a state of transitory turbulence and
distortion.

The self-image may be considered to consist of two principal processes, namely the self-cherishing thought or attitude
(Tibetan: *bdag-gces 'dzin*), and self-grasping (Tibetan: *bdag-
'dzin ma-rig-pa*), sometimes referred to as ego-grasping or
self-grasping ignorance. Buddhists regard these as the two
main threats to psychological health and well-being against
which strategies are to be developed in the practical work
described below.

The self-cherishing attitude refers to the strong phenomenological experience of 'I' or 'me' as typified when for

example we are under emotional threat or embarrassment, which may evoke a strong sense of tightness or holding in the area of the chest. Such an experience is the self-cherishing attitude par excellence! However, this may be regarded as an extreme instance of the general condition which pervades most people, though sustained extremes in self-cherishing would, from the Buddhist viewpoint, tend to typify the mental disorders found in anxiety states and depression. In his book *Meaningful to Behold* Geshe Kelsang Gyatso, a highly realised meditation master and teacher, states that 'All the fearful aspects of *samsara*,[175] from the greatest down to the smallest, arise from the self-cherishing attitude.'[176]

The second process, namely self-grasping, is the principal subject under investigation in Buddhism. Self-grasping (or ego-grasping) has been defined as 'the compulsion, arising from ignorance, to regard one's own personality or 'I' as permanent, unchanging and existing self-sufficiently, independent of all other phenomena and the process of conceptual imputation.'[177]

This self-grasping tendency then generates the solid base upon which the self-cherishing attitude depends. Buddhist enquiry strongly challenges the widely held assumption of an inherently existent self, as it challenges the status and nature of all phenomena. Such a view is deemed to be 'ignorant' or lacking in wisdom and is considered to be the root delusion and primary cause of all suffering. Why is it considered to be the root delusion? Simply put, where there is no self there is no sufferer. The construction by our psychological apparatus of a solid inherently existent self is considered in Buddhism to be a fundamental distortion of reality which gives rise to a wide range of psychophysiological consequences, one example of which is a state of extreme vulnerability to changing circumstances which may culminate in mental disorder or physical ill-health.

Such a distortion of perception gives rise to a deeply held dualistic and dis-integrated view of self and other and as such may be considered to underlie mental states which range from the ambitious drive for worldly power to the confusion and incoherence of psychosis. Buddhist psychology regards the issue of errant perception of self to be so crucial that one may describe all of its practices as in some way having a bearing upon this problem.

From this central error, secondary distortions, delusions, are likely to arise and these include craving/desire, aversion/anger, pride/arrogance and jealousy. If self-grasping forms the container or flask of ignorance then the self-cherishing attitude may be likened to the malevolent genie rising from it.

This view of self-cherishing as troublemaker has a long history in Tibetan Buddhist practice. Earlier Tibetan practitioners have called it the 'devil with the head of an owl':[178] monks and nuns may throw up their hands in dismay when it manifests in their heart and it has been described in the Tibetan Thought Training tradition (see below) as 'the one object of every blame, deserving to be banished.'[179]

The problem of self-cherishing is most effectively tackled through the development of its principle antidote, namely love and compassion, whereby the narrow self-boundaries associated with self-cherishing are widened through empathic involvement with others.

Traditional approaches to the problems of self-cherishing

The methods of working within mental health care described here are based mainly upon traditional teachings given by Geshe Kelsang Gyatso and other eminent lamas over a period of several years. An appreciation of the traditional lineage of such methods of working with the mind is important, especially during these still pioneering days, as any attempt to abstrace certain seemingly useful methods will inevitably distort the appreciation of a subtle and complex whole. So a brief description of this background is in order.

The traditional works upon which the described methods are based include principally the *Bodhisattvacharyvatara* (*Guide to the Bodhisattva's*[180] *Way of Life*) by Shantideva, the basis for Geshe Kelsang Gyatso's commentary and the *Seven Point Thought Transformation* by Geshe Chekawa. It is salutory for present day therapists to consider that Shantideva lived in the eighth century and Geshe Chekawa in the twelfth.

There are two established strategies for tackling the self-cherishing attitude. One is known as the 'Six causes and one effect,' the other 'Exchanging self with others.' However, an essential preliminary to both approaches is the practice of equanimity, that is the development of an unbiased attitude towards all beings. For example, by analysing deeply the basis of our positive and negative conceptions of people we may discover that our belief that some individuals are always positive and others negative is a distortion. Over time some 'friends' may become 'strangers' or even 'enemies,' while we may become friends in the future with someone who presents us with difficulties and problems at present. In worldly existence everything is changing, relationships come and go, develop and decline in a continual flux. Our dearest child today was an unknown entity to us prior to their birth and may become a problematic young adult tomorrow.

This perspective then forms the basis for the first of the six causes, which is to consider that we have had and continue to have a close relationship with all beings and forms of life. In essence one feels that all beings have been a 'mother' to us and as such have cared for us and have been kind to us.

Clearly such a view sits more easily within a culture where reincarnation is an indigenous belief and where mothers are traditionally revered. However, the psychological power of such an outlook is to make us profoundly aware of the positive effects others have upon us, many of whom will be complete strangers. We can begin to notice, for example, the complex interdependence of life on this planet and the contributions of other humans and animals in providing us with food, shelter, warmth and so on. Similarly a more balanced appraisal of the continuous care which most of us have received since infancy would be considered to be fruitful.

This recollection of the kindnesses, direct or indirect, which we have received from others comprises the second cause, namely, 'remembering the kindness of all sentient beings.' Within such a positive frame of mind a practitioner will naturally initiate the third cause leading to the 'awakening mind of *bodhicitta*,' the development of the strong wish to repay this kindness.

This gives rise to the fourth and fifth causes, 'the development of affectionate love' and 'the development of great compassion.' Gyatso[181] states that the development of affectionate love towards all beings will develop naturally as a result of meditating for a long time on the first three causes. A sign of such development is to spontaneously feel heart-felt love towards anyone and not merely to those who are nearest and dearest.

The fifth cause, the development of great compassion, again is considered to arise naturally when we contemplate the sufferings of those we care for. To appreciate their problems, difficulties and so on leads easily to the generation of great compassion, the strong wish that they be free of suffering.

Then because of the depth of feeling for all people and for all life the aspirant will personally feel powerfully committed to act to alleviate others of their distress and suffering. This stage forms the sixth cause leading to the principal effect of the meditation, namely the complete abandonment of the self-cherishing attitude and the evocation of the awakening mind of *bodhicitta*. One may note that not only is the self-cherishing attitude eventually abandoned through such successful training and contemplation but also leads in Buddhist terms to the development of the realisation that the capacity to benefit others completely can only be achieved if one becomes enlightened oneself.

The second strategy or antidote to self-cherishing is the

practice of exchanging self with others. In some ways this method is regarded as being a somewhat more subtle and more powerful practice than the first.

In exchanging self with others the trainees will, initially via the process of meditative imagination, psychologically identify themselves with an acquaintance. In so doing they will immerse themselves in that person's qualities, hopes, fears etc and may actually view their 'former' self from this other perspective. This is considered helpful in empathising with others' psychological distortions or delusions (for example, jealously, anger, craving etc.) thereby facilitating the development of compassion. Several different examples may be taken and rehearsed, rather as in social skills training, and then applied in daily situations. Gradually, over time, the psychological centre of gravity of the motivated practitioner will begin to shift from 'self' to 'other.' In this way not only will mundane preoccupations with 'self' be discouraged but empathy and compassion will develop providing the basis for love − the active wish for others to be happy.

Supportive strategies for the successful development of this practice are available. One has already been mentioned: aspiring *bodhisattvas* strive to develop a strong sense of equality between themselves and others. To this may be added the suggestion to contemplate and appreciate that all beings without exception do not want suffering and do want happiness. Thus all beings are equal and are in the same plight of having to face recurring suffering and therefore are deserving of our compassion and love.

As we are in the same predicament as the great majority of living beings, we also are worthy of our own love and care. This raises the important point that love towards oneself is not the same as the self-cherishing attitude. In Buddhist terms true love towards oneself is the antithesis of self-cherishing, in that effective concern for one's well-being leads to the taking of steps to weaken the attitude of self-cherishing.

An additional important supporting strategy for this prac-

tice is the sustained reflection upon the negative consequences of self-cherishing. As already mentioned all negative
experiences are laid at the door of the self-cherishing attitude
whether it be craving or the desire for circumstances to be
different, or irritation/anger at what befalls us, or fear and
anxiety over loss, death, or whatever. All misfortune is considered to begin and end with the self-cherishing mind.

The central point, then, in the Buddhist perspective is to
appreciate that conventional approaches to well-being only
serve to sustain the self-cherishing attitude and as such only
serve to perpetuate the primary cause(s) of suffering.

Practice may also be assisted by observing a model of a
bodhisattva's love either through the personal example of a
qualified teacher, or by likening it to the love a parent has
for their only child. Such a love is clearly very intense and the
bodhisattva may be described as having far more love for each
being than we have for ourselves. This commitment to others
then serves the practitioner in two ways which may be
relevant to professional helpers. The problems inherent in a
narrow self-absorbed view are placed in abeyance for both
practitioner and client and energy becomes available for
benefitting others.

This process can be enhanced further through the practice
called Taking and Giving (Tib. *Tong len*). This highly regarded
practice requires the trainee to develop an intention to
willingly and joyfully relieve others of their suffering. Such
an intention can be fostered by visualising the suffering and
difficulties of others as black smoke which aspirants, in their
imagination, inhale, and experience as dissolving their own
self-cherishing process or attitude, usually considered to
be located at the heart. Then, from this heartfelt sense of
spaciousness arises, in the form of white light, all the tem-
poral and spiritual energy and wisdom which others need,
thereby releasing them from their suffering. Following sufficient practice such a perspective begins to manifest in
everyday life by willingly and happily taking on others
problems etc.

Therefore, whatever problems or difficulties arise in one's own life or in the lives of those with whom we have relationships, one may take the psychological initiative by enthusiastically utilising adversity in order to become free of self-cherishing. The skill in this approach lies in the apparent paradox that the very circumstances which are conventionally likely to evoke unhappiness, frustration or whatever, can actually provide the impetus for dissolving the root of all problems.

An interesting offshoot of the practice of Taking and Giving lies in its use in Tibetan culture in the treatment of physical illness and as such was known as the 'leprosy dharma.' Such an application derives from the Buddhist view that physical illness derives ultimately from the psychological distortions surrounding the processes of self-grasping and self-cherishing. Taking and Giving may be similarly recommended for dealing with personal problems of a psychological nature.

APPLICATIONS OF TRADITIONAL PRACTICES WITHIN A MODERN SETTING

The outlines above present some of the frameworks available for tackling self-cherishing. Next to be considered is how such strategies may be utilised within a modern Western setting.

Buddhist teachers can be very skilful in illustrating how novices may put such principles into practice. For instance Sogyal Rinpoche in a talk given in 1985 advised that one could try regarding one's own suffering, difficulties and so on with an attitude of kindness. Also the nature of the experience of suffering itself may be transformed by regarding it as being light or cotton wool-like in nature, rather than the more typical experience of denseness or heaviness.

Through such practice one's mind becomes identified with the actual antidote to self-cherishing whilst the suffering itself becomes more peripheral. Also the subjective experience of love and compassion is more open than the tight sense of 'I' which often arises during suffering and it is this open, even boundless, state which Buddhist psychology regards as being more naturally valid. (When working with clients or patients with tendencies toward self-deprecation, attempts to diminish self-cherishing may merely intensify self-hatred, in which case it may prove worthwhile to use the 'kindness towards one's own suffering' approach. Such a gradual approach may be more effective than attempting a full blown commitment to love oneself.)

This simple advice, by invoking the antidotes of loving-kindness and wisdom (or valid perception) for the problems of self-cherishing and self-grasping, integrates the two main practices in the *mahayana* tradition[182] of developing the awakening mind of love and compassion (*bodhicitta*) together with the practice of wisdom (*prajna*).[183]

The development of kindness in the face of suffering can be extended to fully making friends with oneself, regarded as an essential prerequisite to the development of love for others. Therefore the 'equanimity meditation' in which the meditator visualises groups of individuals within the three broad categories of 'friends,' 'strangers' and 'enemies' can be developed to include a visualised image or at least an impression of oneself within the array.

This practice — learning to actively regard oneself as 'just another human being' — can serve to ground oneself in one's own reality, and thus help to abandon unrealistic expectations. If in addition to developing a more balanced perception the meditator is also training in loving-kindness, for example by imaging sending out feelings of warmth to others, it may prove therapeutic to direct such feelings towards oneself as well. Several times in workshops individuals who found it easy to feel warm and positive towards images of their own children discovered they were blocked when attempting to generalise a similar feeling towards an image of themselves.

Positive attitudes towards those who cause us difficulties are also problematic. The Tibetan traditions place considerable emphasis upon the role which an 'enemy' or similar negative individual may have upon our spiritual development. For example His Holiness the Dalai Lama has often stated that 'our enemy is our greatest teacher.' To develop love for those whom we care for is rather different from loving our antagonist. But psychologically there is considerable benefit to be obtained by working on the development of loving-kindness towards those who regard us negatively. One strategy for achieving this is to appreciate that those who disregard us are in actuality suffering themselves. Patients may be perceived as suffering from their condition rather than specifically attacking us. This may provide some psychological space for the helper wherein a more positive, balanced and mutually beneficial state of mind may arise.

Buddhist practice fosters a constructive outlook upon adversity in general. That such an attitude is not merely a 'rosy outlook' or 'putting a brave face on things' can be appreciated by the fact that an essential part of Buddhist training is to deeply consider the drawbacks of general existence until what is known as 'the mind of definite emergence'[184] develops which vigorously seeks a solution to such difficulties.

Skilful practitioners have several options available when faced with any form of adversity. They may be reminded of the shortcomings of worldly existence; may choose to practise patience, an essential quality in the control of anger; choose to contemplate the causally dependent consequences of previous unskilful actions (*karma*) or may use the situation to work upon the self-cherishing attitude through the practice of Taking and Giving.

The problems of anger can be tackled in various ways. As an example the Dalai Lama has described anger as a loss of courage, so that the practice of patience becomes an act of bravery, of not being pushed into anger. In the practice of mindfulness, thoughts or feelings of anger may be merely observed and allowed to pass. Other approaches include using the energy of anger positively and creatively,[185] or merely to regard oneself as an inert block of wood when provoked.[186]

The world view implicit in a spiritual tradition or culture may subtly influence therapeutic work. For instance the Buddhist teacher Chogyam Trungpa,[187] recalling his observations upon coming to the West some twenty years ago, was struck by the pervasive world view of guilt and the notion of 'original sin' which carried with it the feeling that present misfortune was in some way a punishment for a mistake in the past. A subtle difference between this view and the Buddhist perspective of *karma* would be the tendency, found in Western therapies such as psychoanalysis, to over-emphasise the past and be somewhat 'backward looking.' Perhaps in Western psychology the approaches of Rogers, Maslow and Fromm come closer to the Buddhist view, particularly with respect to the emphasis upon developing positive regard for oneself. If all beings possess 'buddha nature' there is no merit in guilt or self-deprecation, which from a Buddhist viewpoint can appear quite ludicrous.

The twin attack outlined so far on self-grasping and self-cherishing may lead to more positive functioning, being more in touch with reality and without typical distortions of perception and feeling. High levels of psychological well-being then would tend to be associated with low levels of self-cherishing whilst low levels of psychological well-being and mental disorder in the Buddhist view would be identified with high levels of self-cherishing. Instances of the latter are readily identifiable in cases where the individual's self-image tends to be ineffectual or incapacitating, such as various anxiety states. One may note though that Buddhist psychology would tend to describe anyone with high levels of self-cherishing as being mentally disordered irrespective of their apparent success in the world.

The themes discussed so far suggest that Buddhist theory and practice may be equally appropriate for both practitioner and client. Such an orientation is to be found in the Maitri project in Colorado, USA. This extremely interesting venture is an application of the principles of Tibetan Buddhism to the problems of mental disorder. Founded by Chogyam Trungpa, Maitri is a therapeutic community wherein both therapists and patients are essentially realising their own human potential through living and working with each other. Within such a context the term 'neurosis' could be applied to anyone in the community, whether staff or patient, since from a Buddhist view any unenlightened person may be regarded as being in some way neurotic. Through living in such a way any therapist would have opportunities to mount an assault upon self-cherishing and in so doing expand their own self-boundaries.

Additionally, both therapists and patients would be practising the development of mindfulness and gaining an appreciation of the workings of their mind through sitting meditation. (For those patients for whom sitting meditation is inappropriate, alternative and more active practices have been developed.[188]) The Maitri project then provides a practical example of how the traditional principles of *bodhicitta* training may be implemented within a modern setting.

If our aim is to become psychologically healthy and to have clear and undistorted perception, then the Buddhist advice to helping professionals and their clients would be to know your own mind! This task of knowing the mind takes as its foundation the practice of mindfulness (*satipatthana*), which is to be found in all traditions of Buddhism. To be mind-ful is to be fully aware in the present and mindfulness is a highly regarded practice in its own right as well as being an essential prerequisite for many other practices. Even a brief taste of this practice will reveal its therapeutic benefits and potential. Its simplicity reveals its purity and there is no need for religious trappings. A common form of the practice is to concentrate on the breath entering and leaving the nostrils, and the difficulty experienced in attempting to follow this practice for any period of time reveals the state of our minds to us. Yet the beneficial effects of this practice may often occur quickly and relatively easily.

In addition to being useful to both client and practitioner as a stress-reduction technique, Deatherage[189] has described several ways in which mindfulness training may be incorporated into clinical practice. For example, one patient with poor concentration was asked to practice looking at the second hand of an electric clock. Another, preoccupied with thoughts from the past was asked to apply the label 'remembering, remembering' when she discovered herself having such thoughts during the day. And a third example was of a young woman, clinically considered to be 'unfeeling,' who was instructed to try breathing meditation and also requested to note any emotion that might arise and interrupt attention to her breathing. This led to the discovery of a wide range of strong feelings which apparently had been previously outside of awareness.

Whilst many subtle processes may be noted during sitting meditation, valuable clinical material can arise if a patient attempts to become more mindful of their psychological processes when engaged in daily life. From this procedure some 'distance' arises within the mind which facilitates disentanglement from psychological turmoil. Whilst a Buddhist view may ultimately question the nature and status of a 'self' that observes, to be able to stand back from personal emotional dramas is a valued psychological development.

The above examples parallel my own pilot work. During 1979–81 a series of self-awareness groups were started at St. Crispin's hospital, Northampton. The first two groups were conducted with psychiatric staff, the third and fourth with patients. The staff groups involved about ten people in each group, comprising clinical psychologists, consultant psychiatrists, mental nurses and psychiatric social workers. Nurse members of the groups varied according to shift rotation.

The aims of these self-awareness groups were stated as follows: 'To find out the extent to which individual control and awareness can be increased in our responses to situations and others. The more we increase our sense of well-being the more energy is available for benefitting others.'

Exercises were practised for a period of one hour, once a week in a group setting. The following exercise may serve as an example: 'Observe and note your own thoughts from time to time as you go about your daily activities. Whilst doing this try not to hold on to the thoughts. Just identify them. Are your thoughts more concerned with the past, present or future? Just note 'past,' 'present,' 'future' By way of linking the self-awareness sessions to other therapeutic approaches established within the hospital, principally behaviour therapy and social skills training, empathy and compassion were presented as skills capable of development and refinement.

One exercise on empathy required group members to visualise a patient in mental distress and then to notice their own reactions to the needs of their patients. They were then asked whether they felt able to really help them. The next stage was to visualise actually being able to help. Again staff were asked to note how they reacted to such change. The exercise was extended to explore how empathy was affected by disappointment as when for example they met the above patient the following day only to find that he or she had relapsed. Again they were to be aware of how they responded. The exercise could be extended to include several stages of improvement and deterioration.

To cope positively with such fluctuation seems to correspond with the Buddhist training which integrates loving-kindness with patience. Trungpa speaks of developing the quality of fearlessness, of being open with others and their neuroses yet never giving up on them. He states 'If you have patience with people, they slowly change. You do have some effect on them if you are radiating your sanity. They will begin to take notice, although of course they don't want to let anybody know.'[190]

Bearing in mind the demands made upon staff it became evident during the group sessions that many staff would benefit from nurturing a more positive attitude towards themselves. Part of this process of 'making friends' with oneself meant avoiding treating ourselves more harshly than we do others. Whilst we might force-feed ourselves with junk food when pressed for time we would rarely adopt the same attitude towards colleagues. A clear instance of such harshness would be an intolerance towards any less than perfect performance.

In the lives of the staff there appeared to be a variety of frustrations from several sources. Rather than analyse any particular situation, one approach was to work with the reaction of frustration itself. Each group member was asked to imagine as vividly as possible any frustrating situation which they had recently experienced and to include as much detail as possible. The feeling of frustration was to be felt as deeply as possible including all of its physical and mental aspects.

Next they were asked to just label or note this experience as it arose in imagination (that is, as frustration, tension, etc.) and to be aware of their response. This was followed by imagining that their complete response had switched from frustration to peace and relaxation. This was to be felt as fully as possible. The switch of feeling was experimented with further by going back to the feeling of frustration and thence back again.

The aim was to enable any particular individual to gain some choice and control over their emotional reactions. Such a playful attitude to what may be experienced as a heavily laden feeling may seem to be rather 'irreverent' but is in accord with Buddhist views on the potential flexibility which we have in our reactions to situations. Staff were also encouraged to generalise strategies from the group to the work setting.

The attitude of staff towards this venture was on the whole one of cooperation. They were forthcoming, warm and welcomed a change in their daily routine. Only one member of the two groups stated that they felt sceptical about the motivation behind having such group sessions.

Of the various exercises used those which seemed most appropriate and interesting to staff were the labelling and noting of one's own experience, especially of negative and unwanted states; changing one's perception of others by becoming more positive and seeing how this affected one's own behaviour; and experimenting with feeling compassion for oneself and again observing the consequences of feeling more relaxed and so on when with others.

Visualisation as a learning method requires practice, so in the exercises emphasis was placed more on 'sensing' a particular situation than on visual detail. Subjective reports suggested that well-being could be influenced in the initial sessions even with rather rough visualisation skills. The methods do require rehearsal on a daily basis along with reinforcement in daily situations for well-being, flexibility and empathy to become increasingly rewarding. Staff did mention that they considered such training to be useful for any helping professional.

On the basis of the work carried out with the staff groups it was proposed to introduce broadly the same range of exercises to two groups of long stay patients in a rehabilitation ward. Some of these patients were in the stage of preparing to move into flat-type accommodation, firstly in the hospital and then in the community. Their programme was wide ranging and included social skills groups, psychodrama and occupational therapy.

Given the situation of the patients it was felt appropriate, after consultation with a senior clinical psychologist, to apply those Buddhist practices which emphasised calmness, mindfulness and positive social attitudes (that is, the *bodhicitta* type of training). Two main aims were to help patients cope with the variety of circumstances likely to occur outside of the hospital setting and to facilitate rapport with others. Therefore the focus was very similar to that of the staff groups with exercises being selected to foster greater personal autonomy and well-being in the face of changing circumstances, and to develop more positive social attitudes towards others. Given that each group met for the self-awareness session only one hour each week emphasis was laid upon the need for practice in daily settings inside and outside the hospital. Nurse staff on the wards were also encouraged to remind the patients to do some of the exercises, such as mindfulness and relaxation, when they were in their rooms.

Attention and concentration were clearly a difficulty. One approach was to ask each patient to bring in something that could serve as an object of concentration. The exercise took the form of attending to details of the object, say an ornament. After a few minutes of observation patients would describe the object to each other. In this way both motivation and sustained attention to detail could develop. Also, when back in their rooms patients could use the objects again in exercises on concentration. Another possibility was to suggest to patients that they spend a few minutes a day developing concentration by attending to the second hand of a clock. Emphasis upon training in the conscious control of attention was also linked with increasing positive perceptions in general. Positive qualities in fellow patients, oneself or staff could be perceived more consciously and reinforced. Also, warmer feelings in general might be nurtured which could shift a person's psychological 'centre of gravity' away from the self-cherishing attitude.

Some examples may be of interest. One patient suffered from a stream of self-deprecating thoughts and was over-whelmed with thoughts of the past. He claimed no compassion, no enjoyment in life, and was full of self-hatred. Upon practising mindfulness breathing for a few minutes with the instruction to just note those thoughts and distractions which may arise he reported some relief and peace. As well as verbally reporting that he felt better, the patient did appear calmer and more collected. The suggestion was also made that he try to recall positive acts which occurred in daily situations. However, by the end of the session the patient would often be as restless as before.

One amusing comment by another patient doing the same exercise was 'This reminds me of Buddhist meditation.' Apparently her daughter had previously introduced the same method to her. In her case, the mindfulness practice led to an enhanced awareness of her predominant emotional state: fear of leaving the hospital. The fear was tackled through the development of warmth and compassion towards oneself and others, along with learning to perceive others as non-threatening. As this woman had faith in God and loved nature, these attitudes were encouraged as sources of nourishment for her.

A third example was a male patient, who like most of the others was in his late forties or fifties. He responded very well to the empathy type of training where one rehearsed sending out feelings of warmth and caring to others. This was helped by considering that all people have problems and difficulties, including staff, and do not want suffering. He made an effort to generalise from the group sessions to the occupational therapy section where he had a supervisory role. This was supported by discussing the interdependent structure of a hospital and the general environment.

About eighteen months after the first series of awareness groups it was proposed that a team consisting of a senior clinical psychologist, psychiatric social worker and myself develop the exercises so that they might be integrated with cognitive problem solving strategies.[191] This time most of the patients were female and short-stay. Occasionally other patients, including one or two men, would join the group. Sessions were to be one hour long, twice weekly, over twelve weeks. Again this was to be a pilot exploration working with new approaches rather than monitoring specific changes in patients.

A similar range of exercises was used as in the earlier groups with emphasis upon relaxation and concentration, the development of empathy and warmth towards oneself and others, together with training in the choice and direction of emotional responses. The exercises were to be alternated with the cognitive problem solving sessions for the first few weeks. Progressively sessions would become shared to help patients to integrate both lines of approach. Given the differences between the two perspectives, it was considered helpful to develop common concepts as far as possible. For example, the concept of 'focussing' was introduced to describe to patients both the attention necessary to become aware of one's breathing and the attention required when rehearsing a cognitive behavioural sequence such as taking a trip to town. Both approaches might be involved in a particular behavioural sequence. Role-playing going into a shop and asking for a specific item might include focussing upon being mindful, developing positive attitudes towards self and others, plus awareness and control of feelings.

Also practised was the choice and change of emotional responses based upon approaches outlined by Tarthang Tulku. He stated, 'For example, every time you think you are not happy, say, 'I am happy.' Say it strongly to yourself, even if your feelings are contradictory. Remember, it is your self-image and not you. Just as fast as a fish can move in the water, you can instantly change to a happy, balanced attitude. Keep yourself there. Believe yourself...You have the choice.'[192]

This approach was used to practise changing feelings in the shop role-play by contrasting the effects of positive and friendly behaviour with a negative and withdrawn response. The aim of such rehearsal was to gain some direction and confidence over our emotional life whilst realising that we need not identify with nor be dominated by our feelings.

The range of material developed in the awareness groups was also used in the professional training of nurses and social workers and in weekend workshops for helping profess-ionals in general. The context was a course of professional training in stress management and counselling. As with the previous groups, the emphasis was upon the mindfulness and empathy/warmth exercises. The latter included an ap-preciation of difficult clients/colleagues as being victims of their own psychological states. Also included was the devel-opment of choice and control over emotional reactions. The exercises were introduced in several ways. Sometimes they accompanied other awareness exercises relevant to counselling training, such as the effects of positive/negative feedback upon others. On other occasions it was appropriate to introduce Buddhist perspectives on mental health in their own right.

It was often useful when working with self-image from a Buddhist perspective to use self-drawing techniques derived from other therapeutic approaches such as gestalt therapy. These 'self-drawings' would be more in the nature of spontaneous doodles rather than artistic constructions. In fact from the point of view of the exercise the more intuitive and spontaneous the drawing the better. The approach used was rather similiar to that used by Kubler-Ross in her work with terminally ill patients and their families.[193]

The self-drawings would only take a few minutes to do and the interesting work occurred often when students described their drawings to others who were 'counselling' them. As in Kubler-Ross's work the great majority of people were able to do the exercise, even if initially hesitant, and the material was often extremely interesting and profound. The exercise could be extended by working with an ideal self-image through asking the question 'How I would like to be?' Comparison could be made with the present self image and links might be developed between the two. By using this method Buddhist approaches to the self can be explored and if appropriate one may use the drawings as a framework for exploring the expansion of self-boundaries. Specific delusions such as anger, fear, craving or clinging may also be explored in a similar way.

One variation of the exercise with direct bearing on the work in the psychiatric staff and patient groups was to depict the self helping others. This was often useful in that the sense of boundary between self and other could be worked with or at least observed in a topographical form. In such a way one's own fears or sense of inadequacy in relation to others may be usefully explored in terms of the boundary between self and client/patient. One might then work upon extending or dissolving this boundary to allow the flow of warmth or positive energy towards ourselves and others, rather as in the visualisation methods described above.

My own feeling is that the potential for applying the essence of Buddhist wisdom in the helping professions is considerable. Trungpa[194] speaks of the 'basic sanity' of the spiritual traditions, and it is largely by using the techniques and ideas that these traditions offer us, as tools for self-examination, that we may hope to recapture some of the sanity that we seem to have lost.

CONCLUDING REMARKS

My aim here has been to try to demonstrate how some aspects of Buddhist knowledge and wisdom may be applied in a practical way within a clinical setting. The attitude of loving-kindness appears an excellent protection for the helping professional. Not only is it an antidote to the problems which accompany the self-cherishing attitude, thereby enabling the practitioner to become more effective and balanced, but loving-kindness also serves as a protection against the stresses of the helping relationship itself. As mentioned in the traditional practices such as Taking and Giving, the attitude of love and compassion also becomes a great source of energy.

There is an optimism in Buddhist psychology with respect to both training and counselling/therapy in that qualities such as loving-kindness can be acquired or enhanced. Therefore the human potential of both practitioner and recipient in the helping relationship can be developed.

12
Buddhism and Behaviour Change: Implications for Therapy

Padmal de Silva

Padmal de Silva is a Lecturer in Psychology at
the Institute of Psychiatry, University of
London, and Principal Psychologist at the
Maudsley and Bethlem Royal Hospitals.

FEW OTHER ANCIENT spiritual traditions have aroused greater interest and curiosity among modern psychologists and psychotherapists than Buddhism. The psychological relevance of much of Buddhist teachings had been recognized from the time the pioneering English translations of the canonical texts began to appear, a little over a century ago, under the aegis of the Pali Text Society. The popularity achieved by Zen Buddhism in the West in the last few decades both reflects and has further contributed to the interest in, and indeed the serious study of, Buddhism by Western psychologists and therapists. The common ground between the ideas and practices of Buddhism on the one hand, and those of Western psychology and psychotherapy on the other, has been discussed quite extensively.[195] A recent issue of a Japanese psychology journal was devoted entirely to this topic.[196]

CONCEPTS OF THERAPY

In considering the relevance of the Buddhist tradition to modern psychological therapy, it is necessary to examine, briefly the concept of therapy. While in general the term 'therapy' is easily and unambiguously understood, it is important to recognize that it can be used in several senses.

Firstly, and most commonly, 'therapy' refers to a systematic attempt to put matters right when something has gone wrong with a person's health. In the context of psychological health, abnormalities or aberrations of behaviour and/or experience (such as depression, anxiety, phobias, obsessional thoughts, compulsive rituals) require correction, with standard procedures. Most practising therapists use the term 'therapy' to refer to this exercise. It is a moot point as to when to consider a behaviour or experience normal or abnormal; suffice it to say, for the present purposes, that when such a development causes interference with people's normal functioning and is thus distressing to them and/or their family and friends, it becomes a problem requiring therapy. Such problems may include, in addition to clearly unusual behaviours or experiences, deficits (for example, lack of social or communication skills) as well as excesses (for example, overeating, uncontrolled drinking). Therapy in this sense is *remedial*.

Secondly, one can conceive of therapy in a future-directed sense; that is, therapy can be *prophylactic*. Steps can be taken with the intention of preventing a dysfunction, or any other problem, from taking place. Consider, for example, counselling offered to a family with a seriously ill person. This is prophylactic therapy in that the family is being prepared, among other things, to cope with the loss that is impending. The preventive use of therapy can be aimed at warding off problems totally (for example, stress inoculation training), or at preventing a condition getting worse, or at stopping a condition or problem leading to further difficulties.[197]

Thirdly, one can consider therapy not for what is generally recognized as a problem, but as an endeavour aimed at improving one's well-being and functioning. This can at times overlap with the first two senses of the term 'therapy,' especially the second, but should be seen as conceptually distinct. For example, if we consider that normal human existence in the hectic industrialized world of today is ridden with all sorts of anxieties, worries and disappointments, and therefore an unsatisfactory state, then one might wish to take steps towards alleviating not any specific symptom or problem but the entire unsatisfactory condition, by altering one's basic responses to one's surroundings. This is particularly relevant in discussing Buddhism, as the Buddhist concept of *dukkha* (usually translated as 'suffering') presents us with just this kind of radical standpoint with regard to what we take for granted as normal existence. The aim of attempting to help people deliver themselves, *via* a process of personal development, from this unsatisfactory state is, it can be argued, broadly a therapeutic one.

INFLUENCE OF BUDDHISM ON THERAPEUTIC PRACTICE

The recent years have witnessed a shift in the interest of psychologists and psychotherapists in Buddhism. It is no longer purely an academic interest; it has now moved into the arena of actual clinical practice. Attempts are being made to apply, in clinical settings, what Buddhism has to offer. There is, for example, a considerable literature today on the use of various Buddhist meditational techniques for common clinical problems. Both case studies and, more importantly, controlled trials have been published showing the utility of the applications of meditation. The clinical uses of meditation as a form of psychological therapy have spread into such diverse areas as headaches, insomnia, general tension, chronic fatigue, drug abuse, excessive self-blame, pathological bereavement reactions, separation anxiety and low frustration tolerance.[198] In Japan, not only meditation but other traditional Buddhist practices as well have begun to be systematically used in the context of psychotherapy. Professor Kishimoto, for instance, has reported on the use of what he calls 'self-awakening psychotherapy' as an essential and integral part of his therapeutic package for neurotic patients.[199] Of particular interest is his use of the practices of the different Buddhist schools and sects or sub-schools (Rinzai-Zen and

Soto-Zen of the Zen school; and Jodo and Jodo-Shin of the Jodo school) to suit each individual patient. Kishimoto has described, for example, the treatment of a seventy-eight year old housewife presenting with anxiety and compulsive neurosis, with a therapy package which included the Naikan method of meditation — this being one of the distinctive techniques associated with the Rinzai sect of Zen to which the patient belonged. Such use of traditionally-derived practices that match the belief system of the patient is beginning to gain ground in clinical practice in other settings as well. The use of the Hindu concept Karma Yoga in the behavioural treatment of a Hindu woman has been described recently by Singh and Oberhummer in the US.[200] Such matching of therapy to patient may not be always feasible, but if judiciously used it can undoubtedly contribute to greater acceptance of and compliance with therapeutic instructions. More importantly perhaps, it can also be argued that it can turn the experience of therapy for a particular problem into a wider and more rewarding experience of personal improvement and growth, within the secure context of one's belief system.

This entry of Buddhist ideas and practices into the arena of modern psychological therapy makes it necessary to examine, closely and critically, both the potential contribution Buddhism can make to therapy, and the possible ways and means of effecting this contribution in a meaningful and systematic way. Some writers have expressed the ambitious notion of developing an integrated new system, which encompasses both Buddhist and modern therapeutic ideas,[201] while others have argued for more limited goals.[202] In practice, what is required is the development of a rational basis for the use of Buddhist notions and practices within the context of therapy to suit each individual and each setting. Such a development will take some time and a great deal of effort to accomplish, but it remains a legitimate goal.

An essential first requirement in this exercise is to undertake a close examination of the concepts and strategies of behaviour change that are found in Buddhism. Behaviour change is, in the ultimate analysis, the most important factor in the therapeutic enterprise; this applies not only to the end product of therapy, but also, to a considerable extent, to the specific steps that are taken in the quest for that end product. After successful therapy, a person would be expected to show behaviours that are different from those prior to therapy (for example, a previously social phobic patient would be able to face social situations without fear and cope with such occasions productively). Equally, the process of therapy itself would often involve new and different response patterns (for example, a spiderphobic patient receiving exposure therapy would engage in increasingly more approach behaviours in the presence of spiders during the therapy). Behaviour change is thus of prime importance in psychological therapy.

NOTIONS OF BEHAVIOUR CHANGE IN BUDDHISM

Let us now examine, briefly, some of the concepts and strategies of behaviour change found in Buddhism. There are many and diverse schools and sub-schools of Buddhism, each with its own literature and tradition. In the following sections, our discussion will be confined to Early Buddhism — that is, the form of Buddhism, usually called Thervada, which is contained in the canonical texts and their early commentaries in the Pali language. The canonical texts are the books of the *Tipitaka* (*Sutta*, *Vinaya* and *Abhidhamma*), and the commentaries considered here are those that were in their present form by the fifth century AD. These represent the Buddha's original teachings and their elaboration and analysis by the earliest disciples and scholars within the Theravada tradition.

ATTAINMENT OF PERFECTION: THE ARAHANT STATE

Buddhism accepts that behaviour change is possible, and encourages and extols change in the right direction. Such change, in the form of personal development, is indeed essential for the main aim of the religious endeavour, which is the attainment of *Nibbana*.[203] The ultimate personal perfection is the state of being an *arahant* ('the worthy one,' 'the perfected one') and is aspired to by all Buddhists. What does it mean to say that someone is an *arahant*? *Arahants* are those who have extinguished the cycle of births and deaths. They have severed the cankers and fetters that bind one to the cycle of *dukkha*, or suffering. They have understood the three qualities of impermanence, suffering and selflessness that pervade all existence. An example of a short description of an *arahant* in the Canon (there are numerous such descriptions) may be cited:

> The *arahant* has destroyed the cankers, lived the life, done what was needed to be done, set down the burden, won self-weal, shattered life's fetters, and is freed by perfect knowledge. He has applied himself to six things: to dispassion, to detachment, to harmlessness, to the destruction of craving, to the destruction of grasping, and to non-delusion.[204]

In psychological terms, *arahants'* actions no longer emanate from the common motives of greed or lust, malice and delusion, though they are capable of joy or positive sentiment. They have loving kindness (*metta*) to all, and compassion (*karuna*). They indulge in nothing, and are restrained in their behaviour. Nine standards of behaviour are given which *arahants* can not and do not transgress (*Anguttara Nikaya*): taking life; stealing; sexual contact; uttering falsehoods; enjoying comforts of wealth; and going astray through desire, through hate, through delusion and through fear. They contribute to society by being teachers and advisors, and they are no burden to their fellow beings.[205]

How does one reach the state of *arahant*hood, which as seen above is characterized by, among others, a certain set of behaviours and experiences? According to the texts, the actual attainment or occasion of this state is a sudden and abrupt change. There are numerous examples of disciples reaching this state while hearing the Buddha's preaching. Other examples refer to some major triggering experience which causes a significant impact on the person. For instance, in the *Theragatha*, the Elder Kulla is reported as describing his attainment of *arahant*hood when he came upon a rotting, untended and worm-infested human corpse in a field. Seeing this, he said to himself: 'Behold, the four-compound, diseased, impure, dripping, exuding – the pride of fools!' He then contemplated the corpse, relating it to his own self, and attained the *arahant* state.

Although the attainment itself is sudden, this can take place only in a person prepared and ready for the change, having gone through a process of self-development involving restraint in conduct, word and thought, and in meditation. Meditation of both the *samatha* (calm) type and the *vipassana* (insight) type are considered relevant. The texts refer to the various stages that many disciples go through, before attaining *arahant*hood. Three prior stages are described, characterizing those who have made spiritual progress but not yet attained the final state (*sotapanna*, *sakadagami*, *anagami*). Those who have not reached even the first of these are the *puthujjana*s: the truly lay, or uninitiated, ones. These are, of course, the vast multitude.

It is important to emphasize that the attainment of *arahant*hood is the result of preparation and endeavour. This involves behaviour change based on restraint, and on self-development which in turn is based on meditation exercises. In short the final, global, personal change encompassed in the state of *arahant*hood is achieved by a process of systematic behaviour change as a means to it.

SPECIFIC BEHAVIOUR CHANGES AND STRATEGIES FOR ACHIEVING THEM

An even more significant point, in the present context, is that the Buddha also considered the well-being of oneself and of one's fellow-beings as an important aim in a layperson's life. This was not merely as an early prelude to the preparation for *arahant*hood, but as a goal in its own right. The Buddha preached explicitly on the need to improve the quality of one's day-to-day life. This involved restraining oneself from behaviour that harmed others, and from excesses, and conducting oneself dutifully towards one's family, neighbours, teachers, elders and others. Behaviours that were likely to lead to unhappy consequences, such as drinking alcohol, womanising and gambling, were discouraged (see, for examples, *Sigalovada Sutta* of the *Digha Nikaya*).[206] The Buddhist lay ethic is a strongly pragmatic one; what is recommended is what is conducive to the individual's and others' well-being. Its basis does not lie in dogma or doctrine. Alcohol abuse, for example, is discouraged on the grounds that it can lead to ill-health, loss of wealth, derangement of mind, proneness to socially unacceptable behaviours and increased quarrels.[207]

The corollary of this position is that Buddhism recognizes the importance, and the feasibility, of specific behaviour changes when and where required. This is a much-neglected aspect of Buddhism, but an extremely important one. The Buddhist concepts and strategies of behaviour change are not confined to the major spiritual training that is required in a committed religious life, with the ultimate aim of attainment of *arahant*hood, but include specific and well-defined ways of changing day-to-day behaviours as well.

Examples of such behaviour-change strategies found in early Buddhism are varied and numerous. Interestingly, some of these are not very different from the corresponding techniques used in modern behavioural psychotherapy. The Buddha and his early disciples both used and recommended such techniques where suitable. These are essentially behavioural techniques, with no recourse to insight or inner factors. They involved specific behavioural steps aimed at directly changing the response in question, in exactly the same way that modern behaviour therapy operates.[208]

Some of these techniques found in Early Buddhism are: (1) There are numerous references to modelling as a way of influencing, and thereby modifying, the behaviour of others.[209] (2) The principle of reciprocal inhibition, along with graded exposure, is acknowledged on at least one occasion as a fear-reduction technique.[210] (3) The modification of undesirable habits by multiple behavioural techniques is acknowledged. The clearest case illustrating this is one of over-eating (see below.) The techniques used include the graded acquisition of control over the target behaviour, use of cues, response cost, and involvement of a family member to implement the programme. The package is remarkably similar to what a modern behaviour therapist would offer for a similar problem.[211] (4) Stimulus control as a means of eliminating undesired behaviours is mentioned.[212] (5) The systematic use of rewards is referred to, as a means of inducing and encouraging desirable behaviours.[213] (6) There is at least one clear account of what is best described as social skills training.[214] (7) For the control of unwanted intrusive cognitions, several techniques are recommended which include: thought-stopping, thought-switching, distraction and overexposure.[215] (8) Self-monitoring, by way of training in mindfulness, is advocated as a strategy for dealing with such problems as poor sleep and fears.[216] (9) A graded stimulus approach is recommended for the development of loving kindness, much like the hierarchical approach used in many modern behavioural strategies.[217] (10) A strategy very similar to covert sensitization is used for both the control of unwanted thoughts and for controlling and eliminating lust and attachment.[218] (11) Several cognitive and cognitive-behavioural methods are also found, including the use of parable and analogy, and the repeated exposure to disconfirmatory experiences in dealing with false beliefs, not unlike some of the strategies of modern cognitive therapies.[219]

For reasons of space, we shall not discuss the above in any detail here. Fuller accounts of these, and of their clear similarity to modern behaviour therapeutic techniques, have been given elsewhere.[220] One example, however, will be cited, in order to give the flavour of these specific behaviour-change tactics used in Buddhism. This account is from the *Dhammapada Commentary*.[221]

> For a period in his life, King Pasenadi of the Kingdom of Kosala used to eat boiled rice by the bucketful, with equally large amounts of curries and sauces. One day after breakfast, feeling slothful as a result of overeating, he went to see the Buddha. Overcome with drowsiness he sat down on one side. 'What is the matter, King, did you not sleep well last night?' the Buddha asked. 'Oh no, Lord,' the King replied, 'but I always have this problem after eating.' Then the Buddha said: 'King, overeating causes problems. Anyone who lives indolently, eats large quantities of food, sleeps all the time, so that he rolls like a pig fed on grain, such a man is a fool because it is bound to lead to suffering.' The Buddha further said, 'King, one should observe moderation in eating, because that leads to comfort.' He then called the King's nephew, Prince Sudassana, and requested him to help. He was asked to memorize a verse containing advice on moderation in eating, and then gave him the following instructions: The prince was to watch the King whenever the latter had a meal. The moment the King was about to take the last handful of rice, the prince must stop him and recite the verse to remind him of the Buddha's advice. The King, thus distracted and reminded of the Buddha's advice, would then not eat that handful. Then, for the King's next meal, the prince should fetch only that much rice as he had been allowed to have the previous time, and so on. This programme went well, with the King co-operating enthusiastically in his training. In fact, if he had to be reminded by the prince of the Buddha's advice by reciting the verse at a meal, he

would give away (not part of the Buddha's programme!) a thousand pieces of money in alms. The
regime made the King lean and energetic again, as
he began to eat a limited amount of food daily. Later
he went and thanked the Buddha.

Summary

To recapitulate, then, the Buddhist theory and practice of
behaviour change encompass different kinds of change.
Firstly, there is the ideal of *arahant*hood — a state of human
perfection that signifies a basic transformation of the person,
thus entailing a radical change in behaviour. This state is
achieved by a gradual process of development, of which both
restraint in motor, verbal and cognitive behaviours and
meditation exercises are significant components. Secondly,
the importance of changing specific behaviours in day-to-
day life, when and where required, is acknowledged. This is
not only as a preliminary preparation for the cultivation of
virtues necessary for the eventual development of the *arahant*
state, but also because the Buddha recognized the value of
healthy, dutiful and productive living in its own right. While
prescriptive but reasoned teaching was one way of attempting to induce these changes, we have seen that there was also
a wide array of specific behavioural techniques employed for
this purpose. In addition, meditation of certain types was
considered relevant in this domain, too, for achieving change
in certain specific behaviours.

BUDDHISM AND PSYCHOLOGICAL THERAPY: CONCLUDING COMMENTS

In attempting to answer the question: 'What contribution can
Buddhism make to psychological therapy?', both the above
concepts of behaviour change have to be taken into account.

Personal development, via the means recommended for
the attainment of the *arahant* state, has much potential value;
perhaps not so much as therapy in the remedial sense, but —

more importantly — as therapy in the prophylactic sense. Those who have reached a state of personal change of such a radical nature as to be able to react to the incessant flux of stimuli that assail them with calmness and equanimity, are clearly less vulnerable to the effects of stress and change around them. They are alert to their own experiences and responses, and here control over them. They are detached, compassionate and relaxed. Goleman[222] has written of *arahant*-hood as an ideal state of mental health, and of meditation — which is essential in the quest for this state — as providing a general pattern of stress-responsivity which is less likely to trigger the establishment of specific maladaptive responses. This is prophylactic therapy in the sense of primary prevention. It must be recognized, however, that the state of *arahant*hood is a difficult ideal to attain, and requires not only meditation but a life of great restraint, committed to the renunciation of worldly pleasures and attachments. In the context of today's world, very few if any would be willing or able to undertake such a path of total renunciation that necessarily negates much of what we normally take as essentials of life, including basic attachments, and aggression in self-defence. On the other hand, this does not preclude the feasibility of undertaking systematic meditative and self-development efforts in order to improve and enhance one's functioning, in terms of greater alertness, sharper acuity of perception of one's subjective states, a more relaxed attitude, and an enhanced ability to tolerate stress, frustration and loss. In other words, while *arahant*hood (which is a perfect state where the person is free from vulnerability to psychological afflictions, and is thus an ideal state of mental health) cannot be an immediate goal for a lay person, some of the self-management efforts that are recommended as essential in the quest for this state can still be of much use. They will contribute to developing a greater ability to face problems, worries and stresses of living and reduce the chances of these causing maladjustments and dysfunctions.

In the more directly remedial sense, the specific behavioural strategies found in Buddhism have clear relevance to current therapy. In fact the efficacy of many of these techniques, in their present form as independently developed methods of clinical behaviour therapy, is well-documented.[223] The existence of these techniques in the Buddhist literature two thousand years before the advent of modern behaviour therapy is not only a matter of historical interest; it also has clinical implications. If specific techniques found in the Buddhist tradition can be used in, or incorporated into, the psychological therapy offered to Buddhist client groups, it is likely that the therapeutic endeavour will on the whole be facilitated; it is not unreasonable to assume that the acceptance of therapy, and compliance with therapeutic instructions, will be greater. Therapy will not be seen by clients as an alien form of intervention, but received as something that fits well into their cultural tradition and belief system. The usefulness of offering therapy that matches the client in this way has already been commented on.

It will also be useful to subject to empirical investigation those specific behavioural techniques, including cognitive-behavioural ones, which up to now have no direct parallels in modern clinical practice. What is needed is the systematic testing of such techniques as interventions for the problems for which they are claimed to have been useful. This process of empirical testing may lead, hopefully, to the widening of the repertoire of behavioural and cognitive-behavioural therapies at the disposal of today's practitioners.

Before concluding this chapter, a final comment needs to be made. We have shown here, *inter alia*, the relevance of Buddhism to *behavioural* psychotherapy; this is in contrast to much of the previous literature and practice, which have highlighted its relevance to insight-oriented therapy. In fact, the behavioural aspects of the Buddhist theory and practice of behaviour change have been neglected until quite recently. It is clear, from our analysis, that Buddhism has much in common with the behavioural tradition of therapy, and has a contribution to make to this field.

13
Bankei — Seventeenth Century Japanese Social Worker?

David Brandon

David Brandon is a director of the mental health organisation MIND in the North West of England, and the author of *Zen in the Art of Helping* (Routledge and Kegan Paul, 1976). He is a Zen meditation teacher.

PEOPLE IN THE helping professions have a poor sense of their own history. Reading most contemporary texts, you might assume that helping people in any systematic way began with the Charity Organisation Society or the modern Welfare State. But priests have a long history of paid helping. For example we have detailed records of Bankei Yotaku's 'case-work' with ordinary people mainly from the year 1690.

Bankei was a Master in the Zen school of Buddhism. He was born in Japan in 1622 and died in 1693. At the core of Zen is a direct pointing into the heart through quiet sitting (*zazen*) and the eventual attainment of *satori* (awakening).[224] Bankei achieved satori when he was only twenty-six.

The records kept by his attendant Itsuzan show him to be a man of great wisdom and humility. He spent most of his life outside the monasteries. He was very popular with ordinary people, who flocked to hear him speak. The problems they brought are very familiar to modern social work and counselling services. His replies owe little to Hollis or Biestek but allowing for three hundred years and eleven thousand miles, the differences are not vast.

Bankei stressed ordinary work as a means of meditation, establishing a harmony and balance in life.[225] 'If your normal walking and standing, your sitting and reclining, are the work of a living Buddha, nothing remains to be done.'[226] He had a direct experience of the unborn mind. 'For Bankei's Unborn is the root of all things and includes not only the sense-domain of our daily experience but the totality of all realities past, present, and future and filling the cosmos.'[227] This is close to Carl Jung's notion of the collective unconscious.[228]

Bankei's teaching was based on his own suffering. The very young Bankei left school and returned home early to avoid a calligraphy class, which he disliked. His elder brother (the head of the family as his father was dead) ticked him off without effect. The brother told the ferryman not to take Bankei across the river between his home and school if he should return early. When Bankei was refused entry to the boat, he said 'The ground must continue under the water,' strode right into the river and struggled to the other side. Later he decided to kill himself to avoid further conflict with his brother. He swallowed a mouthful of poisonous spiders and shut himself up in a small Buddhist shrine and waited for death. After a while he realised he was not going to die and went home.[229]

Here are some extracts from Bankei's talks, which convey some sense of his understanding of human suffering, its causes and how they might be healed.

'At birth, each person receives a Buddha-mind from his parents. He is born with not a single other thing. Yet his illusions he produces by himself through his own one-sidedness...'[230]

'In spite of the fact that you all came into this world with an unborn Buddha-mind and with nothing else, you are partial to yourselves, so you want to make things move in your own way. You lose your temper and become contentious. Then you think: 'I have not lost my temper. What that fellow says is so unreasonable that he has *made me* lose it...'[231]

'...even a man who was until yesterday a great scoundrel, the object of everyone's contemptuous pointing and whispering, if from today on he recognises his past misdeeds and lives in accordance with the Buddha-mind, from this day forward he is a living Buddha.'[232]

'No matter how many different thoughts arise, let them remain right where they are. Don't give thought even to what you may find delightful. You mustn't make your one mind into two. If your mind is always set like this, it won't think about what is good and what is not good. It won't think it should not think about such things, or that it should cease to think about them, and therefore thoughts of good and bad cannot help cease naturally. The same is true of displeasure and pleasure, which are both merely bred from your self-centredness.'[233]

Here are some ideas familiar to modern social workers. 'He has *made me* lose my temper' shows an understanding of what just over 200 years later was to be described as 'splitting' and 'projection' — the psycho-analytic defence mechanisms. The idea of bringing different parts of the mind into unified consciousness is an essential element in the gestalt therapist's armoury.

Of especial interest are the accounts of Bankei at work. His teachings are based on the experiences of ordinary people. 'I never quote the words of the Buddhas or Patriarchs when I teach. I need only to examine directly the personal affairs of people themselves.' He would have failed any professional social work course on the grounds of inadequate theoretical and philosophical understanding.

A woman asked, 'I have a fear of thunder which is far out of the ordinary. Whenever I hear it, immediately I feel sick and suffer great anxiety. Please, tell me how I can somehow put an end to this fearfulness.'

Bankei said, 'When you were born you had no mind to fear things, only the unborn Buddha-mind. The illusion of fear for something is a figment of thought that was produced after you came into the world. Thunder benefits man by bringing rain into the world. It doesn't harm him. Your going afraid because you contend with the thunder is the work of that figment of thought; it doesn't come from outside yourself. When you hear the sound of thunder, trust single-mindedly in your own mind and Buddhahood.'[234]

Many people who came to Bankei were concerned with

dying and death. Often he saw that as an important and genuine gateway to experiencing real mental health and spirituality. The priest Jozen said, 'I'm greatly troubled about death. That's why I'm always coming here to see you. I don't think there could be anything of greater importance for a person.' Bankei responded, 'That mind is the fundamental source of Buddhist practice. If you come to think like that and do not lose your determination, you'll soon conform to the Way.'[235]

During the long winter retreats many women travelled from all parts of Japan to see the great Zen Master. Some came grieving inconsolably having lost a parent or child. They believed that Bankei could help lessen their grief. Bankei talked quietly to them: 'The sorrow of a parent who loses his child, or of a child whose parent dies, is the same throughout the world. It is a matter involving the depth of the karma binding together the relation of parent and child and making us parents and children. It is in the nature of things for parents or child to grieve when death takes one from the other. Even so, for all grief and sorrow, the dead do not come back. In their ignorance, people lament continually with all their heart what cannot be undone. Was ever the return of a dead man achieved because of the zeal with which he was lamented? No.'[236]

Some men came to see Bankei about their uncontrollable anger. Here he uses a family therapy technique — paradoxical imperative or something very like it. A monk addressed him: 'I was born with a short temper which is always flaring up. My Buddhist teacher has done his best to help me, but without success. I realise myself it is not good, and I try to correct it, but it is something I was born with so I have not been successful...'

Bankei responded: 'You have a very interesting inheritance. Is this short temper here now? If so, bring it out right this instant. I will cure it for you.' The monk said: 'I don't have a temper now. It appears suddenly when something irritates me.'

Bankei said: 'Then you weren't born with it. You precipitate it yourself on account of some chance cause. Such causes may arise, but still, where could the temper come from if you did not generate it...? Your parents gave you a Buddha-mind when you were born, nothing else. From the time you were a tiny child you have watched and listened to people in their fits of ill temper and you have learned from them and imitated them, until irascibility has become a part of your own disposition too.'[237] That is fairly close to a seventeenth century exposition of learning theory.

Bankei has like most Zen Masters a profound disrespect for the intellect as a source of real and fundamental human change. Here he pulls the rug from under the feet of this amateur psychologist. A layman said, 'Last year, when I was beset upon by confused and disordered thoughts and asked you how I could put an end to them, you told me to let the thoughts arise and cease without bothering about them. I accepted that. But later I found that it was almost impossible to do.'[238] (It is just like Monday morning in Preston West Social Services office. The duty officer is confronted with 'I did what you told me on Friday and it didn't work...') Bankei despatches this client with 'It's difficult because you think there's a teaching that you should let thoughts arise and cease without bothering about them. You cannot get through personal turmoil through the imposition of yet another rule, even if you think it comes from me.'

A layman asked, 'When I get rid of a thought that comes into my mind, another appears right afterwards, and this continues on repeatedly. What can I do to overcome it?'

Bankei expounds on the same theme: 'Cutting off occurring thoughts is like washing blood off in blood. The original blood might be washed off, but you're still defiled by the blood you wash in. You can wash it as much as you like, the bloodstains won't go away. You don't know that your mind is originally unborn and undying, that it is free of illusion, and you think that thoughts really exist, so you revolve in the cycle of birth and death. You must realise that thoughts are temporary, changing appearances, and neither seize on them or hate them, just let them occur and cease of themselves. It's like the image reflected in a mirror. The mirror is clear and bright and reflects whatever is placed before it. But the image does not stay in the mirror...'[239]

In the next story Bankei shows an understanding of what we would now call alcoholism — dependence on *sake* (rice wine). A layman said, 'I don't doubt that my thoughts are fundamentally without substance. Yet they keep popping endlessly into my head all the same, and I find it almost impossible to be the unborn, even for a short time.'

Bankei said, 'That's because although at the time you arrive in this world there's only your unborn Buddha-mind, as you grow up you become accustomed to seeing and hearing the manner in which ordinary people engage thir minds, until, habituated to illusion over a long passage of time, the delusion of your own mind gets to be completely free and unrestrained, so if the mind trusts and affirms the unborn Buddha that it originally is, they will disappear.

It's like a man who loves *sake* but must abstain from it, because of bad health. The thought that he wants to drink still arise in his mind whenever he encounters a chance for a drink. Yet because he abstains from drinking it, he doesn't get ill, and he doesn't get drunk; he remains a non-drinker in spite of the thoughts of *sake* that arise in his mind, and ultimately he becomes a healthy man, cured of his illness. Illusory thoughts are like this. If you just let them arise and let them cease, and don't put them to work or feel any aversion to them, before you know it, they will disappear into the unborn mind.'[240]

Bankei had little time for the formal trappings of religious practice — the temples, the incense, the long hours of austere meditation. He would have been impatient with social services bureaucracies. He grasped the heart of human suffering. In criticising his Buddhist teachers he got close to my feelings about modern social work. 'I am deeply grateful for all the teaching I have received from Buddhist teachers. It is not at all that I don't agree with what they say. Only somehow or other, the feeling I get is one of scratching at an itchy foot without taking off my shoe. They don't get directly to the itch. Their teaching does not strike home to my inmost being.'[241]

Bankei not only expressed compassion, he *was* compassion. During one of his retreats, a student was caught stealing. Others reported it to Bankei and asked for his expulsion. Bankei ignored it. Later the student was caught stealing again and once more Bankei ignored the request for expulsion. The other students were angry and drew up a petition asking for the thief to be sent away or they would leave. He read the petition and called everyone before him. 'You are wise brothers. You know what is right and what is not right. You may go somewhere else to study if you wish, but this poor brother does not even know right from wrong. Who will teach him if I do not? I am going to keep him here even if all the rest of you leave.'

A torrent of tears cleaned the face of the brother who had stolen. All desire to steal had vanished.[242]

14
Meditation: Psychology and Human Experience[243]

Michael A. West

Michael West is a Research Fellow at the
Medical Research Council/Economic and
Social Research Council Social and Applied
Psychology Unit at the University of
Sheffield. He has been conducting research
on the psychology of meditation for some
thirteen years and has published widely on
this subject. His research and activities also
include studies of the transition from school
to work, adolescent drug use, work role
transitions and stress and creativity among
helping professionals.

SCIENTIfic RESEARCH ON meditation represents a meeting of psychological methodologies from two quite distinct philosophical and theoretical backgrounds. Meditation may be described as the methodology of Eastern psychology in that it is a means to experiential knowledge of mind and self, whereas Western psychology has adopted the scientific approach to understanding, relying on procedures which are publicly observable and verifiable. The irony of this meeting is perhaps that we have learned little about meditation and more about our methods of enquiry.

In this chapter I shall describe the history of psychological research on meditation and briefly summarise the research results. Then taking a broader perspective on the history and type of research, it will be argued that our understanding of meditation has been as much restricted as developed by these endeavours. The results of in-depth interviews with long-term meditators in the West will be described and the implications for research discussed. It will be argued that existing methodologies have been allowed to determine our questions, rather than psychological theories (both Eastern and Western), and that this has further limited our appreciation of meditation.

PSYCHOLOGICAL AND MEDICAL RESEARCH ON MEDITATION

Among the earliest studies on meditation were those carried out in the 1950s by Das and Gastaut,[244] Bagchi and Wenger[245] and Kasamatsu and his colleagues.[246] Their interest was primarily in physiological changes occurring during the practice of meditation, and they chose as subjects expert practitioners — yogis and Zen Buddhist monks. Indeed, Bagchi and Wenger transported sophisticated recording equipment around temples, monasteries and even into remote caves, to contact these meditators. The research showed unusual patterns of brain wave activity during meditation, especially during periods of 'samadhi' or ecstasy. While methodologically crude these early attempts to understand meditation were significant in their focus on accomplished practitioners of meditation rather than on novices.

Physiological changes associated with meditation

Few studies were conducted in the West until the 1970s, though as early as 1960, Peter Fenwick, of the Institute of Psychiatry in London, reported at a conference in Marseilles[247] on his studies of brain wave patterns during meditation. In 1970 Keith Wallace[248] published details of physiological arousal levels during the practice of Transcendental Meditation (TM), creating a stir of interest among both psychologists and doctors. Wallace, Benson and Wilson[249] argued that they had evidence of a fourth major state of consciousness (after waking, sleeping and dreaming) which was characterised by very low levels of physiological arousal. They reported significant and dramatic decreases in heart rate, respiration rate, oxygen consumption and skin conductance. However, with further studies and more careful research methods, the reliability of some of these results has been thrown into doubt. There is much doubt about whether for example, heart rate and oxygen consumption decrease during meditation.[250] Some reviewers see meditation has having no effects that distinguish it from simply sitting quietly,[251] whereas others claim that meditation is important in bringing about a generalised reduction in many physiological system.[252] What is clear is that studies of meditation have failed to establish that it is a fourth major state of consciousness — at least in physiological terms. The evidence suggests that there are decreases in arousal during meditation but these are not significantly different from decreases in arousal that can be achieved by other relaxation practices.[253]

Little research has been carried out to assess the long term physiological effects of the regular practice of meditation. In one six month longitudinal study,[254] people learning and practising meditation showed significant decreases in spontaneous skin conductance responses (a measure correlated with anxiety) outside of meditation. This study also showed greater decreases in arousal during meditation as subjects practised regularly over the six-month period. Goleman and Schwartz,[255] on the basis of their research, argue that experienced meditators show faster recovery from stressful experiences than do other people.

There has been much research interest in patterns of brain wave activity during meditation. The results of some studies suggest that meditation might simply be sleep by another name, while others suggest that meditation is a basis for creative ability and holistic growth.[256] Overall the EEG research indicates that there is a pattern of lowered arousal during meditation and that it may be possible to differentiate meditation from other relaxing activities and altered states of consciousness by reference to patterns of EEG activity.

In summary, research on the physiological effects of meditation reveals decreases in arousal during the practice of meditation though it is not possible to isolate these as due specifically to the mechanics of meditation. Some remarkable changes in physiological functioning have been observed among expert practitioners of meditation but these have been single case studies rather than controlled studies of groups of meditators.[257]

Meditation and personality

It was shortly after the publication of Wallace and Benson's research[258] that psychologists began to examine the effects of meditation practice upon behaviour and personality. Comparisons of meditators and non-meditators revealed the former to be less depressed, less anxious, less irritable, more self-actualized and happier.[259] Furthermore, long-term meditators were significantly less anxious than short-term mediators. Longitudinal studies have confirmed a causal relationship by showing decreases in anxiety and neuroticism over time among those learning and regularly practising meditation.[260] Three characteristics of this research should be borne in mind. First, almost all the research focused on TM rather than other types of meditation. Second, only three studies examined changes in personality over a period greater than three weeks. Third, that a number of studies[261] have shown that those attracted to TM are more anxious and neurotic than the general population and are therefore more likely than other groups to exhibit large changes on such measures.

Meditation as therapy

Of the three major areas of meditation research — physiological changes, personality changes and therapy — therapy has been the least productive. Early interest was aroused by the possibility that meditation might be a useful treatment for drug addiction and irresponsible claims were made by researchers and meditators alike on the basis of inadequate research.[262] While meditation has become increasingly popular as a therapy over the last 20 years, most studies evaluating its effectiveness have failed to overcome the methodological problems which dog research on psychotherapeutic outcomes. Benson and others[263] in one of the more careful studies, compared self-hypnosis and meditation as treatments for anxiety. Thirty-two patients practised their techniques daily for eight weeks. Change in anxiety was determined by psychiatric assessment, self-assessment and physiological test-

ing. Overall improvement occurred as a result of both interventions. The authors concluded that meditation is effective
in the treatment of anxiety and is simple to use.

Woolfolk and others[264] found meditation to be more effective
than no treatment and equally effective as progressive relaxation in the treatment of insomnia over a six month period.
The use of meditation in the treatment of hypertension has
been carefully investigated. Most studies show only short term
decreases in blood pressure, dependent upon regular meditation practice, suggesting the importance of sustained practice
for beneficial outcomes.[265] There have been no large scale and
careful studies of the effectiveness of meditation as an adjunct
in psychotherapy, though there are many interesting anec-
dotal reports of its use.[266]

A major problem of interpretation of this research is that
measurable effects may be created by the beliefs of meditators in the efficacy of meditation, that is, a kind of placebo
effect, and that any technique, given similar credibility,
would have similar effects. The use of the TM technique in
investigations has compounded these problems since the
teaching maximises attribution, placebo and expectancy effects. People learning TM are exposed to 'scientifically backed'
claims for the benefits of the technique. The individual is also
taken through a religious ceremony, asked to pay a sizeable
sum of money and to participate in group discussions of the
effects of meditation. Such a series of influences is likely to
increase both expectations and subsequent belief in the
efficacy of the technique. These beliefs are powerful factors in
themselves in producing behaviour change. Such problems
beset all research evaluating psychotherapeutic outcomes but
are particularly difficult to overcome in this area.

So, some fifteen years of sustained research on meditation
and over 1,000 published research articles[267] reveals the following: (1) During meditation the body becomes a little quieter, a
little stiller; (2) Regular practice of meditation is associated
with decreases in anxiety though whether this is due specifically to meditation rather than simply sitting quietly is not

known; (3) Meditation is as effective as selfhypnosis and progressive relaxation in the treatment of problems such as insomnia and anxiety, though regularly of practice seems important for effects to be sustained.

Why has meditation therefore been practised for thousands of years in a variety of cultures and religious and philosophical contexts if this is all that it accomplishes? Even a cursory knowledge of the practice of meditation in the East will testify that meditation is not viewed as simply a prophylactic for stress. The aim is usually to achieve a state and trait of consciousness which is an expression of fundamental religious beliefs about ways of being. Below I consider the reasons why psychologists have been so little concerned with these subjects and so much concerned with outcomes only marginally relevant in the traditional context of meditation.

THE HISTORY OF MEDITATION RESEARCH

When research into meditation first began in the late 1960s and early 1970s it was regarded by many psychologists and doctors as a rather esoteric and fringe area. Consequently those who pursued this interest may well have attempted to make their studies more respectable by using reputable methodologies which employed well-established dependent variable measures such as oxygen consumption, brain wave patterns, heart rate and even rectal temperature. To measure more complex changes in behaviour standardised questionnaire instruments such as the Eysenck Personality Inventory or Cattell's 16 PF or other paper and pencil tests were used. Many of the researchers were themselves 'new' meditators with an investment in discovering positive effects of meditation in their research. Conceptual analysis often sits uneasily with experiential knowledge and perhaps these researchers were eager to ease their own doubts about meditation. Hence, much of the research is on short-term easily demonstrated outcomes such as physiological parameters and gross personality change.

The research tended very much to follow a conventional 'medical model' approach. Those who participated as subjects in this research were viewed rather like patients with an illness, for which meditation was the hypothesised cure. Thus, measures of personality were taken before they began meditation practice and again after a short period of practice. 'Improvement' on these measures was then assessed. Meditation came to be seen as a kind of therapy for current maladies such as hypertension, drug abuse, insomnia, headache and even as an aid to memory and scholastic performance. Such concerns with short-term gains accruing from meditation practice have a peculiarly Western materialistic rather than Eastern orientation.

The emphasis on short rather than long-term effects of meditation is also apparent when we look at the studies examining physiological changes. Almost all have examined changes during meditation, rather than longer term changes outside of meditation or changes during meditation but over a long period of practice. Personality is a term used to describe relatively stable and consistent patterns of behaviour, yet researchers in this area were looking for change over periods as short as three or four weeks. Similar criticisms apply to studies of meditation in therapy.

Perhaps part of the reason for this orientation is the marketing of TM in the West as a powerful and effective antidote to stress, with promises of a more effectively functioning nervous system and relief from psychosomatic disorders. Many scientists simply set out to evaluate the claims of the TM organisation rather than deriving their own hypotheses from theories or from examinations of the Western or Eastern psychological literatures. This is not of course a criticism of the method of marketing TM. The Maharishi's ability to combine the marketing of the West with the practical wisdom of the East has brought hundreds of thousands to the experience of meditation.

A final criticism of the research is its almost exclusive emphasis upon the experience of relatively novice practitioners and yet in the East meditation is a path to be followed for years in pursuit of such qualities as clarity, wisdom and compassion. This emphasis on novice practitioners is a pragmatic response to the perennial difficulty of finding sufficiently large numbers of volunteers for research studies. The experiments of psychologists are populated predominantly by undergraduate psychology students – a captive audience. Similarly, it has been because TM meditators are the easiest sample of meditators to contact that we find so few studies of long term practitioners of techniques such as Zazen. The consequence of this bias has been a concern with short-term gross effects of meditation, compounded by the fact that many of those who take up TM lapse in their practice in the first three to six months and meditate only sporadically, if ever, thereafter. Estimates vary, but probably fewer than one third continue meditation with any regularly, that is, four or more sessions per week.[268]

In conclusion, there is a clear need to go back to the basics and reconsider what we are examining and how we wish to understand it. It may therefore be instructive to talk with meditators about their experiences, their motivations and their practice to discover better the most appropriate directions for our research endeavours. Good longitudinal research is difficult to conduct in terms of time and effort but short-term studies have been of limited value. Study of meditation in its Eastern context suggests there is probably more to be gained by study of longer term practitioners than relative novices. Finally it is time that study of meditation went beyond TM to explore the experiences of those from a variety of meditative traditions.

The lives of meditators

The rest of this chapter reports preliminary results and observations from an ongoing longitudinal study of the lives and meditation 'career histories' of people who have been practising a variety of techniques over a period of at least three years. The study uses intensive interview data which are tape-recorded, transcribed and then content-analysed. The methodology is similar to case study analysis and is also based on the explicit recognition that the interviewer plays an important part in the process of the research through interaction with the interviewee.[269]

The meditators who have participated in this research are drawn from a variety of backgrounds and are not intended to consitute a representative sample of long-term meditators. A number are psychologists, some are doctors, one is a teacher and others are social workers, engineers and unwaged women. The interviews are semi-structured around accounts of meditation career histories; experiences during meditation and changes in them over time; comprisons of the methods and experiences of different kinds of meditation; changes in daily life associated with the regular practice of meditation; significant experiences (good or bad) associated with meditation; the philosophical or religious context of the practice of meditation; whether a particular teacher or guru has been influential in the individual's meditation career; how meditation practice may have affected social relationships, relationship with self, attitudes to life and death; whether meditation is practised socially or in isolation; and why the individual practises meditation now.

Meditation career histories

Those who have participated in the research have meditation histories spanning, on average, thirteen and a half years, with a minimum of four years and a maximum of nineteen years. These figures do not always represent a period of sustained practice, since people sometimes stop meditating for a number of years or limit the frequency with which they practice. Nevertheless, in all of these cases, meditation practice has been sustained and regular for a period of at least the preceding two years and in most cases considerably longer.

Descriptions of meditation career histories reveal a number of dimensions upon which each individual can be placed:

Intermittent versus Sustained

Some meditators do not practise with any long-term regularity. As one interviewee said: 'I find it hard to sustain any ongoing commitment for very long. It suits my style more to delve into things intensely and then come out and be relatively normal for a while.' Such a pattern seems particularly characteristic of the early years of meditation practice. Another said: 'I used to come back to doing it. . .if I was sitting at my desk and was very tired I would do it. It was a relaxing thing to do. If under stress I would do it for a little while and then stop. I felt better, but I didn't know if that was due to meditation or not.' Others are more sustained in their practice. Sarah, for example, has been practising meditation since she was 12 years old and for only one brief period in her 20s has she lapsed, though her meditation methods have varied considerably. There is some indication that periods of particular stress and turmoil may disrupt meditation practice. Barbara suspended her meditation practice during such a period: 'I feel there are great troughs in people's lives and meditation is just not always appropriate.'

Unimodal versus Multimodal

All of the meditators have practised more than one technique of meditation, with longer-term meditators being more likely to have experience of a rich mixture of methods. Julia began at the age of sixteen with breathing meditation at the end of her yoga practice and subsequently would focus on visual objects such as a candle, a stone or a flower. Later her meditations were on short pieces of reading material: 'I would read something like 'The Prophet' and then think about it, sitting and contemplating it for about half an hour.' Richard learned TM while at University and since then has begun to learn Tai Chi. His sitting meditation now involves meditation on breathing. Anna however is determined to limit her experimenting:'...there is a time for exploration, but then at some point you have to take your trolley out of the spiritual supermarket and commit yourself to one discipline or you will never make progress.'

Group versus Solitary

Some come to meditation through groups such as the TM organisation and their careers are marked by moves from one such group to another. For others meditation is a solitary affair. Alistair taught himself a breathing meditation from a book and practised this for fifteen minutes daily. Since then he has attended a few lectures at the School of Meditation but disliked the 'bombastic and dogmatic teachings.' He still practises breathing meditation and also uses a mantra during his daily life, especially when walking. Recently he has met other meditators but is unsure about whether his involvement in a group will be sustained.

Social Support versus Social Conflict

Meditation can be solitary and even conflictual since some meditators are surrounded by family members and friends who regard their practice as odd or are even hostile to it. Richard's wife 'couldn't sit still to meditate and doesn't know what meditation is all about. She can't see any effect it has on me, and doesn't understand why I can't be natural, being a spontaneous person herself and far less self-conscious than I am.' For others there is much support and acceptance, especially if both partners in a relationship are meditators. Daniel says his family are 'very sympathetic and supportive and tolerant of individuality. I am very fortunate as they see meditation as simply something that I do. My wife goes to yoga classes although she herself is not a meditator. She practices yoga at home but it's not something I interfere with anymore than she would interfere with my Tai Chi practice.'

Taught verus Acquired

This dimension overlaps to some extent with the Group-Solitary dimension and refers to whether the meditator has developed his or her own practice of meditation or whether formal teaching has been involved. For example, most of Jim's experience in his seventeen years of intermittent meditation practice has come from exposure to teachers. One of his first experiences was with TM and then he joined Bhagwan Shree Rajneesh's movement and learned a variety of different meditations. In visits to Zen Buddhist centres he learned Zazen, and has developed other meditation practices through similar contacts.

Effortful versus Gentle

Meditation can be a rigid discipline which involves finding time and practising with diligent efforts difficult meditations such as Zazen. Anna for instance feels the need for greater discipline and values the pressure of a group because '. . . one of the troubles about practising on your own is that I think I'm doing it, but when I go to a weekend session, I see how slack I've become, so I'm evolving a more rigid context now.' Jim has approached all forms of meditation '. . . in a very gentle way. My attitude has been very non-grasping from the beginning.' He is much easier with himself being less concerned to maintain regular practice and adopting a more permissive attitude than Anna to the wanderings of his mind during meditation.

Spiritual versus Secular

For some meditators their practice is intrinsically part of a religious or spiritual life, while others reject religion. Jim falls somewhere in between. When asked whether he had any notion of a deity or spiritual entity, he replied: 'No certainly not. Because to have any such idea is to create a distinction between the creator and the created. And my image of God is not like a painting but like a dance. One is the whole thing. One is not controlling it. One is it. The dancer is the dance.' Daniel is a Christian and attributes to meditation his 'very strong love for God, a much clearer more genuine love. I feel you can come to a much more direct experience in spiritual life through meditation, not just an academic thing you talk or think, but you actually feel something of the love which holds the world together.'

Advanced versus Novice

This dimension could be simply used to place the individual on the basis of years spent in regular meditation practice but this would imply that advancement comes from 'doing meditation time.' Alternatively one could rely on the individual to give an indication of their advancement at any one point in time (perhaps through standardised self-reports) but some will always describe themselves as 'spiritual babes' while others seem convinced by each new sensation that they are teetering on the brink of enlightenment. As interviewer I bring my prejudices to each situation, but I am sometimes left with a feeling that a person has some stillness, a clearer vision and maybe a greater certainty than is usual. Perhaps this is too vague and subjective, for one can imagine other observers making different assessments. But then as Shapiro and Walsh argue: 'intellectual understanding in this area requires an experiential basis and what was incomprehensible at one stage may subsequently become understandable once an individual has sufficient experience of the meditation process.'[270] These issues require much discussion and pose perhaps insurmountable problems for researchers. Nevertheless Eastern psychological theories challenge us to tackle them.

The value of the notion of the meditation career is in placing meditation in the context of the individual's life over time and broadens our attention to the longer timespan of experience rather than evaluating effects in terms of only short-term sensations and outcomes. The career dimensions also help to differentiate between meditators with different career patterns. The tendency to see meditators as a homogeneous group dominants the research literature and has obscured the large and real differences in people's experiences. As we shall see below, it is often the uniqueness of each individual's experience of meditation and not the commonality which seems most significant in the lives of meditators.

What is meditation?

Most of those interviewed have practised a number of kinds of meditation and could identify some common essence across them. Sarah, who has been one of the most consistent over the years says it involves controlling the mind and always bringing it back to the object of meditation. This produces 'A feeling of centering and gathering your thoughts . . . just being really, being in that moment.' Jim says the most important component is 'the watching, the witnessing, being aware that you are aware, allowing the rise and fall of experience.' Jeffrey finds all meditation is a way of 'getting the mind to stop still. . . hooking the mind off its habitual concerns. The mantra gives the mind a job to do instead of fussing about with thought trains. The outcome is calmness and when the mind is calm, there it is.' For Julia meditation is 'any way of watching.'

Why begin meditating?

In 1975 I asked this question of eighty-three people who had learned TM and the vast majority were attracted by the possibility of gaining benefits such as relaxation, calmness and freedom from worry.[271] Other reasons mentioned included desires for self-realisation and self-awareness. In the current series of interviews, Daniel, who has been practising for sixteen years on and off, but very regularly for the last five years says 'I had always been drawn towards it, because the study of one's mind seems to me crucially important. It was part of religious exploration.' For Julia the roots can be traced into childhood: − 'I can trace a religious interest right back. When I was about eight I built an altar in my room and had pictures up and sat in front of it...' Sarah too began meditation when quite young, at twelve and taught herself yoga and meditation from a book: 'The meditation would be things like imagining a candle flame or focusing on the feeling that no matter what went on around me, no one could take away the inner self. Maybe it's because I was an only child and I spent a lot of time alone.' Barbara had apparently more practical reasons for her initial interest: 'I had back problems and after reading a book on yoga began to practice both yoga and meditation.' For Alistair: 'It's a feeling of having an indirect experience of something you sense is there and want to reach. An intuition that there is something one is missing and meditation is a route to it.'

Jeffrey relates his interest to a spontaneous mystical experience in childhood in which 'I had the answer delivered to me on a plate and the whole of my intellectual and then practical interest in Zen Buddhism has been concerned with the recovery and understanding of the experience. It was a feeling of being totally overwhelmed in something utterly magnificent and extraordinary − an emotion filled with gratitude, wonder and incomprehension.'

Meditation experience over time

The experience of meditation also appears to change in a consistent way over time. Meditators report greater ease of concentration and more stillness. Daniel, for example, is convinced that the experience of meditation changes over time: 'I think the awareness, the consciousness is clearer, so that if thoughts come up you remain aware of the breathing.'

Jeffrey too sees a change: 'It just gets easier to reach that state. When I began meditation using a technique of wall-gazing it was very difficult, a real fight, not only the sitting but the thoughts of 'what am I doing here? Why am I sitting in a room with a Buddha image anyway? What is all this crap, this unscientific nonsense? Why not do something active like be a doctor? And then feeling imprisoned by the wall, wanting to punch it. But there is none of that now. I sit down and the practice will emerge fairly quickly, providing I'm not overtired, when it's better to sleep.'

The effects of meditation

The effects of meditation appear both subtle and pervasive in the lives of meditators. Anna tells how, when she initially began to meditate, she would read a Zen poem and explore the ideas in silent sitting which 'calmed me down and lifted me up.' Now she uses breathing meditation and Tibetan Buddhist meditations. The breathing meditation she finds 'does still the mind, does detach me from thought processes and reactions, from the events of everyday life. Meditation also deepens the feeling that it is OK to be me and that makes life a good deal more bearable.'

Daniel found that meditation helped him in the writing of his first book '. . . because by meditating just before I started writing I was able to clear the mind. . . and the writing became much more spontaneous.' Later there were more pervasive benefits: '. . . anger or fear or impatience. . . these are much less marked, less sharp. . . the smaller fears and anxieties that come along can be dealt with in a more detached way. By looking at them they go. . . looking as an observer, as a watcher, their impact is not so central. Julia too has found that her perspective has changed and she is less affected by 'these little things that niggle people. . . there seems to be so much more. I do think the world's a wonderful place and meditation enables you to see things as they really are in a still way.' Jeffrey finds his years of meditation practice have helped him to 'sustain an attitude and insight into life that the world just is and it's alright, and that the unseen is perfect in the fact of the ghastly social world of our times, and that even death doesn't matter.' But this experience of a broadening perspective is reported by even the relatively short-term meditators. Alistair, a relative novice, talks of feeling more relaxed and being less 'enmeshed in things that are not important.' This enables him 'to be more concerned with the moment.'

Jim talks at length about a change in the quality of his awareness and receptivity as a result of meditation practice. He experiences greater clarity: '...of thought, people and decisions and a sense of being very efficient when I want to be.' Along with this has come a subtle but profound change in his experience of himself 'in the sense that my experience and thought emerges as if there is a fountain or spring within me, the source of which is completely opaque to me. I experience myself as a conduit or a screen perhaps and less and less as a perpetrator...which has led to an attitude of interested passivity towards myself...a feeling of not being responsible for the generation of things...and a real interest and amazement and humour about myself and an attitude of friendliness and indulgence towards myself...my funny little ways...even the judgements I have about people.'

Perhaps such changes have adverse effects on those around. The interviewees do not think so. Jim feels more empathic: 'I can put my judgements on one side and see people and have a love for them and a compassion for them in the moment.' Jeffrey feels 'much less paranoid and more tolerant of other people, while Alistair sees himself becoming more intuitive in his relationships. Sarah's meditations on love, compassion and equality have had a 'very, very powerful effect in changing relationships and making me see other people in a different light. Without any sort of conscious change of mind, just by doing the compassion meditations regularly, you find yourself wanting to help other people and really caring just that little bit more. Before becoming a Buddhist, Sarah 'always felt that my happiness depended very much on other people and the relationships I had with them, and not so much on myself and the negativity I was carrying around. I had very much a feeling of self and other and other being different from self. Now I have an appreciation that self and other are not different...'

Changes in relationships and activities are experienced in work life too. Jeffrey cites his relationship with his boss. 'Tibetan Buddhism and the meditations have taught me to take on the problems of others instead of feeling angry...to see it from his point of view and think of him as a brother. That's part of the method of taking on the offending person as a loved relative. It doesn't work all the time...in emotional relationships it's much more difficult.' Anna is a doctor and meditation has proved useful for her work because '...the tools I have been given help me to face the pain and suffering in my job...I used to feel terribly helpless...now I don't feel guilty that I can't solve the whole thing, and I can offer something human.'

But what all the meditators say is that changes occur gradually. Julia says that for this reason it is hard to say what effects meditation has, because 'it just creeps up on you over a long time, so it's a gentle accumulation of calmness, stillness, perspective and an ability to help others.'

Some meditators emphasise quite different effects from others, while some effects, such as a sense of perspective and ability to remain detached from minor upsets are shared by all. But another theme which emerges with constancy is the sense of 'being in this moment here and now.' Keith talks of moments of clarity which occur throughout the day and Barbara talks abstractly of '...it's not just you being more... you are changing, the 'beingness' also changes as you come to encompass it.' Matthew too talks of his self-awareness more continually becoming the object of his own awareness '...it intrudes in conversations, during sleep and even when I relax but it's taken a long time for these little twinkling experiences to become the object of my attention...but it is happening.' Both Barbara and Julia describe how daily activities have become meditations and Jeffrey talks of even the washing-up sometimes feeling like an offering '...if you can stop and just gaze out of your eyes, with a sort of settling, the visual world just settles into itself. If you persist in it, it is almost as if the thinking mind stops and there is simply the acoustic, visual world just manifesting itself, which I find so powerful at times it almost brings me to tears — maybe tears of relief. You can drop all the socially tiresome stuff and there is nature in itself.' Julia too talks of cutting off, being still and at one with everything: 'it allows you to be in touch with things as they really are. Things unfold in their own time, and it stops this awful Western way of wanting to make the world how you want it to be.'

The common elements in people's experience are striking but what also impresses is the variation depending upon the context of meditation practice. Thus Tibetan Buddhism with its emphasis partly on relationships with others seems to evoke feelings of compassion and love. But even within a tradition each individual reports quite unique effects of meditation and the richness of their reports may be lost in attempts to group or summarise them. But there is a feeling too that the more meditators attempt to communicate their experiences in words, the more difficult it is for non-meditators to appreciate and understand the significance of the experience.

Significant experiences associated with meditation

Of course these people may simply be deluding themselves and rationalising hours of meditation sitting. If we asked those around them how their practice of meditation had changed them as people, we might find little corroboration. More objective research is needed. Such doubts perhaps prompted my expectations that many would report significant experiences, because I have the prejudice that some who are drawn to meditation techniques, unusual practices and traditions are perhaps sensation seeking. However, the majority of those I interview deny any significant experiences associated with meditation practice, telling only of gradual and subtle changes. Jeffrey says that he has come to develop an attitude of offering his life throughout the day and how with this has come a sense of gratitude and calmness 'which is far more enduring than that in enforced sitting...'

But Sarah is able to give an example, having recently returned from a two week solitary retreat. She found her meditations varied between being '...diabolical and those where I'd finish and somehow my whole environment was transformed. For a few moments quite genuinely seeing things in a different way...a very light quality about everything...very beautiful quality. It's the first time I've ever felt that meditation has transformed the way I look at things directly and not just intellectually.' And Daniel talks about driving in his car and '...becoming aware that I'm seeing something in a direct way instead of with concepts...seeing the world with the freshness of a child and a sort of blissful feeling.'

Why do they meditate now?

This was the most challenging questions for the meditators and it is the answers to this question which perhaps provide the clearest glimpse of what meditation means to these people. To Barbara 'It's my central belief, the heart of me. I feel I should honour that part of me...all of it leads up to the purest expression of me.' Jim enjoys meditation because 'physically it feels good...interesting in terms of the insight that I get into myself and the more I can watch all this stuff going on and accept it, the more I can reveal myself to others.' Anna says '...it's the heart of life...It makes life whole... you can make it take in the whole day or everybody you know or everything you have to do...it has that sense of pulling everything together, so it's a real centre.' Sarah meditates because it calms her down and she sees it as 'the only real hope to get rid of suffering by gaining complete control over the mind so that eventually your thoughts, feelings and actions are totally positive.' Julia finds it '...a way of being in touch with the universe.' One person emphasised the importance of the space that meditation provides her. She finds it a time of caring for herself, free from demands and needs and a time of being still and peacefully alone 'to allow her pure and perfect self to open more and more.'

CONCLUSIONS

By discussing with long-term practitioners their meditation career histories many questions of research interest arise and the paucity of the existing research literature in this area is underlined. Short term investigations based on novice practitioners using only one kind of meditation fail to capture the deep significance of the place of meditation in people's lives. Research on meditation would seem to be best advanced by careful (though time-consuming and difficult) longitudinal studies, guided by careful theorizing. The current research, as an example of a methodology, will be extended to include more long-term meditators and those already interviewed will be recontacted at intervals to chart the changes in their meditation and life experiences.

So many meditators talk of effects of meditation manifesting slowly, almost imperceptibly over time, confirming the importance of adopting longer term perspectives in research. And in this respect the notion of the career may be useful since it locates meditation in the context of the individual's life and helps us to recognise the need for studies of how it affects life attitudes and work experience. It becomes clear from this notion too that careers vary between individuals and simply grouping people on the basis of their shared interest in meditation may hide important differences. The interviews also suggest that research might explore the difference between types of meditation. And the aims of meditation should also be taken into consideration since interpretation of experience is likely to be much influenced by initial motivations. Finally for those who adhere to a religious or philosophical conceptual system, meditation has particular significance and functions which differ according to the system of belief and which have consequent impacts upon the interpretation of experience. These factors too must be considered in research.

The value of qualitative research at this time lies in helping to formulate new issues and problems which can be investigated systematically by more structured methodologies. It would, for example, be useful to explore the extent to which people bcome calmer outside of meditation and more detached from minor problems, and to compare different methods in this regard. Changes in patterns and quality of social interactions and in relationships among those who take up and sustain practices of meditation over a long period of time might also be plotted. Here too a focus on the context is important, since those from Buddhist traditions which emphasise compassion, love and equality may be more likely to experience changes in the quality of their social interactions. Reference to Eastern philosophies provides sophisticated conceptual frameworks to guide hypothesis development and within contemporary psychology many potentially useful theoretical orientations exist such as theories of self awareness,[272] reversal theory,[273] self concept theories, [274] symbolic interactionism, theories of social judgement and attribution theory to name but a few.[275]

The questions posed above entail difficulties of investigation, but over-simplifying questions may produce answers which only trivialise the experience. Research on meditation has often sampled the banal in meditators' experience and has illustrated the limitations of the nomothetic approach in areas of subtle and subjectively significant behaviour. The glimpse these interviews give us of the significance of meditation in people's lives illustrates how an ideographic approach at this stage provides unstructured but very rich data. Perhaps one of the consequences of this meeting of methodologies of East and West is that we are forced to turn back and examine psychological methodology more carefully.

A repeated criticism of psychology is that the discipline focusses on phenomena which seem far removed from everyday subjective experience and that the most important experiences and events in people's lives are all too infrequently the subjects of inquiry. The study of meditation perhaps confirms both the need for a science of human behaviour to engage in exploration of people's most profound experiences and the importance of recognising the individuality of such experience and its place within the person's life.

15

The New Religions and Psychotherapy: Similarities and Differences

R. Guy Fielding and Sue Llewelyn

Guy Fielding is a Principal Lecturer in Communication Studies at Sheffield City Polytechnic. His teaching and research is concerned with communication skills, particularly those concerned with persuasion and influence, and he has published widely in the area of persuasion and attitude change.

Sue Llewelyn is a Lecturer in Psychology at the University of Nottingham. Her research interests include the experience of psychotherapy from the subjective viewpoint of both therapists and clients, the mental health of women, and also group psychotherapy. She has written widely on psychotherapy processes and group therapy, and is currently involved in co-authoring a book on women's life choices.

INTRODUCTION

ONE OF THE most noticeable areas of individual growth and development over the past few decades, primarily amongst the affluent, young and self-aware, has been the search for self and for meaning in life, as witnessed by the growth of interest in two distinct fields of personal enquiry. These are the new religions (or at least new versions of old religions) often referred to as cults,[276] and psychotherapy. While the growth of psychotherapy has been on the whole welcomed by observers, the growth in the new religions has frequently been greeted with widespread alarm and condemnation. In this chapter, we shall look at this growth, and we will consider some of the differences and similarities of the two approaches. We will take as our primary focus of interest the new religions, rather than psychotherapy, as an adequate examination of the research concerning psychotherapy is outside the scope of a chapter such as this.

Unlike psychotherapy, cult phenomena have been the focus of much popular attention in recent years. The names of some of the new religions, such as the Moonies, the Orange people, Est, Hare Krishna, the Children of God, and Scientology, have become household words. They have been widely commented upon by the media, politicians, the church, and also by various social scientists. They have particularly fascinated social scientists and psychotherapists, probably because of the striking psychological phenomena purportedly associated with them. These include the adoption of deviant life-styles, the rejection of the cult member's family, and extreme and occasional tragic occurrences such as the mass suicide/murder at Jonestown. They have also fascinated social scientists, we believe, because one of the grounds on which they have been criticised is their use of psychological techniques of persuasion and influence. These are techniques studied, even developed, by psychologists and psychotherapists, and which have been assembled, perhaps purposefully but often on an apparently ad hoc basis by the cult recruiters and trainers, and turned into avowedly irresistable procedures for 'brain-washing' their victims. The fascination for social scientists is quite possibly that of seeing their techniques actually at work; while the interest for therapists is perhaps alarm that major personal change is being effected in the recruits without the professional label of respectability which is usually accorded to psychotherapy, or the protection which is at least theoretically available to the consumers of a professional service.

The underlying theme of our chapter is that there is a need to re-examine at least some of the prevalent beliefs about the new religions, and in particular the popular evaluation of them hinted at above. We will do this by examining each of the grounds on which the new religions have conventionally been judged and criticised, and in each case look at whether these judgements are in fact justified and can be sustained, especially in the light of their similarity in processes and outcomes to the more 'respectable' procedures used in psychotherapy. In addition, we shall examine the issue of whether in fact many of these new religions actually function as religions, as whether in reality they act as a form of psychotherapy for many of their followers.

Let us say at the outset that we are *not* arguing that the new religions are 'a good thing' because they may resemble psychotherapies. We will be trying to show that the verdict of 'guilty' that has so far been passed on the cults is, we believe, based on an inadequate consideration of the evidence. However, we don't think that that makes the new religions 'not guilty.' Rather, we think that *some* of them are profoundly 'guilty,' and are destructive towards their members, but that it is not possible to understand which ones, why, or how to respond and deal with them and their victims until our own thinking about them has been clarified. That is what we shall be trying to do in this chapter, by examining them alongside and in comparison with psychotherapy. Similarly, in considering this parallel between the two types of activity, we are not making a claim that psychotherapy is necessarily a 'good' thing in itself, either. Psychotherapy, like the cult groups, may help some people in some ways at some times during their lives. We intend to argue that the way in which the new religions are effective relates quite closely to the ways that psychotherapy is effective, and it may well be the case that for at least some individuals, involvement in a new religion is no more harmful than involvement in perhaps a rather prolonged and intensive form of psychotherapy.

In addition, we do not wish to deny that there are some very big and significant differences between the two types of practice. For example, most therapy patients do not give away many of their material possessions to the therapist (although they may in some cases pay out considerable sums of money in fees). Nor do they tend to change their names or country of residence in order to be near the therapist, as cult members sometimes do. The families of therapy patients tend not to get so upset about the changes that occur as do those of cult members (although the changes that may take place in therapy do sometimes cause family problems). However, the order of magnitude of involvement is clearly different, as is the extent and nature of the reaction to those changes.

DEFINITIONS

Before proceeding further, we need to define exactly what we mean by 'the new religions,' or cults. In Webster's 1966 Third New International Dictionary, there are three definitions of the word 'cult': (1) A system for the cure of disease based on the dogma, tenets, or principles set forth by its promulgator to the exclusion of scientific experience or demonstration; (2) great or excessive dedication to some person, idea, or organisation; and (3) a religion or mystic regarded as mysterious or unorthodox. Each of these definitions implies that members of what we call cults typically: (1) adhere to a consensual belief system which is deviant in at least some particular with respect to the dominant cultural context; (2) sustain a high level of within-group cohesiveness, and reject participation in the majority culture; (3) are strongly influenced by group behavioural norms (that is, are conformist); (4) impute charismatic (or divine) power to the group or its leadership; and (5) are deviant with respect to the dominant religion.

Obviously, all-encompassing definitions such as the above are inadequate: for example, we may not be justified in treating all of the groups as equivalent, and as having similarly characteristic ways of behaving. (The same point must also be made about the psychotherapies.) Nevertheless, these definitions all point towards a key aspect of groups which are labelled as 'cults': they reject the values and norms of the popular culture in favour of their own unorthodox views. It is the suggestion of some writers[277] that this fact provides the key to understanding the common reponse to the cults: their unorthodoxy threatens the power and control of the orthodox religions and therapies, which must reject the value of the new religions largely because they are dangerous competitors and rivals. Indeed, it is interesting to note that some of the main sources of condemnation have been therapists as well as churchmen. It therefore seems to us that in many ways new religions and therapies are 'competing' for the same groups of people: the young, affluent, and self-questioning.

In order to examine the argument that the processes by which the cult groups function in many ways parallel those by which psychotherapists function, we shall examine a number of aspects of the new religions: their mode of operation; their content; their recruits; and their consequences. In each case, we shall look at the ways in which the new religions have ben castigated, to see whether the objections to them are in fact reasonable or not.

PROCESSES USED BY THE NEW RELIGIONS

A simple-minded comparison between the processes and methods employed by psychotherapists, and those employed by the new religions, might suggest that the one is carried out on a voluntary basis, in the interests of the patient, whereas the other is carried out using techniques of brainwashing, and is not in the interests of the cult member. It is not hard to find accusations of this kind, by sampling typical newspaper stories. For example: 'How love-bombed Mrs Olsen needed to be deprogrammed' (from The Guardian, 9th November, 1983); 'Cult Drove My Kevin to the Grave' (from Bradford Telegraph & Argus, 4th December 1984); 'German Industralist abandons all for Christ' (The Guardian, 21st February 1985); and perhaps the most famous headlines of all: 'The Church that breaks up families' and 'They took away my son and raped his mind' (from the Daily Mail, May 29th 1978). The Times (1st April 1981) reporting on the outcome of the libel case brought by the Moonies against the Daily Mail as a result of these headlines and the articles that accompanied them, used the following headline: 'Cult's "love bomb" that was better than a gun'; and The Guardian, in rather more measured terms, reproted that: 'Jury agree that Moonies cult is brainwashing' (Guardian, 1st April 1981).

The accusation of brainwashing is clearly a key one, and one which needs examination in more detail. The term 'Brainwashing' was first used by an American Journalist, Edward Hunter, as a translation of the Chinese colloqualism

'Hsi Nao,' which literally means 'Wash Brain.' It was used to describe the processed by which prisoners of war in Korea and elsewhere were assumed to have been persuaded to become sympathetic to the views of their captors. The popular image of brainwashing was that it was an enormously successful operation, by which innocent soldiers were turned into mindless communist sympathisers. It is used nowadays to explain the way in which recruits are said to be coerced into rejecting family and friends, and become devoid of individual personality or personal responsibility.

Now, if the new religions can be said to be brainwashing their recruits, most people would probably say that they cannot be understood to be acting in the best interests of their members. Instead, they must be acting in the interests of the cult, which is presumably destructive of individual personality. Brainwashing is assumed to be an all-powerful technique, which is somehow achieved by imposing the will of the evil collective or ideology on to the unsuspecting and unwilling victim.

An important component of this view of the process is that it is irresistible. Yet evidence shows that this is far from being the case. For example, in Korea, of the 7190 American prisoners who were taken and subjected to 'brainwashing,' only twenty-one remained in Korea after the war, and the majority of these returned after eighteen months or so. Likewise of the British, out of 980 prisoners of war, only one remained behind in Korea. So even if the charge of brainwashing were to be sustained, this does not mean that the new religions thereby possess an iresistible means of conversion. So how in fact do the cults fare as 'brainwashers'?

The answer is, not very well. But an immediate qualification which has to be made is that it is obviously difficult to generalise about all of the new religions together, so we shall therefore consider those new religions at whom the charge of brainwashing has been most frequently levelled. The Unification Church (the Moonies) are perhaps the clearest case to consider, for as we have seen, the British courts have upheld the claim made by the Daily Mail that the Unification Church employs brainwashing techniques in its recruitment activities. Barker[278] reported that of every 100 people who attended an introductory weekend workshop, only thirteen affiliated in some way to the Church, and only eight of these joined as full-time members. Less than four people remained as members after two years. If we examine figures presented by the Unification Church itself a similar picture emerges. At the end of August 1981 it was announced that the Moonies' 300 strong team of 'specially-trained' missionaries was leaving Britain. They claimed that during their three-year stay in Britain they had converted 2000 people (Guardian, 26th August 1981), a success rate of 2.2 convertees per recruiter per year. These figures seem to compare rather unfavourably with those achieved by the average insurance salesman. Thus, the impression of an all-powerful recruitment technique seems to fade, and to be replaced with a more realistic image of a social movement using conventional (if somewhat unsuccessful) techniques of persuasion to recruit people to its view of the world, and to membership of the group.

Of course one of the objections to the new religions is not only the way in which they actively encourage the process of conversion, but the way that they even more actively discourage members from seeking disconfirming evidence for the group's theology or values. Most observers confirm that the process of recruitment to one of the new religions involves a intense, emotionally charged period during which time the person's existing ties with the world are challenged, and replaced by new structures, which are more in line with the beliefs held by the religious group.[279] But it should also be noted that many members of the cults, including members of the Unification Church live, not in sealed, isolated and restricted communities but as ordinary members of society. We should also note that an examination of the experience of patients in psychotherapy suggests that parallels exist between the process of conversion to one of the new religions on the one hand, and successfully engaging in psychotherapy on the other. If individuals seek psychotherapy, they are usually expressing some form of discontent with an existing way of behaving and thinking. Hence the first job of any competent therapist is to help patients let go of some of their troublesome, although safe, current ways of behaving. This has to be done by challenging the patient's current understanding of themselves and the world, and encouraging the patient to develop new ways of being in the world. The only way that patients can possibly allow this to happen is if they trust the therapist, and are prepared, at least for a while, to suspend their commitment to current ways of acting and thinking. The therapist then has to encourage patients to experiment with new and hopefully more effective ways of behaving: ways which tend to be informed by the therapist's own view of the world, as well as the therapist's professional theories about what is desirable or 'mature' behaviour. Understood in this way, the role of the therapist is that of an encourager and persuader, who attempts to help the patient to see things more like a mature person (such as the therapist) sees them. In effect, the therapist persuades the patient to become more like the therapist.

According to Frank,[280] the process of psychotherapy is simply a modern version of healing which has been happening throughout the centuries, in all human societies. Frank identifies six key features of healing, which he believes bring about change, largely through the process of persuasion. These features include the presence of socially sanctioned healers who have a rationale or myth to explain their actions; a willingness on the part of the 'patient' to submit to the healer's wisdom; and a set of rituals which mark the 'patient's' acceptance of his or her role. It seems that at least some of these features are also present during recruitment to the new religions. In addition, recent work on the effectiveness of psychotherapy has suggested that the way in which it works is primarily through the operation of non-specific factors, which include features of the therapeutic relationship such as hope, faith, the opportunity to express feelings, and so on.[281]

Such components may also be said to be present at least in the conversion phases of recruitment to cult groups.

As we have seen, during psychotherapy patients submit to a process by which their existing way of making sense of the world is systematically dismantled, so that a new, more effective way of functioning can be assembled. Patients entrust themselves to the therapist, and allow the therapist to learn all sorts of personal and intimate information. There is ample evidence[282] that therapists have considerable influence over their patients, and, despite protestations to the contrary, systematically persuade their patients to change in a variety of ways. Yet the new religions are castigated when they appear to do the very same thing.

Although a reasonably similar change process can be observed in individual therapy and cult involvement, the parallels between the operation of the new religions and psychotherapy can be most clearly seen in group therapy. Group therapy is a process by which the therapist uses the power of group dynamics (such as conformity pressures, group loyalty, modelling and so on) to reinforce change in the individual.[283] Many group leaders consciously make use of the very human tendency on the part of group members to want to belong and to receive approval from others, in order to establish a group norm of sharing and supporting which is part of the process of therapeutic change. A number of researchers have pointed out that a key feature of effective therapy groups is cohesion.[284] Such facts have not passed unnoticed by the cult recruiters, who also use group loyalty, conformity pressure, and plenty of positive reinforcement for conforming to group norms, both to recruit and maintain membership.

CONTENT OF THE NEW RELIGIONS

The next way in which the new religions are often attacked is on the basis that they have bizarre, inhuman beliefs, which are unreasonable and factually inaccurate. Although it is difficult to make general statements about the belief structures of the new religions, one thing is fairly clear. Many if not most critics do not actually know what many of the cult religions believe, so that the majority of judgements are based on prejudice rather than knowledge. But given particular content, how are judgements to be made? For example, the Moonies believe that God intended Adam and Eve to marry and have perfect children, thereby establishing the Kingdom of Heaven on Earth. The devil intervened, in the shape of the snake and seduced Eve. Eve passed her impurity on to Adam, bringing about the Fall. But how do we judge whether this is good or bad? It is our opinion that this is largely a matter of values and social consensus, not of fact.

Furthermore, such beliefs which may seem peculiar taken out of context, can easily appear reasonable or even logical, within the appropriate context. It is perhaps important here to compare such a belief with other, more conventional beliefs. For example, the traditional Christian belief holds as a sacred truth that the Son of God was born of a Virgin, performed a number of miracles, was crucified and was clinically dead for three days, after which He was resurrected from the dead, and ascended to Heaven. In His name, believers regularly eat and drink symbolic representations of His blood and body. The point of this is simply to demonstrate how bizarre common beliefs may appear when taken out of context, and without the mythic richness which is given by a community which understands the symbolic truths represented in the simple story. The same doubtless applies to many of the truths espoused by some of the new religions, although most critics do not take the time to enquire.

However, there are beliefs and practices espoused by some of the cults about which we do feel able to make judgements, and which appear to us to be morally bankrupt: for example the belief that the ends justify the means. This belief underlies and justifies strategic behaviour, such as lying to new recruits, manipulating and deceiving members of the public and so on. In no way do we want to be understood as condoning such behaviour. But we also believes that in acting in this way, members of the new religions are not behaving differently from members of many other groups who also believe that the end justifies the means. For example, many groups believe in the use of violent revolution, or in censorship during warfare, because these acts are said to be in the long term interests of the group. Indeed, the Christian religion is a good example. In the name of Christ, believers have tortured and murdered thousands of non-believers throughout history; here too the ends were said to justify the means. Another example might be the involuntary incarceration of some patients in mental hospitals, for treatment against their will, which is assumed to be in their long-term interests.[285]

It is most important to reiterate here that we do not wish to suggest that the beliefs or practices of any particular cult are morally acceptable to us, or in particular that we in any way support Moonie beliefs and practices. However, we do want to argue that if we condemn the Unification Church, the Scientologists, or any other sect on the basis that their beliefs are irrational and inhuman, or that their actions are unethical and intolerant, then we must also apply these self-same standards to our own beliefs and actions. And if we apply the same standards to other areas of life we find that some of our most respected institutions may be equally 'guilty,' as are some of our therapeutic practices.

CHARACTERISTICS OF THOSE JOINING THE NEW RELIGIONS

One of the most frequently heard accusations made of the new religions is that they tend to attract people who are in need of psychological help, and those who are inadequate or even psychologically disturbed. A number of researchers have looked at the characteristics of recruits to the new religions, and have reported evidence which seems to confirm this. For example, whilst it appears that most recruits come from middle class families, and may well have above average educational level,[286] a common antecedent of those joining is some sort of trouble in the family.[287] Another background variable seems to be excessive anxiety about the approach of adulthood.[288] Typically, recruits are at a stage of life in which they are open and receptive to new ideas and experiences. The stereotyped picture of the rather lost-looking young person en route for nowhere in particular and being picked up by recruiters at the railway station, is not without some basis in reality. Levine[289] reports that cults do tend to attract individuals who are in some psychological pain before joining, and Etemad[290] has described cult recruits as 'depressed, inadequate, or borderline anti-social youths.' According to Galanter[291] 'their preoccupations with purpose and destiny are closely associated to a dissatisfaction with interpersonal relations, leading to loneliness and a sense of alienation.' A marked degree of use of illegal drugs prior to recruitment has been noted by other researchers.[292]

Although most researchers are agreed on the finding that many recruits are looking for some deeper meaning and purpose in their lives, they dispute whether there are more than the average number of deeply disturbed individuals amongst their ranks. Some researchers[293] have failed to find evidence of an excess of serious mental disturbance amongst members of the new religions, and point out that like any population, there are bound to be some with psychiatric disorders. On the other hand, others suggest that there does seem to be some evidence of a greater than normal level of psychopathology amongst recruits: for example, several report a higher than average number of cult members with some pre-existing degree of psychiatric disorder.[294]

Of course there are considerable methodological problems with retrospective reports, in that people may obviously colour their accounts according to the particular view that they currently wish to espouse. Nevertheless, it does seem likely that the new religions do attract a substantial number of people who are in some psychological distress and yet who also have some degree of willingness to change. Prior to joining the group, such people seem to be dissatisfied with their personal circumstances, and to be ready to do something about them. Given the nature and extent of the personal and social changes involved, it would be surprising if circumstances and motivations such as these did not exist amongst recruits. As such, the new religions obviously appeal to people similar to those who are attracted to psychotherapy, and want to change something about themselves. Interestingly, some writers have noted an increasing tendency for some individuals to try out both sources of help, and to progress, possibly rather indiscriminately, through a number of different therapies and religious groups until they find one which suits them.[295] But it is hard to understand how the new religions should be held responsible for the alienation and human confusion that they are seeking to alleviate, any more than doctors should be held responsible for the illnesses that they are seeking to cure.

CONSEQUENCES OF JOINING ONE OF THE NEW RELIGIONS

If as suggested above, the impetus for seeking either psychological help or membership of a religious group is reasonably similar, so the outcome of both types of involvement are to some extent parallel. In brief, although some individuals do appear to be harmed by the experience,[296] the majority appear either to gain psychologically from their involvement, or to be relatively unaffected.[297] Galanter[298] points out that in 1920, William James wrote of religious conversion as a process whereby a person who is confused, inferior and unhappy, becomes certain, superior and happy. The consequences of joining a cult religon can be similar to those of conversion to any other belief system: increased certainty, confidence and contentment.

Of course, as in the psychotherapies, the outcome is likely to be different for different people: for the lost and lonely the new religions may provide a structure of meaning and a community of like-minded people; while for the deeply disturbed, they may provide a form of asylum. Levine[299] concludes from a clinical examination of research into cult group membership that 'Cults do significantly reduce symptoms of anxiety, depression, (and) confusion in members who experience these.' She also points out that 'Cults do at times serve as a haven, and even a therapeutic milieu for members with serious psychiatric behavioral disorders.'

In addition, Levin and Zegans[300] report the case of a schizophrenic youth who was profoundly helped by his unconventional religious beliefs, and conclude that: 'Many of the members of the new religions are seeking what has always been available to the shaman, a structure of meaning into which his own idiosyncratic experiences can be fitted, a tradition which guides and shapes otherwise bewildering and frightening psychological states. For these participants in the new religions, cults sustain the legitimacy of their experiences and provide a viewpoint from which they can be interpreted.'

On the other hand, it is without doubt true the *some* individuals are harmed by cult group membership. Levine[301] concludes that 'Cults do contribute to the appearance of emotional problems in a significant number of ex-cultists,' and Singer[302] believes that ex-cult members are likely to suffer from depression, severe passivity, indecisiveness and loneliness, in addition to considerable fear of the cult. Conway and Seigelman[303] talk of the dangers of 'snapping' into a robot-like state, in which the individual is unable to think or act for themselves. However, Galanter[304] points out that these negative reactions are much more common amongst those who had been forcefully 'de-programmed' than those who chose to leave of their own accord.

But the same is also true of some psychotherapies. Recent research on the outcome of psychotherapy suggests that while many patients will benefit from therapy, a small proportion actually appear to be harmed by the process.[305] In addition, Lieberman, Yalom and Miles[306] point out that some psychotherapy groups produce 'casualties': individual who leave their therapy much worse than when they initially sought help; while Llewelyn[307] provides details of some of the unethical practices which sometimes occur in psychotherapy, particularly of a sexual nature, and which can cause longlasting and serious problems for therapy patients.

Even more seriously, some psychotherapy groups can themselves become rather like cults, and while purporting to be devoted to increasing an individual's psychological health, they can in fact do the opposite. Temerlin and Temerlin[308] describe how a number of professional therapists have abused their professional position to set up groups which encourage obedience and adoration by the 'patients'; likewise, Hochman[309] provides details of some of the coercive and destructive activities which have been labelled 'therapeutic' by a number of therapists who work well out of the way of professional scrutiny and study.

CONCLUSIONS AND IMPLICATIONS

The above analysis of the process, content and outcome of involvement in the new religions, points to the fact that a judgement is being brought against them which is based not so much on objective, psychological evidence, as on a criticism of the beliefs and values of these religions. Yet it appears that many commentators are saying that cults should be condemned and restricted, *not* because they disagree with what the cults believe, but because of the consequences which they imply follow from the way in which the cults present their beliefs. However, as we have shown, it is not clear that this evaluation is based on a rational analysis of any objective evidence characterising the cult phenomenon: recruitment, content or consequences.

One clue to what in fact could be the basis of this criticism is given precisely by the fact that no distinctions are made between the different new religions. It is precisely what they have in common that is the basis of criticism. And what they have in common is an opposition to the status quo: both the status quo in contemporary religion, and in the psychotherapeutic establishment. Hence one way of understanding the pervasive negative evaluation of the new religions is to see it as self-interest on the part of commentators and even researchers who see the cults as threatening because they represent 'unfair' competition. An additional clue is given when we compare the evidence and interpretations offered by different kinds of researchers. Broadly speaking, the most 'hostile' research has been presented by researchers working within psychiatry and psychotherapy, less hostile research has been presented by psychologically-orientated researchers, and the least hostile, most temperate analyses have been those produced by sociologically-influenced researchers. But as we noted at the beginning of the chapter, the new religions and psychotherapy are competing for exactly the same client group; the young, the affluent, and the self-aware. Could this hostility then be related to simple social and economic competition, a pressure not influencing the judgements of psychologically and sociologically orientated researchers, who are thereby able to adopt a more truly disinterested perspective? In a revealing article in the 'house-journal' of the American medical profession, Clark[310] argues:

> ... [the physician] may not immediately appreciate the degree to which the medical profession as a whole is under attack by these organisations. For one thing almost all embrace magic in many forms, including faith healing, and in their general rejection of their surrounding culture discard scientific linear thinking: thus, they reject modern medicine and consider physicians as enemies. In practice even those cults which occasionally use medical facilities

are extremely reluctant to seek this help or *to pay
their bills* (our emphasis).

The response of the leaders of the established religions can
also be understood as, in part at least, a reaction to the
challenge posed by the new religions to their moral and social
authority. The importance of the challenge posed in terms of
simple competition for converts, and the economic power
that these converts represent, should also not be underes-
timated. By extension, the response of opinion leaders within
politics, the law, the media, etc should also be seen in the
light of the need to defend the existing social order. Viewed
in this way, reactions to the new religions can be seen as
another example of the 'moral panics' described by Cohen[311]
and characterised by outrage and over-reaction (as well as
confusion). In the perspective of history and social change,
many of today's most well-respected religions, for instance
the Society of Friends (Quakers), the Mormons and even the
Moral Re-armament movement within the Church of England,
were subjected to, and have survived similar attacks.

However, as we have hinted throughout this chapter, our
personal evaluation of the new religions is a generally negative
one, and we feel that we should state the criteria against
which we have formulated our judgement. These are: (1) Do
we agree with, and approve of, the teachings of that particular cult? (2) Do we believe the teachings of that particular
cult to be true and correct? (3) Do we believe that the cult, and
its agents, act morally in their dealings with its own members,
and with non-cult members (for instance, does it lie, cheat
and deceive)? Against these criteria, there are few cults which
we personally find attractive. However, the essential point to
be made is that these are non-psychological criteria and
judgements. They are criteria which concern personal values,
beliefs and attitudes, and we accept that our evaluations are
in this way subjective and value-laden. What we hope we
have demonstrated is that this is the only legitimate basis on
which such evaluations can be made.

The attempt to invoke psychological perspectives, theories and evidence as the basis for, and as the legitimation of, criticism of new religions also has a number of implications for psychology (and for the other social sciences). The first of these is that it is important that those involved in any debate of this kind should make explicit the ethical/value issues that are involved, and if this is not done willingly, it should be one of the first issues addressed by any psychologist invited to comment on, or wanting to take part in the debate. The second implication is that, if we offer criticisms, based on psychological analyses, of the worth of particular phenomena, we should also be prepared to consider the ethical issues raised by our own technologies, and we should be prepared to judge ourselves by the same standards. This would force us to spell out, for instance, in the areas of individual and group psychotherapy, the nature of, and the relation between process, content and outcome in terms of their ethical con- sequences. At the present time the ethical acceptability of these practices appears to be one of the 'taken-for-granteds' of the psychotherapeutic enterprise. An additional implication is that, whilst the citing of psychology and psychologists in controversies over the new religions is in many ways a positive trend, indicating the acceptance of the psychological perspective as an important and useful one, it also has its dangers. These are the readiness with which acceptable standards of evidence and analysis can be abandoned in 'the rush to judgement,' and the related way in which the professional and critical role of the psychologist can be so easily misappropriated.

We would like to end on a positive note, which we have found useful in our evaluation of the claims of both the supporters of the new religions, and of various therapeutic theories. The following quotation was used by Vaughan[312] in her discussion of the new religious movements, and we have found it as apposite as she did. The words are those of Buddha, in the Kalamas Sutra, and in our view, should represent the attitude of the careful and scientifically minded observer of the new religions.

Do not believe in what you have heard; do not believe intraditions because they have been handed down for many generations; do not believe in anything because it is rumoured and spoken of by many; do not believe in anything merely because the written statement of some old sage is produced; do not believe conjectures; do not believe merely in the authority of your teachers and elders. After observation and analysis, when it agrees with reason and is conducive to the good and benefit of one and all, then accept it and live up to it.

16
Psychotherapy and Techniques of Transformation

Paul Heelas and Rachael Kohn

Paul Heelas is a Lecturer in the Anthropology of Religion in the Department of Religious Studies, University of Lancaster. His research is in the areas of the cross-cultural study of emotion and the new religious movements, particularly Rajneeshism and Exegesis.

Rachael Kohn is currently Visiting Leverhulme Fellow at the Department of Religious Studies, University of Lancaster. She has conducted research on the new religious movements, particularly in Canada.

'DOES THERAPY LEAD lead to spiritual life?' asks Frans Bakker, an adept of Da Free John, and many have answered in the negative. But if participants in a fair number of new religious movements are to be taken seriously, psychotherapeutic techniques *do* have an important role to play in the spiritual quest. Indeed, if this testimony is counted as evidence, those who see therapy as incompatible with spirituality have got it wrong. For example *est*, as Werner Erhard's initiatory seminar used to be called, draws techniques from the Western psychological tradition which are put to the service of 'enlightenment.' The flourishing nature of Erhard's organization and the testimonies of participants appear to belie the incompatibility thesis.

Positive assessments of the role of psychotherapy within spiritual contexts are backed up in the final sections of this chapter. One argument is that 'secular' psychotherapies can work on the 'ego' in ways which almost demand their employment in spiritual paths. However, some of our discussion of what it is about psychotherapy that has allowed it to be used as a technique of transformation should also please the advocates of incompatability. But because spiritual matters lie beyond the province of academic proof (they fall outside the scope of logic and empirical assessment) we limit ourselves to presenting different interpretations as alternatives. There are a number of ways of understanding the relationship between psychological techniques and spiritual realization. We leave it to those who have first hand experience, or second hand prejudices, to make the choice they desire.

INCOMPATABILITY

Psychotherapy, many would argue, is scientifically informed. The medical approach is often to the forefront. Scientifically grounded methods are employed to enable people to change themselves. The goal is to acquire self development, or rather self normalization, in a fashion which accords with what is scientifically (and socially) possible. With this frame of reference, religion or spirituality is the enemy. It is positively harmful to rely on religious 'mumbo jumbo' in a desperate effort to find salvation. Crutches have to be knocked away. What matters is strengthening the ego, many still agreeing with Freud's view that 'where there was id, there shall ego be.' Surrender to father figures or to oceanic spiritual experience can only be damaging. Such reliance is bound to threaten what is all important, namely scientifically demonstrated means of obtaining socially defined ego identities.

Therapists such as Freud argue the incompatability thesis from the side of science and society. However some advocates of the spiritual path, now treating the ego as the enemy, argue to the same end. Bhagwan Shree Rajneesh, for example, hates conventional psychotherapy. Cultivation of the ego is intrinsically damaging:

> Western psychology still thinks in terms of a healthy ego. But ego can never be healthy. It's a contradiction in terms. Ego, as such, is ill.[313]

Cultivation of the ego attaches people ever more strongly to the limitations of the human sphere. Lying 'beyond' the ego, realization of the freedom and natural virtues of the spiritual domain is ruled out of court. The spiritual domain can only be realized when people go to a master, someone who works to an end which stands in stark contrast to that held by the psychotherapist. For, continues Bhagwan, a master

> doesn't help you to attain a stronger ego. He makes you feel that the ego you have is already too much. Drop it! Let it go!

Only then can you be 'whole and flowing.'

How on earth can psychotherapies, aiming to handle fear, guilt, anger and the like by developing a functional ego structure, be of any use to the spiritual enterprise? It certainly looks as though ego identification simply enhances the very thing which cuts us off from spiritual experience. It certainly looks as though going *to* the ego to diminish unhappiness is a very different enterprise from going *beyond* it. How can we expect to detach ourselves from our egos when success is defined in terms of how our egos should be? In short, it looks as though psychological and spiritual growth aim at entirely incompatable states of affairs: the ego, and that which cannot be identified with it. Furthermore, it looks as though attempts to combine the two kinds of growth can only be counterproductive. There might be talk of enlightenment in *est*, for example, but use of techniques drawn from western psychology ensure that only the ego is affected. As Skynner puts it, approaches of this variety 'mix levels' and so

> stand in danger of offering a half-truth sufficiently like the real thing to satisfy this deeper (spiritual) hunger without leading to anything more real and even of simply increasing the attachment to the ordinary self.[314]

COMPATABILITY

If participants in the new religious movements are to be believed, however, a very different picture emerges. It could of course be the case that an awful lot of people and the movements with which they are associated have got it all wrong. This possibility is discussed later. For the present we introduce historical and testimonial evidence suggesting that psychotherapy can be put to spiritual use; that psychotherapies *are* transformative. We will see what lies behind the observation, reported by Needleman, that:

> The shrinks are beginning to sound like gurus, and gurus are beginning to sound like shrinks.[315]

The general setting is provided by the quite strong tendency for 'secular' psychotherapies to generate or otherwise become associated with spirituality. Contemporaries of Freud – Jung, Groddeck, Reich and Assagioli to name but four – bear witness. So does the increasing extent to which those interested in effecting personal growth have broadened their frontiers. First humanistic psychology (discussed by Vitz in a work with the revealing title *Psychology as Religion*),[316] then the growth or human potential movement, and then, yet more spiritually orientated, transpersonal psychology.

Clare and Thompson go so far to write of 'the inexorable thrust which propels every new therapy into a creed of salvation.'[317] More specifically, they claim:

> Reichian message, Moreno's psychodrama, Rogerian psychotherapy – they each began as a relatively circumscribed approach to helping the mentally distressed and ill and ended up as a programme for living, a philosophical statement and a religious message.

Their overall conclusion is that what was devised as a way of freeing humans from the hold of religion has been put to service in the religious enterprise:

> A search for a way to live, a search which in this century led first to the early, tentative steps of psychoanalysis... now, seventy years later, leads

back to the religious sensibilities and mysticisms
psychoanalysis was intended to supplant.[318]

The tendency for 'secular' psychotherapies to generate spirituality can be yet more vividly illustrated. It seems certain
that a not inconsiderable number of new religious movements have in measure been generated by the spiritual
potentials of psychotherapy. Dianetics, basically a Freudian
psychotherapy, rapidly became subsumed by the Church of
Scientology. Much the same kind of development can be seen
in the history of Psychosynthesis, Silva Mind Control, Rebirthing, the International Society of Analytical Triology, and even
in some manifestations of Primal Therapy and Co-Counselling.
Other therapies which have become religious movements
include Dianology (Church of Eductivism), Abilitism (Sana-
tana Dharma Foundation) and Compulsions Analysis (The
Process). All these movements might have owed much to the
Freudian legacy — but all have transcended it. We can also
think of Synanon Foundation Inc., founded in 1958 as an
Alcholics Anonymous alternative, and proclaimed as the Synanon Religion in 1974. Other drug rehabilitation units, especially those employing the Minnesota model, have also
developed spiritual features. One well known unit in London
appears to be well on the way to becoming the home of a new
religious movement.

The most arresting evidence for compatability, however, is
provided by movements which have been specifically established as ways of utilizing psychological techniques to bring
about enlightenment. Self religions, provided for example by
Bhagwan and Erhard, draw on western techniques to advance
spirituality as envisaged in Eastern terms. More exactly, techniques are used to handle the ego, the entity which stands in
the way of monistic realization of the self itself — the witness
of experience, of truth, of the source, of ultimate unitariness.

In this context it is not possible to distinguish between
psychological and spiritual growth. The former works to the

end of handling the ego in spiritually efficacious fashion. As Bhagwan says,

> This whole life is a challenge to growth. That is the true religion and true psychology, too — because a true religion cannot be other than a true psychology. I call that psychology the 'Psychology of the Buddhas.' It gives you a great challenge to be more than you are. It gives you a divine discontent. It makes you aflame with a desire to go higher and higher — not higher than others but higher than yourself.[319]

Indeed, what are called 'spiritual therapies' have worked to bring many to Bhagwan's path. At least until recently, non-sannyasins (Bhagwan's initiates are called 'sannyasins') have come to ashrams to take courses in Rebirthing, Primal, Rajneesh Dynamic Bodywork, Body Awareness, Self Exploration, Hypnotherapy, the 48-Hour Marathon (including bioenergetics, gestalt work and dance), and so on. For many these courses trigger conversion. They lead participants to see what lies beyond the ego.

Werner Erhard's claim is that his seminars facilitate 'de-identification.' In the words of this master,

> The person de-identifies with his mind, de-identifies with his body; he de-identifies with his emotions, he de-identifies with his problems; he de-identifies with his *maya*, he begins to see that he is not the Play.[320]

Techniques employed are highly reminiscent of those found in more secular contexts. Confrontational processes, encounter, gestalt, guided fantasy, catharsis, positive thinking, cognitive therapy, transactional analysis, psychodrama, to name but some, are variously employed. And as with conversion to Bhagwan's path, techniques appear to work. A number of studies show a high incidence of reported benefits.[321] And research on a movement not dissimilar to Erhard's, namely Exegesis, shows that many of those who follow the path report experiencing the 'god' that lies within.[322]

Casting his eye over the American scene, Kornfield surmises that 'psychology is a big part of our country's religion right now.'[323] It is difficult to estimate figures, but a conservative guess would be that at least ten million Americans are currently involved with psychospiritual paths, ranging from spiritually significant encounter groups to fully-fledged self religions.[324] Together with the fact that psychotherapies help effect conversion, their spiritual potential, we have seen, is suggested by a number of psychotherapies having generated religious movements. It certainly looks as though psychotherapy can do more than simply strengthen the ego.

OPTIONS

We can now look at different ways of explaining how the supposed enemy of spirituality has come to be put to the service of enlightenment. Our question, it will be recalled, is: 'What is it about psychotherapy that has allowed it to be used in this fashion?'

One answer, which will please advocates of the incompatability thesis, is that far from allowing people to go beyond the bounds of personal development psychotherapies are employed to attach participants to a new kind of ego identity — that of dependency on their master. Participants are broken down and made to feel guilty (confrontational techniques); participants are rendered suggestible (cathartic techniques); participants are built up again (positive thinking); and participants are built up in such a way that they can be used to further the ambitions of Bhagwan, Erhard or whoever.[325] Spiritual teachings to do with the self as ultimate or god-like have nothing to do with true spirituality. They are used to motivate participants, to strengthen their egos in accord with the masters' plans, to give religious gloss and santification to what are essentially capitalist ambitions.

A related theme is that spirituality has been added to

psychotherapy in order to attract, and then keep, those who are interested in bettering themselves. Some time ago Mowrer wrote,

> Psychiatry is wonderful, religion is wonderful, put them together and you get something better still![326]

People are attracted to psychotherapies — such as Dianetics, for example. They experience benefits. They go so far, but still feeling dissatisfied they want more. Those who run the therapies therefore engage in the strategy of adding that something more — in the case of Scientology, the possibility of becoming an Operating Thetan, a god-like being. But because Scientology (and most other self religions) continue to present themselves in ways likely to appeal to those interested in psychological growth, they are able to continue to draw their clientele from the psychotherapeutic subculture. Psychotherapeutic presentation, combined with the suggestion that here is something more, functions to ensure numerical success. It is thus not without significance that according to one study, eighty percent of those attracted to the growth movement have previously been in more secular forms of psychotherapy.[327]

Another theme to do with how psychotherapy can be used in conjunction with spirituality to attract and then keep those interested in perfecting themselves leads us to consider the dynamics of psychotherapeutic processes. It seems clear that many processes are powerful, generating intense and unusual (emotional) experiences. From the work of Schachter and Singer,[328] as well as a number of other experimental studies, we know that experiences of this variety are open to interpretation. What this means is that the relatively inchoate experiences felt during a sannyasin-led group or during an *est* seminar can be moulded or transformed into experiences which accord with the teachings of the movement in question. As a non-sannyasin taking part in a Primal group has told us:

> I felt a gap appear in my mind. It was powerful. Then Bhagwan appeared.[329]

He interpreted his experience in terms of the meanings closest to hand — and so quite naturally felt the presence of Bhagwan. Conversion took place.

It seems incontestable that one of the most important characteristics of psychotherapy which has allowed it to be put to use in the service of enlightenment lies with its capacity to generate unusual experiences. This goes a long way towards explaining why 'secular' psychotherapies can become more spiritual; and why psychotherapeutic techniques are employed in enlightenment seminars. The incompatability critic sees this as generating inauthentic spiritual experiences. Emotions bound up with the ego, in that they 'flood' when the ego is threatened, are the real basis of whatever 'spirituality' is experienced. However, it could equally be the case that psychotherapeutic techniques designed to 'shake' or 'strip' the ego do in fact reveal dimensions of experience which lie beyond the ego and which are of genuine spiritual worth. Whether or not this option is valid cannot be settled from the academic perspective. The possibility that experiences are of the self itself, are of god, cannot be assessed by academic methods of inquiry. However, it perhaps worth nothing that the testimony of major religious traditions, and of a number of interpreters (such as Martin Buber and Victor Turner), apparently support claims of this variety.[330]

Bearing in mind that we cannot arrive at a final decision on the subject, more evidence suggestive of the compatability thesis is that 'secular' psychotherapies often address the ego in ways which accord with what self religions aim to do. Consider Scientology, where an aim is to become 'clear' by eradicating 'engrams.' Although traditional Freudian therapies aim to strengthen the ego by eradicating emotional traumas, the fact remains that the processes involved appear to be perfectly compatible with the different aim of going beyond the ego ('engrams,' including emotional traumas) to become 'clear.' Dianetics-Scientology shares with Freudian psychotherapy the idea that traumatic incidents are stored until 'relived' ('abreacted'). The psychodynamic process works in both settings to free the ego of harmful influences.

Another illustration of compatability is provided by the importance many psychotherapies and all self religions attach to the act of becoming aware of the operations of the ego. For Erhard 'awareness' is the key to transformation. In the words of an *est* trainer,

> An asshole is a machine that thinks he's not a machine; an *enlightened* man is an asshole that *knows* he is a machine.[331]

It is thus hardly surprising that such seminars draw on psychotherapies (Transactional Analysis, gestalt, confrontational techniques, etc.) which strive to display the extent to which peoples' lives are conditioned by the games they play; by their 'strategies for survival,' unconsciously adopted and now in control. Neither is it surprising to find that Freudian derived psychodynamic theory is here put to use in order to advance self knowledge.

Where scientology might hold that 'engrams' can be erased by catharsis, Erhard, as we have seen, holds that the ego is with us for ever − so instead of using catharsis to get rid of distressful experiences processes are employed to make people fully aware of their emotional life. We can best illustrate by reference to the 'platform process' which occurs in most dramatic form in the Exegesis Standard Seminar. After a group catharsis session, which leads participants to feel that they can exorcise painful emotions, small groups are lined up on a platform, in front of a large audience, and are told to 'cathart.' They do, sometimes half-vomiting. The seminar trainer then tells them that they have been ridiculous, performing like that in front of so many, taking pride in their ability to break convention in order to get rid of their painful emotions. The trainer goes on to reveal what is really happening:

> If you carry on piling up a load of shit in front of yourself the pile will just get larger and larger.

The point of catharsis, it transpires, is to enable participants to get to know their emotions.[332]

There is much more to be said about compatabilities between psychotherapies and self religions. One obvious point, for example, is that the theory of ego employed by the self religions is virtually identical to that found in behavioural psychology and therapy. Gurdjieff, the father of self religions, taught that 'man is a machine,' and he took great delight in meeting J.B. Watson, the father of behavioural psychology. Another important similarity which could be explored is that between cognitive therapy and the role played by 'on the spot' psychoanalysis during psychospiritual seminars. But what of the argument that psychotherapies strengthen the ego?

All we can say on this crucial point is that this does not seem to happen in the self religions. First, the presence of a realm of experience beyong the ego, experienced when the ego is 'cleared' or rendered fully conscious, ensures that ego attachment is not enhanced. The realm ensures that the ego is put in perspective. And second, the presence of such a realm means that the nature of therapies can be transformed. They can be effected by Enlightened masters. This theme is clearly in evidence in Bhagwan's path. Rajneesh spiritual therapy, it is held, goes beyond therapies which allow participants to 'hang on' to their identities, lifestyles and the like. This is because they occur in the 'context' of Bhagwan. It is his spiritual energy which opens up 'the meditative space' in participants. It is his spiritual energy which transforms conventional therapies into techniques which bring people to god. Thus we are told,

> Rajneesh spiritual therapy is humanistic psychology that has been transformed through being in the hands of an enlightened Master. The way (spiritual therapists) conduct their programs has its source in the meditative space within themselves that has opened up through being with Him. This inner space is His context.[333]

Most of the self religions reject the term 'psychotherapy'. Representatives claim that their techniques might be derived from mainstream psychotherapy but work in different fashion by virtue of their being utilized by skilled masters or 'context-setters.' Who knows? — other than participants and critics, of course.

Part II: Psychology as religion

Now let us come at the question from the other side, and look at the spiritual or religious elements that may be present in what is conventionally described as psychotherapy. The most influential psychotherapies, especially those deriving from Freud, are not exactly devoid of religious characteristics. If this is true, the deployment of psychoanalytically based therapies for spiritual ends is an ironic but not an entirely surprising phenomenon. The following interpretation of these therapies will resonate strongly with themes which appeared in the first part of this chapter. Our aim is to show how short a step it is from believing in Freud to believing in the message of self religions. Granted the impact that Freud has made, the religious ingredients of his message go a long way towards explaining why psychotherapeutic techniques are felt to be compatible with, indeed to facilitate, the spiritual search of many in the west.

The first remarkably religious element of psychoanalysis is Freud's theory of the origin of neurosis, in which the psychological downfall of man is given a prehistoric ancestry and eternal significance not unlike the Biblical story of the fall of Adam and Eve. In *Totem and Taboo*[334] Freud recounts the primal drama which has been imprinted on the human psyche as the prototype of the Oedipal conflict. The son kills the father in order to take possession of a woman he has gathered to himself. Repressed because of its forbiddenness, the conflict is doomed to reappear in the emotional development of every child, and if unresolved will be the cause of adult neurosis. Freud's theory of the primal deed bears an obvious resemblance to the Genesis story, in which the shaping of human character is a consequence of the original sin of rebellion against the Father. And the role of psycho-analysis in society is also parallel to that played by religion. Whereas salvation in the Judaeo-Christian tradition is dependent on the knowledge of humankind's sinfulness, cure in the psychoanalytic tradition is founded on the unmasking of the origins of human neurosis.

If *Totem and Taboo* did not play a central role in the complex theory of psychoanalysis, the concept of the unconscious, wherein lie the repressed secrets of humankind's forgotten origins, is crucial to the entire Freudian perspective. As well as being the repository of repressed events, wishes and unregenerate instincts, the omniscient unconscious was believed to retain all impressions from earliest experience[335] as well as bearing the imprint of the cosmic death and life urges. The unconscious is therefore a source of mental conflict whose subversive power is weakened by the release of its secrets into consciousness.

The disarming of the unconscious is not a simple matter of 'confession,' for the conscious self (ego) actively represses the traumatic and the immoral. 'Infantile amnesia,' for example, 'hides the earliest impressions of our mental life from *all of us.*'[336] 'Memories' of disturbing dreams or past events are distorted in an effort to evade the truth. Yet the ego's defensive measures point indirectly to the truth, and Freud believed that 'every former state of memory content may thus be restored.'[337]

It is here that the psychoanalyst takes on the quasi-religious role of the 'seer,' for it is he alone, and not even the sincerest of patients, who can understand the true meaning of narratives and dream symbols.[338] In a maxim that precludes the conscious self from guilelessness, Freud stated, 'it is the presence of resistance that is the test of significance, the best clue to the importance of the material under consideration.'[339] Nothing of importance will readily be disclosed by the patient, and the key to the matter is likely to be concealed under layers of self-deception. Only the psychoanalyst possesses the power to discern it. As 'seer,' therefore, the psychoanalyst becomes the *uniquely qualified mediator* between humanity's conscious self, which is rooted in the construction of social expectations, and its unconscious reality, which contains a mixture of primordial and primary experience.

That such a process of discernment requires the patient's absolute faith in the powers of the analyst, as much as a willingness to lay bare the contents of his or her unconscious, is unquestionable.[340] The intellectual submission is underscored by the belief that a patient's critical self-reflection hinders the process of cure.[341] In contrast, the analyst, according to Freud, appears as invulnerable as a religious ascetic, whose 'severe discipline,' 'courage,' and generally 'irreproachable character,' is presented to the patient in an inpenetrable facade of opacity and 'coldness of feeling.'[342] The gulf between patient and analyst is as important in the process of cure as it is in the purely medical situation, for the principle known as the placebo effect, in which faith in a doctor and his medicine can cure an illness, is undoubtedly paralleled in the psychoanalytic situation. Indeed, Jerome Frank's editorial on 'The Two Faces of Psychotherapy,' in which he compares the techniques of psychoanalysis with those of 'religio-magical' healers, makes the same point.[343]

It is finally to Freud's view of religion that we turn to find the most potent comparison of the psychoanalytic experience with the religious one. Freud's attack on religion was basic to his indictment of the church's outworn dogmatic authority and the individual's submission of his rational mind to it. Yet Freud curiously may have reinforced the already prevalent Nineteenth Century romantic view that both disparaged organized religion as false and authoritarian, and recognized religious *feeling* as a pristine state of the soul, observed most authentically in children. In his often quoted response to Romain Rolland,[344] Freud dismissed the 'oceanic feeling' of religious bliss as the consequence of a fixation at the narcissistic stage of infancy, when the child seeks union with the mother. Despite Freud's rejection of this regressive activity, he nonetheless rooted the religious feeling in that great repository of true reality, the unconscious, and identified it with the earliest form of bliss, the selfless union of the child with the parent. Although the moral critique contained in Freud's attack on religion has become history, the fundamentally human source of religious feeling has taken root in the notion of the unconscious.

After Freud, the notion of the unconscious continued to carry religious connotations. In the analytical psychology of Carl Jung, the unconscious as the home of the numinous found direct support. But here, the unconscious is significant less for its experience of religious feeling than for its inheritance of a symbolic universe of religious meaning shared by the human species. Whereas plumbing the unconscious in psychoanalysis aimed at dispelling neuroses and thereby improving social and interpersonal functioning, in Jungian analytical psychology, it is explicitly a method of gaining wisdom and enlightenment.[345]

The specifically European, even Nineteenth Century character of Jungian analytic psychology has had few followers in North America. Several other psychoanalytic offshoots, however — some quite remote from their Freudian roots — have popularized the omniscience of the unconscious, and have sought ways to 'tap' its spiritual, even miraculous, powers.

One variant of psychoanalysis that hovers on the brink of the explicitly religious is Arthur Janov's Primal Therapy, to which we referred in Part I. Positing the existence of a Primal Pain residing in the unconscious, Janov held it to be the cause of layers of debilitating ego defence mechanisms. What is required to get rid of these defences is intensive emotional regression to the universally experienced Primal Pain: the child's fear of the loss of parental love. Reliving the Pain acts to expel it and also to 'shut off' all its attendant neuroses. The patient is often completely cured, it is claimed, in less than three weeks.[346] That a variant of Primal Therapy, called Rebirthing, has established itself in Britain, replete with a supporting system of religious ideas, is predictable. The religious overtones of Janvo's therapy are evident in the beliefs that a primal truth lies hidden in all of us, and that we can vanquish all false ideas and negative behaviour in a ritual catharsis. It could even he argued that rather than cure, what Primal Therapy achieves is conversion.

The similarity of psychological processes and religious conversion is found also in much gentler forms of American psychology. Abraham Maslow's[347] conception of 'peak experiences' in which a broken person is made whole again, brought to a higher threshold of consciousness, and becomes 'god like' in the transcendence of ordinary needs and drives, has much in common with the language of religious conversion.[348] And Erik Erikson's notion of a series of crisis situations, which produce new, ever greater levels of self-understanding, has been shown, in his own biographical accounts of religious figures[349] as well as in appraisals of his developmental psychology, to parallel the gradual process of conversion.[350]

While in many developments of psychoanalysis the religious parallels have remained implicit, in others they have been spelled out clearly. Existential Psychoanalysis, for example, has been directly linked to Zen Buddhism. A leading exponent of this school, Erich Fromm,[351] transmuted the Freudian imperative of 'Where there is Id there shall Ego be,'[352] into a step in the process of enlightenment.[353] Both are methods of dissolving the polarity between the conscious and the unconscious.[354] More important, by positing the unconscious as the authentically universal aspect of being, Fromm believed that its recovery into consciousness 'transforms the mere idea of the universality of man into the living experience of this universality; it is the experiential realization of humanism.'[355]

Concluding comments

This chapter has surveyed some of the many ways in which

religion and psychotherapy seem to interact. The first part showed that, in practice, many of the new religious movements involve techniques that derive from psychotherapy, and that, despite arguments to the contrary, there is a general attitude amongst the adherents of these movements that the therapeutic and spiritual quests are at least compatible, and often mutually supportive. Whilst the second part has shown that even the most orthodox and traditional therapies possess many aspects that can appropriately be termed 'religious.' Whilst we cannot come to a scientific conclusion about the relationship between the two enterprises, it does seem therefore that the boundaries, both conceptual and in terms of practice, are less rigid than has sometimes been argued. It remains likely that psychotherapy does have a legitimate role as at least one subset of possible 'techniques of transformation.'

17
Therapy and Beyond: Concluding Thoughts

Guy Claxton

THE CONTRIBUTIONS TO this book have demonstrated some of the ways in which the ideas and methods of the spiritual traditions have been taken up and used by psychologists and psychotherapists. In the theoretical domain, those interested in understanding better the nature of self and of personality have found much, particularly in the traditional literature of Buddhism, to provoke and further their enquiries. When combined with the Buddhist teachings of 'dependent origination' and 'selflessness,' constructivist theories of perception for example, or systems such as Kelly's 'personal construct theory'[356] take on a new urgency and importance, for we are led to investigate the deep beliefs about our own nature that have become dissolved in our day-to-day processes of seeing and thinking. Buddhist teachings provide a mirror that reflects the insights of perceptual psychologists back onto our selves, and that urges us to apply those insights reflexively.

Forming a bridge between theoretical and applied domains, the spiritual traditions have been used to help us formulate better psychologies of emotion than have previously been available. Buddhism traces very simply the way in which illusions concerning self give rise to attachment (to what is congenial to self) and aversion (to what is not,) and shows us how these in turn call forth the whole gamut of discomfitting feelings — guilt, suspicion, greed, cynicism, embarrassment, defensiveness and the rest — that contaminate our relationships at all levels from the personal to the international. We see in stark relief the double-bind that we create for ourselves: first we commit ourselves to an individual philosophy that, by its very nature, generates these emotions; then we forget what the theory is, simply reacting like robots to its programming; and then we top it all off with a theory *about* emotion within which we construe ourselves as passive victims and recipients of bad feelings, without responsibility for either their appearance or their removal. Whilst our right hand is beating us with sticks the left alternately tries to fend off the blows and to massage away the pain. As Welwood says: 'By alienating our own energy, making it 'other' and then judging it negatively, we may come to believe that emotions are demonic, that we have 'monsters' inside us. By treating emotions as an autonomous power, we grant them dominion over us.'[357]

These theoretical insights, inspired by both conceptual and experiential study within the spiritual traditions, have been influential in bringing into being training courses, such as 'the *est* training,' 'The Forum,' 'Exegesis,' 'Insight,' and 'Self-transformation' that have proven popular over the last decade, and that are somewhere between philosophical seminars, *sesshins* (prolonged periods of meditation and reflection,) and group psychotherapy. Thus another way in which the spiritual traditions have had an impact on psychology is in suggesting powerful new technologies for personal enquiry that are appealing to, and suitable for, ordinary, averagely well-adjusted, passably successful people, who wish to dig into 'the meaning of life.' That some of these 'technologies of transformation' make exaggerated claims for themselves ('Instant Enlightenment in Two Weekends!') while others lack suitably wise and compassionate personnel to deliver them, so that the form persists without the original spirit, is unfortunate, and perhaps inevitable. But this should not lead us to make the complementary mistake of dismissing or caricaturing them, nor of underestimating the value that large numbers of people have derived from taking part in them. Through such courses, some of the wisdom, or at least the flavour, of the spiritual traditions has been made available to people who would otherwise have not come across it. And if they serve to whet the appetites of even a proportion of participants — without doing damage to them: a frequent piece of scare-mongering that has no evidence to support it — then they are doing a useful job.

It is when we look at the impact of the spiritual traditions on psychotherapy as such, however, that we find the most matters of contention. For there are legitimate and increasing doubts about the suitability of, say, Buddhist teachings, or *koan* meditation, for people who are confused or unhappy, or who have not, up to a point, mastered the arts of working and relating. It might be useful, therefore, to summarise some of the points at which psychotherapy and the spiritual traditions seem to diverge, and at which distinctions of method and purpose need to be clearly drawn.

Clients most commonly seek therapy because they want to be happier than they are. The prevalence in their lives of some feeling (anxiety, loneliness) is too great, or of another (liveliness, intimacy) too little. Their premise, which the therapist will, by his or her manner, validate, is that they have a problem, and that the appropriate solution is to adjust the balance of feeling, so that they cease to have 'too much' grief or confusion, or 'too little' happiness. To do this, therapist and client explore jointly what it is that is creating the unwanted blockage or glut, and through insight and awareness, by recalling and feeling the pain of past shocks, or by sinking into the unwanted experience in the present, the problem is resolved or the feeling is accepted, and the pain of resistance diminishes. This is a very rough sketch, but not an unfair one, I think.

At the back of both client and therapist's minds, from start to finish, are certain psychological norms or desiderata that guide their progress, provide a benchmark of therapeutic success, and remain unexamined and unchallenged. Well-people, healthy-people are more-or-less rational; are open to their feelings but do not get overwhelmed by them: can cry, but not all the time for a week; care about world hunger, but do not starve themselves; have a 'realistic and positive self-image'; behave well to their parents; care about others but are fairly self-sufficient; get angry when their rights are violated or property stolen; wear shoes to the office; and so on. The implict contract between helper and helped involves agreement about many such facets of what is normal, healthy and sane — and agreement also that the client needs helping back onto the rails so he or she can live within the guidelines. They spend a limited time together, with a more-or-less specified goal, and an expectation of progress towards it. In most therapeutic schools, openness to experience, self-awareness and self-acceptance are seen as important, or even necessary, means to an end. But the client's aim is to achieve a functional balance between openness and defensiveness. Defences that work, in keeping at bay threatening experiences, can happily be left in place. And the therapist, being the client's servant, should respect his or her wishes and limitations, and not go probing into areas that the client has no felt wish to explore.

On the spiritual path, however, nothing is taken for granted. The premises that underlie the search for happiness, peace, security and self-realisation must themselves be dug up and examined. Nothing can be presupposed, least of all one's assumptions about the nature of Self, or of 'the good life.' The quest is for Truth not Happiness, and if happiness or security or social acceptability must be sacrificed in the pursuit of this ruthless enquiry, then so be it. The spiritual seeker's task is not problem-solving but problem-seeking. Whatever experiences are upsetting must be mounted and ridden in any direction they choose to go, so that the fear that underlies them can be confronted and scrutinised. No thought or feeling or behaviour is 'righter' than any other. It is all grist to the mill — the mill that puts experience to the test, and that relentlessly separates out and discards any belief, however cherished, that turn out to be unjustified.

In particular, the illusions concerning Self will have to go. While psychotherapy, we might say, seeks to expand the boundary of Me, so that previously alien aspects of myself can be re-espoused, and thereby rendered friendly, the spiritual traditions focus on the boundary itself. Their concern is to help us reality-test the separation of Self from Other, so that it slowly wears thin and patchy and may in a moment of *satori* vanish altogether, like a nightmare on waking. The more I carefully collect the data, and catch it before the sense of separateness has been stirred in to it, the more that sense becomes untenable, and unnecessary. In meditations such as *shikan-taza*, or *vipassana*, one cultivates a state of awareness that is intense but choiceless, so that whatever surfaces is experienced fully as it is, neither being clung onto, nor pushed away.

Some of the confusions between what we might call the paths of Happiness (therapy) and Truth (meditation) now become apparent. It happens for example, that people in therapy experience states of selflessness 'by accident': in moments of self-acceptance, part (at least) of the boundary around Self must dissolve, in order to include the previously banished fear or rage or sadness. Whether such moments are seen for what they are will depend on where the client is looking, and on the perceptiveness and leaning of the therapist they are with. Similarly meditators generate greater self-acceptance 'by accident,' as they learn to be able to stand whatever they see about themselves as they sit. And both meditators and therapeutic clients will experience times of serenity as the compulsive patterns of thinking and unease, the products of resistance to oneself, drop away.

In fact it is often not appreciated by beginners on the path of spiritual growth just how central a role their own mucky, petty emotions are going to play. If they anticipate that meditation will precipitate a steady slide into peacefulness they are in for a shock. Though sitting meditation adopts a pose of stillness, it masks frequent periods of inner turmoil. And the rigour of a Zen monastery, or of a long retreat, are designed precisely to create friction with the ego-emotions, bringing to the surface again and again feelings of frustration, resentment and 'I want/don't want.' Irmgard Schloegl, A Zen teacher in London, is fond of quoting the Buddhist precept: 'The buddha nature *is* the passions: the passions *are* the Buddha nature.[358] While the Tibetan master Chogyam Trungpa Rinpoche says:

> Unskilled farmers throw away their rubbish and buy from other farmers, but those who are skilled go on collecting their own rubbish, in spite of the bad smell and the unclean work, and when it is ready to be used they spread it on their land, and out of this they grow their crops. And though it is very difficult and unhygienic, as it were, to work on, that is the only way to start. So out of these unclean things comes the birth of the seed which is Realization.[359]

It can now be seen as well why meditation may not be in the best interests of people who are in therapy. Their 'problem' is that they are struggling not to be overwhelmed by feelings that they are sure are dangerous and bad. To stimulate such feelings fully into consciousness, without having strengthened their ability to disidentify with the self-critical voice, is to plunge them into their own particular horror. It requires courage and commitment to 'keep your seat' (as they say in Zen) when the horse is bolting, and if you have not learnt to do so, then the effects will be anything but therapeutic. The meditator must above all learn to make friends with his or her own fearfulness, and develop the ability to sit quietly in its presence without diving for cover. Furthermore, if one is still committed to the *idea* of being in control, then to appear to lose it is terrifying, and one's only recourse is to use to the full whatever defensive ploys of denial or projection or fantasy one has available. In the extreme case, as Laing[360] has reported, even to be understood by someone else can feel like an invasion and a threat.

Even those who are committed to a spiritual path will be swamped from time to time by fear or doubt, as their experience suddenly takes on unfamiliar forms or hues. It is for this reason that a seasoned meditation teacher — someone whom the meditator admires and trusts — is so important, for in times of difficulty the teacher's calm and reassurance will lend the student courage. The same is true of a therapist: his or her ability to look at the client's experience with, in Carl Rogers' phrase, 'fresh and unfrightened eyes'[361] helps the client to see a difficulty through, and not to jump off into renewed defensiveness half-way. And for both therapist and spiritual guide, the only thing that gives them genuine calm — and thereby makes them genuinely trustworthy — is that they have been there themselves. They have walked through the same dark tunnel, found no monsters, and know it to be safe.

But they differ in the breadth and depth of their serenity. The therapist's is like a river, still pools interspersed with white water. The spiritual guides, who know that nothing can threaten them, not even death, because who they truly are is not bounded in either space or time, have a presence like a vast, flat lake. The therapist's self-acceptance is patchy and sporadic, because it is still located within an unquestioned sense of self. He or she can still be shaken by some buried or unprecedented fear. But enlightened people cannot be disturbed by anything, for there is no longer any vestige of a distinction between self and experience. Identified with nothing in particular, they are free to be anything: the feeling of hunger, the pressure of the chair, the broken glass on the forecourt, the disappointed child. They can be touched by everything, for there is nothing to resist. And they can be touched by nothing, for they are a polished mirror on which no reflection can ever leave a mark.

We might conclude from this that while meditation will be inappropriate for many clients, tending to push them further than they are ready, willing or able to go, it offers an invaluable aid to therapists, that ought to be a part of every therapist's initial and on-going training. The products of meditation are insight, awareness, equanimity and magnanimity, and any therapist who declines to undertake a practice that strengthens and expands these vital therapeutic qualities has some explaining to do. Welwood is certainly in no doubt on this point:

> When I studied Rogerian therapy in graduate school, I felt frustrated because I was never taught *how* to develop 'unconditional positive regard' for the client. I was told that this was essential, and it sounded good to me, but it was assumed that I should be able to feel this way toward anyone who walked into my office. What I discovered many years later was that meditation provided a concrete operational method for developing just those ingredients of acceptance and unconditional friendliness that are most essential for successful therapy. A therapist who sits through the subtle, complex twists and turns of his own thoughts and feelings is unlikely to find many of his clients' problems all that alien, shocking or unfamiliar. The more a therapist trusts his own basic goodness underneath his confusion, the more he can help clients find their way between these two aspects of themselves. And the more he can face his own fear, the more fearlessly he can approach his clients' problems as well... [362]

The spiritual traditions therefore offer an invitation to psychotherapists to see their training as experiential and continuous, and to appraise their value to their clients in terms of qualities of *being*, rather than the skills and techniques of *doing* or the conceptual understanding of *knowing*. Without such qualities as the tradition Rogerian trinity of genuineness, non-judgmental warmth and compassionate understanding, all the skill and knowledge in the world are unlikely to do any

goods.[363] Unfortunately this is an invitation that many psychotherapists will turn down, for they will find it threatening to
both their personal and their professional selves. Personally
they will be unwilling to put at risk the workable patchwork
of beliefs and evasions that constitute their personalities.
While many will also be loath to give up the professional
standing that their claim to knowledge and skill gives them.
Many therapists are deeply attached to a sense of their own
power, control, expertise and understanding, and to accept
that these count for little beside the qualities of basic human-
heartedness that they cannot affect, and may lack, may be too
bitter a pill to swallow. To be asked to inspect and question
their own need to be successful, or to have it suggested that
such a need is itself neurotic, and a failing in a good therapist,
will feel like an attack that must be warded off.[364]

It is probably also true that many therapists are too
attached to the drama of neurosis. The spiritual teachers I
have met have all shared one delightful quality that is easy to
recognise but hard to describe. Seeing both the tragedy of the
suffering we are in, and at the same time the irony of a
situation in which we ourselves are responsible for the pain
we would escape, they are able to communicate both acceptance and humour. On the one hand they can understand our
predicament, show compassion, and do not make us feel
small. But on the other there is a lightness of touch that says
'Come on now. This is all rather silly, isn't it?' They see the
drama clearly but refuse to buy it, and the twinkle in their eye
can somehow help us see for ourselves the home-made, out-
of-all-proportion nature of our upset. In short they behave
like a loving parent with a child with a burst balloon: they can
comfort us without *agreeing* with us. They keep sight of the
big picture. And sometimes they can help us to laugh at
ourselves: to see ourselves as ridiculous, but without putting
ourselves down, and to acquire towards ourselves the same
attitude of gentle, amused affection that they have towards all
emotional absurdity.

Whereas some therapists, like naive parents, get sucked

into the turmoil, and, losing their perspective, come to collude with our point of view about how *serious* it all is, and thereby strengthen it. Such therapists may help patients to see into their predicament, but not to see through it. And, understanding the tragedy but not the comedy, they will find the message of the spiritual traditions unappealing, or even frivolous.

For the enlightened master, therapist and client are both in the same boat, whilst for himself and his students there is a very definite distinction. They are looking for something and he's got it (or rather he knows that he's got it, and they don't yet know that they've got it as well.) And it is very clearly his job to help them look for it, and to prevent them looking for it in the wrong places − in an accumulation of intellectual knowledge, for example, or in the deliberate affectation of some lifestyle. In his students' relationship to him there is therefore a degree of respect and honouring that would be out of place in the therapist's consulting room. The master manifests his dis-illusionment in everything he says and does, though it is not so much the content of his words and actions as the subtle spirit that pervades them that conveys the message. He teaches through his example, his being, as much as through the exercises he sets or the teachings he gives, and as students spend time in his presence, so they hope to pick up something of that quality of being. It simply begins to rub off on them. Thus while they are earnestly picking away at their own misconceptions, discarding that which is false, so at the same time they are being infected with and inspired by a light, lively, loving intelligence. But 'it's a wise man who knows his own limitations' (as Clint Eastwood said to his superior in one of the Dirty Harry movies), and few therapists would prescribe as part of their therapeutic regime that clients should come and watch them eating their supper, or playing with the cat.

The other big difference between the paths of Happiness and Truth is the extent to which they permeate a seeker's life. Therapy, by and large, concerns itself with the domain of feeling and emotion. Though it may be something in the clients' relationships, their actions, their thinking or their perception that is giving rise to their unhappiness, these aspects of their lives are only investigated or altered so that the reading on the Misery-ometer goes down. If we can reinterpret the hallucinations, or get rid of the phobia, you will Feel Better, and that is the point. But for the spiritual seeker these other domains are made problematic in their own right. In all the Buddhist traditions, though especially in Rinzai Zen's use of the *koan*, the status and value of thought itself is questioned: not just some (weird) thoughts, but all thought. Educated Westerners in particular have been trained to be very good at using the tool called Reason, but have been hopelessly mislead about the limits of its usefulness. We are like surgeons who can wield a scalpel with exquisite skill, but insist on using the scalpel to take a temperature, treat a headache or open a tin of sardines. The *koan* is a device for breaking people of the compulsion to use the scalpel of rational thought on inappropriate problems – the problem in question being 'Who am I?' Only after we have blunted a hundred fine-ground blades on the sardine tin, and are blue in the face with frustration and hunger, are we willing to look around, and spot the can-opener that has been on the table the whole time. Beliefs about the nature and function of thought have to be brought to the surface and reappraised.

Likewise our perception of the external world is called into question. Our common-sense attitude to perception is built on the premise that we *receive* it, as a television set receives electromagnetic waves through the air, and turns them into sound and pictures. Embedded in this belief is a clear distinction between inside and outside, Me and Not-Me. But close attention to experience, and particularly to the errors and interpretations it contains, begin to reveal that there is a much closer relationship between Who-I-Am and What-I-See than had seemed to be the case. I am not so much the receiver of my perception as its creator, and therefore I am at some level responsible for it. So in the course of this enquiry the boundary between Self and Other is again eroded and punctured. The sense of self becomes diffused, and 'I' seems to expand to include both other people and, in the limit, everything that I have sensed and known. Where the therapeutic enquiry leads to a reconstruing of the intrapersonal, the spiritual enquiry widens to include the interpersonal and ultimately the impersonal worlds. And as it does so, the seeker's orientation shifts from the predominant concern with personal salvation to a broad sense of authorship of every aspect of experience, and a deep concern for all the creatures that 'I' have brought into being.

In summary, we might say that therapy represents a special and limited case of the more general spiritual search, as Newton's Laws of Motion are special cases of Einstein's broader theory of Relativity. The quests for Happiness and for Truth thus share certain features, but aspects of the former are localized, and must not be assumed to apply across the board. Someone starting in therapy may get a taste for self-enquiry that becomes freed from the pursuit of happiness and deepens into a spiritual journey, and this shifting of focus often happens. But a definite change of gear is involved that should not be expected — or even necessarily encouraged — to occur.

There are echoes of the spiritual traditions in all the brands of therapy: it would be surprising if there were not. George Kelly's personal construct approach[365] highlights the way we create our own interpersonal perceptions (and then take them for gospel); Carl Rogers[366] has much to say about openness to one's inner experience and the value of receptivity; Fritz Perls'[367] gestalt therapy stresses the importance of here-and-now attention to detail; Albert Ellis[368] emphasises the fact that unhappiness is caused by errors in our personal philosophies; many movements pick out the importance of non-judgmental attention; Sigmund Freud, of course,[369] started us thinking about the ploys and evasions we use in order to avoid noticing the absurd or threatening aspects of our experience; and so on. But all of them are brought up short at some point by their adherence to a belief or an unexamined assumption that the inexorable Buddhist bulldozer would continue to batter its way through.

As this book has shown, there are many areas of psychology and psychotherapy that are beginning to benefit from contact with the spiritual traditions. But we must be wary in interpreting and applying those traditions, for they are powerful, and not to be treated superficially or lightly. Wilber[370] has pointed out how the parallels between mysticism and modern physics have been exaggerated and trivialized and we would do well to heed his warning in relating psychology and spirituality. Critical caution should prevent us from polluting the rich harvest of insights that is available with our own overenthusiasm, and half-baked preconceptions.

Notes and References

1. Katz, N. (1983). *Buddhist and Western Psychology*. Prajna Press: Boulder, Colorado.
2. Welwood, J. (ed.) (1983). *Awakening the Heart: East/West Approaches to Psychotherapy and the Healing Relationship*. Shambhala: Boulder, Colorado.

1 *Western Psychology and Buddhist Teachings: Convergences and Divergences*

3. Bandura, (1977). 'Self efficacy: Toward a unifying theory of behavioral change.' *Psychological Review*, *84*, pp.191–215.
4. Seligman, M.E.P. (1975). *Helplessness: On depression, development and death*. W.H. Freeman; San Francisco.
5. Abramson, L.Y., Seligman, M.E.P. and Teasdale, J. (1978). 'Learned helplessness in humans: Critique and reformulation.' *Journal of Abnormal Psychology*, *87*, pp. 49–79.
6. Murti, T.R.V. (1955). *The Central Philosophy of Buddhism*. Allen & Unwin: London.
7. Jung, C.G. (1978). 'Yoga and the West,' in *Psychology and the East*, R.F.C. Hull (trans.). Routledge & Kegan Paul: Princeton, New Jersey, p.83.
8. Jung (1978), ibid, p.81.
9. Boin, J. (1976). *The Teaching of Vimalakirti*. Pali Text Society: London.
10. Jung, C.G. (1962). *Commentary on 'The Secret of the Golden Flower'*, R. Wilhelm (trans.) Routledge & Kegan Paul: London, pp.85–6.

11. Radley, A. (1977). 'Living on the Horizon,' in *New Perspectives in Personal Construct Theory*. D. Bannister (ed.), Academic Press: London.

12. Kelly, G.A. (1969). 'Ontological acceleration,' in *Clinical Psychology and Personality: Selected Papers of George Kelly*. B. Maher (ed.), Wiley: New York.

13. Kelly, G.A. (1977). 'The Psychology of the Unknown,' in *New Perspectives in Personal Construct Theory*. D. Barrister (ed.), Academic Press: London.

2 Mind, Senses and Self

14. Fontana, D. (1986). 'Self-assertion and self-negation in Buddhist psychology.' *Journal of Humanistic Psychology*, 26, (in press).

15. See e.g. Watts, A. W. (1973). *Psychotherapy East and West*. Penguin: Harmondsworth.

16. Jung, C. G. (1956). 'On the discourses of the Buddha,' reprinted in C. G. Jung (1978), *Psychology and the East*. Routledge & Kegan Paul: London.

17. Govinda, A. (1969). *The Psychological Attitude of early Buddhist Philosophy*. Rider: London.

18. Guenther, H. V. (1971). *Buddhist Philosophy in Theory and Practice*. Shambhala: Boulder, Colorado.

19. Ayer, A. J. (1976). *The Central Questions of Philosophy*. Penguin: Harmondsworth.

20. Mead, G. H. (1934). *Mind, Self and Society: From the Standpoint of a Social Behaviourist*. C. W. Morris (ed.), University of Chicago Press: Chicago.

21. Conze, E. (1972). *Buddhist Meditation*. Unwin: London. See also Hamilton-Merritt, J. (1979). *A Meditator's Diary*. Penguin: Harmondsworth.

22. Wilber, K. (1982a). 'Odyssey: a personal inquiry into humanistic and transpersonal psychology.' *Journal of Humanistic Psychology*, 22, 1, pp.57—90; and Wilber, K. (1982b). 'The pre-trans fallacy.' *Journal of Humanistic Psychology*, 22, 2, pp.5—43.

23. Govinda (1969), op.cit.

24. Mascaro, J. (1973). *The Dhammapada*. Penguin: Harmondsworth.

25. Burtt, E. A. (ed.) (1955). *The Teachings of the Compassionate Buddha*. New American Library: New York
26. Masunaga, R. (1972) (trans.). *A Primer of Soto Zen*. Routledge & Kegan Paul: London.

3   *The Light's on but there's Nobody Home: The Psychology of No-Self*

27. Needleman, J. (1983). 'Psychiatry and the sacred,' in J. Welwood (ed.), *Awakening the Heart: East/West Approaches to Psychotherapy and the Healing Relationship*. Shambhala: Boulder, Colorado.
28. Barlett, F.C. (1932). *Remembering*. Cambridge University Press: Cambridge.
29. Loftus, E.F. (1975). 'Leading questions and the eye-witness report,' *Cognitive Psychology*, 7, pp.560–72,
30. Quoted in Allport, G.W. (1961). *Pattern and Growth in Personality*. Holt, Rinehart & Winston: New York.
31. Rinehart, L. (1976). *The Dice Man*. Panther: St. Albans.
32. The discussion that follows is based closely on pages 41–43 of Claxton, G.L. (1981). *Wholly Human: Western and Eastern Visions of the Self and Its Perfection*. Routledge Kegan Paul: London.
33. Wittgenstein, L. (1974). *Tractatus Logico-Philosophicus*. Routledge & Kegan Paul: London.

4   *Who am I? Changing Models of Reality in Meditation*

34. For both approaches, see Davidson, J.M. and Davidson, R.J. (1980). *The Psychobiology of Consciousness*. Plenum Press: New York and London; and Valle, R.S. and Von Eckartsberg, R. (eds) (1981). *The Metaphors of Consciousness*. Plenum Press: New York and London.
35. See Tart, C.T. (1975). *States of Consciousness*. Dutton & Co. and Tart, C.T. (1980). 'A systems approach to altered states of consciousness,' in Davidson, J.M. and Davidson R.J., op.cit.
36. Blackmore, S.J. (1982). *Beyond the Body*. Heinemann: London. (Also Paladin: London, (1983)).
37. See, for example, Hofstadter, D. (1979). *Goedel, Escher, Bach:*

An eternal golden braid. Basic Books: New York. Also
Penguin: London (1980), or Marr, D. (1982). *Vision.* W.H.
Freeman: San Francisco.

38. See Tart (1975), op.cit.
39. Blackmore, S.J. (1984). 'A Psychological theory of the out-of-
   body experience.' *Journal of Parapsychology, 48,* pp.201—18.
40. Blackmore, S.J. (1986). 'Where am I? Viewpoints in imagery
   and the out-of-body experience.' *Journal of Mental Imagery*
   (in press).
41. Green, C.E. (1968). *Lucid Dreams.* Hamish Hamilton:
   London.

5 *Selfhood and Self-consciousness in Social Psychology: The Views
  of G.H. Med and Zen*

42. The historical origins of modern psychology are described
   by E.G. Boring (1950). *A History of Psychology.* Appleton
   Century Crofts: New York.
43. James, W. (1950). 'Principles of Psychology.' Dover: New
   York.
44. Watson, J.B. (1930). *Behaviourism.* (2nd edn), University of
   Chicago Press: Chicago.
45. Harré, R. and Secord, P.F. (1972). *The Explanation of Social
   Behaviour.* Basil Blackwell: Oxford.
46. Gauld, A. and Shotter, J. (1977). *Human Action and its
   Psychological Investigation.* Routledge & Kegan Paul:
   London.
47. Blumer, H. (1969). *Symbolic Interactionism: Perspective and
   Method.* Prentice-Hall: Englewood Cliffs, NJ.
48. Morris, C.W. (1934) (ed.). *Works of George Herbert Mead,
   Vol. 1 of Mind, Self and Society.* University of Chicago Press:
   Chicago. Being notes of Lectures delivered without notes
   by Mead, recorded verbatim by students and edited for
   completeness, *Mind, Self and Society* tends to be difficult-
   going and repetitive. Secondary sources of Mead which
   might form a good starting-point are: Meltzer, B.N. 'Mead's
   Social Psychology,' in J.G. Manis and B.N. Meltzer (eds)
   (1967). *Symbolic Interactionism.* Allyn and Bacon: Boston; and
   the very readable introduction to Social Psychology from

the Symbolic Interactionist perspective of Mead: Hewitt, J.P. (1984). *Self and Society: A Symbolic Interactionist Social Psychology* (3rd edn). Allyn and Bacon: Boston.

49. *Mind, Self and Society* presents a description mainly from a phylogenetic point of view. Some development psychologists have seen the implications of Mead's work from the ontological point of view. See, for example, Richards, M.P.M. (ed.) (1984). *The Integration of a Child into a Social World*. Cambridge University Press: London.

50. Morris (1934), op.cit., Chapters. 7 and 9.

51. See White, L.A. (1959). 'Four Stages in the Evolution of Minding,' in S. Tax, '*The Evolution of Man,' Vol.2 of Evolution After Darwin*. University of Chicago Press: Chicago. White's account is discussed in Becker, (1962). *The Birth and Death of Meaning*. The Free Press: New York; and by Hewitt (1984) (see note 48 above).

52. Berger P.L. and Luckmann T. (1972). *The Social Construction of Reality*. Penguin: Harmondsworth.

53. Harre and Second (1972) (see note 45 above).

54. See Harré, R., Clarke, D. and De Carlo, N. (1984). *Motives and Mechanisms*, Chap.2. Methuen: London.

55. In fact, one could describe the social objects which a particular author creates as having selective advantages or disadvantages. A discussion of the interaction between biology and self-conscious activity can be found in Reynolds, V. (1980) *The Biology of Human Action* (2nd edn). W.H. Freeman: Oxford.

56. Morris (1934), op.cit., Chapter 22.

57. This view closely parallels that of Vygotsky, L.S. (1964). *Thought and Language*. MIT Press. Vygotsky was a Soviet psychologist from a completely different tradition to the North American sociological and philosophical tradition in which Mead participated. Nevertheless, their conclusions on the implication of language in human consciousness are remarkably similar.

58. Meltzer (1967), (see note 48 above), p.9.

59. Watts, A. (1957). *The Way of Zen*. Pantheon Books: New York.

60. Ibid.

61. Ibid.

6   *The Spiritual Psychology of Rudolf Steiner*

62. Wilson, Colin (1985). *Rudolf Steiner: The Man and his Vision*. Aquarian Press: Wellingborough.

63. See R. *Steiner (1925/1977) Autobiography*. Rudolf Steiner Press: New York.

64. R. Steiner, *(1922/1982) West-East Aphorisms*. (English translation published in *The Golden Blade, 24,* pp.15—21.)

65. See Dary, J. (ed.) (1975) *Work Arising from the Life of Rudolf Steiner*. Rudolf Steiner Press: London.

66. Crook, J.H. (1980). *The Evolution of Human Consciousness*. Clarendon Press: Oxford.

67. Steiner's *Theosophy** (1904/1973) is a good source for this general scheme.

68. Davy, C. (1961/1978). *Towards a Third Culture.** On the consciousness soul, see also a helpful essay in Barfield, O. (1966). *Romanticism Comes of Age*. Rudolf Steiner Press: London.

69. See Barfield, O. (1928). *Poetic Diction*. Faber: London. Also Watts, F.N. (1978). 'Beyond Metaphor,' *New Forum, 5,* pp.21—23.

70. See Watts, F.N. (1980). 'The Role of Thinking in Overcoming Psychological Problems.' *The Golden Blade, 32,* pp.91—9. John Davy in *Hope, Evolution and Change* (1985 pp.263—73) has drawn attention to the parallel between them and the stages of dying described by Elizabeth Kübler-Ross.

71. Skinner, R. (1910/1979). *Occult Science.* pp. 245—251.

72. Watts, F.N. (1980), op.cit.

73. See Lehrs, E. (1958). *Man or Matter*. Harper: New York.

74. Steiner, R. (1886/1979). *Theory of Knowledge implicit in Goethe's world conception*. Anthroposophic Press: New York.

75. Lehrs, E. (1958), op.cit.

76. Steiner, R. (1912/1979). *The World of the Senses and the World of the Spirit*. Steiner Book Centre: Vancouver.

77. Steiner, R. (1917/1985). *On the Life of the Soul*. Anthroposophic Press: New York.

78. Steiner, R. (1919/1972). *The Wisdom of Man.**

*See bibliography on p.333 for details.

79. Steiner, R. (1919/1975). *The Study of Man.**

80. Nesfield-Cookson, B. (1983). *Rudolf Steiner's Vision of Love.* Aquarian Press: Wellingborough.

81. Steiner (1919/1975), Lecture IV.*

82. Ibid., pp.100−1.*

83. 'The mission of anger,' in Steiner, R. (1910/1983). *Metamorphoses of the Soul.* Vol. 1.*

84. For example, Harwood, A.C. (1940/1967). *The Way of a Child.* Rudolf Steiner Press: London.

85. Steiner, R. (1909/1976). *The Four Temperaments.* Anthroposophic Press: New York.

86. Steiner, R. (1911/1983). *An Occult Physiology.* Rudolf Steiner Press: London.

87. Steiner, R. (1921). *Man as a Being of Sense and Perception.* Rudolf Steiner Press: London. Also Davy, J. (1985) *Hope, Evolution and Change.* pp.151−63.*

88. On semantic processing, see Craik, F.I.M. and Lockhart, L.S. (1972). 'Levels of processing: a framework for memory research.' *Journal of Verbal Learning and Verbal Behaviour*, *11*, pp.671−84. On links with Steiner's treatment of the senses, see Watts, F. (1981). 'The variety of sense experience' *Anthroposophical Review*, *3*, pp.5−8.

89. Schachtel, E.G. (1959). *Metamorphosis.* Basic Books: New York.

90. Steiner, R. (1909/1946). *Practical Training in Thought.* Anthroposophic Press: New York.

91. Davy, J. (1975), op.cit.

92. Steiner, R. (1917/1946). *Psychoanalysis in the light of Anthroposopy.* Anthroposophic Press: New York.

93. Watts, F.N. (1980), op.cit.

94. Steiner, R. (1910/1979), op.cit.

95. Davy, (1985), op.cit.

96. Steiner, R. and Wegman, I. (1925/1967). *Fundamentals of Therapy.* Rudolf Steiner Press: London.

97. Easton, S.C. (1986). *New Vistas in Psychology: An Anthroposophical Contribution.* Rudolf Steiner Press: London. Also Lievegood, B. (1979). *Phases: Crisis and Development in the*

*See bibliography on p.333 for details.

Individual. Rudolf Steiner Press: London.

98. Steiner, R. (1919/1976). *Influences of Lucifer and Ahriman*. Rudolf Steiner Book Centre: Vancouver.

99. Steiner, R. (1906/1970). *At the Gates of Spiritual Science*. Rudolf Steiner Press: London.

100. Samuels, A. (1985). *Jung and the Post-Jungians*. Routledge & Kegan Paul: pp.116–18.

101. Hillman, J. (1975), *Re-visioning Psychology*. Harper: New York.

ANNOTATED BIBLIOGRAPHY

(a) General books by Steiner

1. Steiner, R. (1904/1973). *Theosophy: An Introduction to the Supersensible Knowledge of the World and the Destination of Man*. Rudolf Steiner Press: London. A general exposition of his model of man.

2. Steiner, R. (1904/1969). *Knowledge of the Higher Worlds: How is it Achieved?* Rudolf Steiner Press: London An account of the meditative path.

3. Steiner, R. (1910/1969). *Occult Science: An Outline*. Rudolf Steiner Press: London. His largest book, which incorporates much material from the earlier books, but also includes much material on the details of the early evolution that some find hard to relate to.

4. Steiner, R. (1984) in McDermott, R.A. (ed.). *The Essential Steiner: Basic Writings of Rudolf Steiner*. Harper & Row: London. A convenient selection of Steiner's work.

(b) General books by other authors

5. Barfield, O. (1957/1965). *Saving the Appearances: Study in Idolatry*. Harcourt, Brace: London. A lucidly written and scholarly Steinerite account of man's current state of development, and his perceptual relationship to the world (though Barfield may be closer to philosophical idealism than was Steiner himself).

6. Davy, C. (1961/1978). *Towards a Third Culture*. Floris Books: Edinburgh. Another readable account of the 'onlooker consciousness,' and the need to integrate the two cultures of

the sciences and humanities.

7. Shepherd, A.P. (1954/1983). *Scientist of the Invisible: Introduction to the Life and World of Rudolf Steiner.* Floris Books: Edinburgh. A good general introduction to Steiner that presents his ideas largely in his own terms.

8. Davy, J. (1985), *Hope, Evolution and Change.* Hawthorn Press: Stroud. Not an exposition of Steiner, but a collection of essays on scientific topics (including psychology) enriched by a Steinerite perspective.

(c) Psychological books by Steiner

9. Steiner, R. (1919/1975). *Study of Man.* Rudolf Steiner Press: London. Of his various lecture courses on psychological topics, this is the most comprehensive and systematic. See p. 266.

10. Steiner R. (1910/1972). *Wisdom of Man, of the Soul and of the Spirit.* Anthroposophic Press. New York. From an earlier period, less comprehensive, but containing his most deailed excursion into the description of basic psychological faculties.

11. Steiner, R. (1910/1983). *Metamorphoses of the Soul: Paths of Experience.* (2 vols.), Rudolf Steiner Press: London. An attractively 'human' and accessible account of miscellaneous psychological phenomena. See p.104.

(d) Psychological books by other authors

12. Konig, K. (1973). *The Human Soul.* Anthroposophic Press: Spring Valley, New York. (Now out of print.) A fairly comprehensive account of Steiner's psychology, mostly in his own terms.

13. Zeylmans van Emmichoven, F.W. (1946/1982). *The Anthroposophical Understanding of the Soul.* Anthroposophic Press: New York. Concentrates on basic psychological faculties, and based mainly on the 'Study of Man' lecture course.

7 *Buddhist Psychology: A Paradigm for the Psychology of Enlightenment*

D   = *Dīgha Nikāya*, PTS
Dhs = *Dhammasangani*, PTS

M   = *Majjhima Nikaya*, PTS.
PED = Pali English Dictionary, PTS.
PTS = Pali Text Society.
S   = *Samyutta Nikaya*, PTS.
SA   = Commentary to *Samyutta Nikaya*, PTS.
SnA = Commentary to *Suttanipata*, PTS.
Ud   = *Udana*, PTS.

102. See especially the *Journal of Transpersonal Psychology*.
103. Popper, K. R. (1972). *Conjectures and Refutations: the growth of scientific knowledge*. Routledge & Kegan Paul: London.
104. Suttas are the discursive or narrational part of the Buddhist scriptures.
105. *Ariyapariyesanasutta*, M.26, I. B. Horner (trans.) *Middle Length Sayings*. Vol. 1. PTS: London. In general, the translations of the Pali texts are not at all satisfactory for use by psychologists. They are, for the most part, quite unaware of psychological theories, and the very few that do take these into account, such as *Buddhist Psychological Ethics*, the translation of *Dhamassangani* by C. A. F. Rhys Davids (3rd edn, 1974, PTS: London) were done at the turn of the century. For this reason I give my own translations with page references to the Pali texts, but only general references to published translations.
106. M i, 163.
107. Ud 80.
108. S.iv 373 and SA.iii 112. An interesting discussion and analysis of Nibbana can be found in Johannson, Rune (1969). *The Psychology of Nibbana*. Allen & Unwin London.
109. D.16. Translated by T.W. and C. A. F. Rhys Davids as *Dialogues of the Buddha*. (1921). PTS: London. Vol.I, 1899; Vol.II, 1910; Vol.III.
110. D.ii.100.
111. It is necessary to use the Pali technical terms in this section because they do not as yet have equivalent concepts in Western psychology.

112. Rahula, Walpola (1964). *What the Buddha Taught.* Gordon Fraser: London. 2nd edn 1967, pp.21–22.
113. Johansson, Rune (1956). *The Dynamic Psychology of Early Buddhism.* Curzon Press: London.
114. Kelly, G. A. (1955). *The Psychology of Personal Constructs.* Norton & Co: New York.
115. *Ariyapariyesanasutta*, etc.
116. D.ii.311–13.
117. D.ii.305.
118. D.ii.308.
119. D.ii.310.
120. D.ii.311.
121. M.2 *Sabbasavasutta*.
122. I am grateful to Peter Connolly for this clear and insightful definition.
123. SnA 128.
124. See PED under *karuna*.
125. An earlier version of this paper was presented to the British Psychological Society Conference, April 1984. I am indebted to Dr Johannes Bronkhorst for many helpful suggestions in the preparation of this paper.

9   *Buddhism and Psychotherapy: A Buddhist Perspective*

126. See Fromm, E., Suzuki, D.T. and De Martino R. (1974). *Zen Buddhism and Psycho-Analysis.* Souvenir Press: London; Watts, A. (1973). *Psychotherapy East and West.* Penguin: Harmondsworth; and De Silva, P. (1973). *Buddhist and Freudian Psychology.* Lake House: Colombo.
127. Being scientific does not necessarily imply being a philosophical materialist, of course, but the two are frequently held to be identical. Materialism often shades into epiphenomenalism and mechanism, related philosophical views both opposed to religious or spiritual doctrines.
128. Berger, P.L. (1973). *The Social Reality of Religion.* Penguin: Harmondsworth.
129. Jung studied gnosticism and alchemy.
130. See Macquarrie, J. (ed.) (1967). *A Dictionary of Christian Ethics.* SCM Press: London.
131. Ibid., pp.229–31.

132. Many will feel that I am being too dismissive of Christian mystical or spiritual practices, but one way to compare ideas of progressive human development and 'therapeutic' practices to bring this about, in Christianity and Buddhism, is to look at their basic scriptures. For example, comparison of the *Majjhima Nikaya* of the Pali Canon with the New Testament reveals sutta after sutta in the former describing human development and the means to achieve it, whilst in the latter there is nothing of the sort.

133. See Karasu, T.B. (1977). 'Psychotherapies: an overview.' *American Journal of Psychiatry*, *134*, pp.851—63. And Block, S. (1982). *What is Psychotherapy?* Oxford University Press: Oxford.

134. Samadhi is a term with various meanings in Buddhism. There can be transcendental *Samadhi* and mundane *samadhi*. Technically, *dhyana* is mundane *samadhi*. In the threefold path as I have described it *sila* and *samadhi* are treated as mundane qualities which lead to the arising of the transcendental. Once the latter has arisen, the mundane threefold path is left behind, and each of its aspects transformed into its transcendental equivalent.

10 *Beyond Illusion in the Psychotherapeutic Enterprise*

135. Suzuki, D.T. (1960). 'Lectures on Zen Buddhism,' in Suzuki, D.T. Fromm, E. and De Martino, R., *Zen Buddhism and Psychoanalysis*. Souvenir Press: London.

136. Suzuki, S. (1970). *Zen Mind, Beginner's Mind*. Weatherhill: New York.

137. Miles, T.R. (1966). *Eliminating the Unconscious*. Pergamon Press: Oxford.

138. Stolorow, R.D. and Lachmann, F.M. (1980). *Psychoanalysis of Developmental Arrests: Theory and Treatment*. International Universities Press: New York.

139. For a discussion of 'quality' of self-image, see May, G.G. (1982). *Care of Mind, Care of Spirit*. Harper & Row: New York.

140. Fromm, E. (1959). 'Psychoanalysis and Zen Buddhism.' *Psychologia*, *2*, pp. 79—99.

141. Krynicki, V.E. (1980), 'The double orientation of the ego in the practice of Zen.' *American Journal of Psychoanalysis, 40,* pp. 239–48.

142. Lederer, W. (1959). 'Primitive psychotherapy.' *Psychiatry, 23,* pp. 255–65.

143. For example, Kondo, A. (1958). 'Zen in psychotherapy: the virtue of sitting.' *Chicago Review, 12,* pp. 57–64. And Maupin, E.W. (1962). 'Zen Buddhism: a psychological review.' *Journal of Consulting Psychology, 26 ,* pp. 362–78.

144. Kutz, I., Borysenko, J.Z. and Benson, H. (1985). 'Meditation and psychotherapy: a rationale for the integration of dynamic psychotherapy, the relaxation response, and mindfulness meditation.' *American Journal of Psychiatry 142,* pp. 1–8.

145. Ibid.

146. Beck, A.T. (1976). *Cognitive Therapy and the Emotional Disorders.* International University Press: New York.

147. Ellis, A. (1962). *Reason and Emotion In Psychotherapy.* Lyle Stuart: New York.

148. Kelly, G.A. (1955). *The Psychology of Personal Constructs.* Norton: New York.

149. Ponce, D.E. (1982). 'Buddhist constructs and psychotherapy.' *International Journal of Social Psychiatry, 28,* pp. 83–90.

150. Kuhn, T. (1970). *The Structure of Scientific Revolutions.* University of Chicago Press: Chicago.

151. Ponce, op.cit.

152. Dogen, E. (1976). 'Fukanzazengi,' in Jiyu-Kennett, *Zen is Eternal Life.* Dharma Publishing: Emeryville, California.

153. Guttman, N. (1977). 'On Skinner and Hull: A reminiscene and projection.' *American Psychologist, 32,* pp. 321–8.

154. Skinner, B.F. (1978). 'Why I am not a cognitive psychologist,' in Skinner, B.F., *Reflections on Behaviourism and Society.* Prentice-Hall: Englewood Cliffs.

155. Skinner, B.F. (1957). *Verbal Behaviour.* Prentice-Hall: New York.

156. Skinner, B.F. (1974). *About Behaviourism.* Jonathan Cape: London.

157. Ibid.

158. Day, W. (1982). 'A Behaviourist Faces Certain Realities Concerning The Self.' *Behaviour Analysis, 3,* pp. 2–12.

159. Suzuki, op.cit.
160. Capra, F. (1975). *The Tao of Physics*. Shambhala: Boulder, Colorado.
161. Bateson, G. (1973). *Steps to an Ecology of Mind. Collected Essays in Anthropology, Psychiatry, Evolution and Epistemology*. Granada Publishing: London.
162. See Stanton, M.D. (1980). 'Family Therapy: Systems Approaches,' in Sholevar, G.P., Benson, R.M. and Blinder, B.J. (eds), *Emotional Disorders in Children and Adolescents*. Spectrum: New York.
163. Palazzoli, M.S., Boscolo, L., Cechin, G. and Prata, G. (1978). *Paradox and Counter Paradox. A New Model in the Therapy of the Family in Schizophrenic Transaction*. Jason Aronson: London.
164. Minuchin, S. and Fishman, H.C. (1981). *Family Therapy Techniques*. Harvard University Press: London.
165. Ibid.
166. Sangharakshita, B. (1967). *The Three Jewels. An Introduction to Buddhism*. Rider: London.
167. Bateson, op.cit.
168. Rogers, C. (1951). *Client Centered Therapy: Its Current Practice, Implications and Theory*. Constable: London.
169. Wilden, A. (1980). *System and Structure: Essays in Communication and Exchange*. (2nd edn), Tavistock: London.
170. May, op.cit.
171. Ben-Avi, A. (1959). 'Zen Buddhism,' in Arieti, S.(ed.), *American Handbook of Psychiatry*. Basic Books: New York.
172. Krynicki, op.cit.

11   *Applications of Buddhism in Mental Health Care*

173. Tulku, T. (1978). *Openness Mind*. Dharma Publications.
174. Op.cit; and Trungpa, C. (1985). The Meeting of Buddhist and Western Psychology. *Tibetan Bulletin*, *16*, p.10.
175. Samsara is the vicious cycle of death and rebirth, fraught with suffering and dissatisfaction, and born from ignorance of the true nature of reality. Gyatso, G.K. (1980). *Meaningful to Behold*. Wisdom Publications: London. p.348.
176. Ibid. p.245.
177. Ibid. p.347.
178. Ibid. p.246.

179. Rabten, G. and Dhargyey, G.N. (1984). *Advice from a Spiritual Friend*. Wisdom: London, p.56.
180. Bodhisattvas are those who strive to attain enlightenment for the benefit of others. They have developed the quality of *bodhicitta*, the motivation to attain full enlightenment for the benefit of all beings. Such a motivation is based on a fully developed love and compassion for all life and is the complete antidote to the self-cherishing attitude with its attendant range of psychological problems.
181. Gyatso, op.cit pp.27, 28.
182. Mahayana is the greater vehicle of those seeking full enlightenment for the sake of benefiting others. Gyatso, op.cit.,p.348.
183. Wisdom (Skt.*prajna*) is insight into the true non-inherent nature of self and phenomena. Antidote to the ignorance of self-grasping.
184. Definite Emergence is commitment to gain freedom from the shortcomings and sufferings of cyclic existence.
185. Trungpa, C. (1976). From a 'Workshop on Psychotherapy,' in *Loka 2: a Journal from Naropa Institute*: Doubleday: New York.
186. Gyatso, (1985). op.cit., Chapter 6.
187. Trungpa, C. (1985). 'The meeting of Buddhist amd Western Psychology.' *Tibetan Bulletin*, 16, pp.10−15.
188. Casper, M. (1974). 'Space Therapy and the Maitri Project.' *Journal of Transpersonal Psychology*, 6, pp. 57−67.
189. Deatherage, G. (1975). 'The Clinical use of "Mindfulness" Meditation Techniques in Short Term Psychotherapy.' *Journal of Transpersonal Psychology*, 6, pp. 133−42.
190. Trungpa, C. (1983). 'Becoming a Full Human Being,' in Welwood, J. (ed.), *Awakening the Heart*. New Science Library: Boulder and London.
191. Spivack, G. and Shure, M.B. (1973). *Social Adjustment of Young Children: a Cognitive Approach to Solving Real-life Problems*. Jossey-Bass: New York.
192. Tulku, T. (1979). 'The Self-image,' in Welwood, J. (ed.), *The Meeting of the Ways: Explorations in East/West Psychology*. Schocken Books: New York.
193. Kubler-Ross, E. (1982). *Living with Death and Dying*. Souvenir Press: London.

194. Trungpa, C. (1979). 'An Approach to Meditation,' in Welwood, *The Meeting of the Ways*. Op.cit., Chapter 10.

12   *Buddhism and Behaviour Change: Implication for Therapy*

195. Katz, N. (ed.) (1983). *Buddhist and Western Psychology*. Prajna Press: Boulder, Colorado.
196. *Psychologic*, 1986, 22, No.2.
197. Forgays, D.G. (1983). 'Primary prevention and psychopathology,' in *The Clinical Psychology Handbook*, Hersen, M., Kazdin, A.E. and Bellack, A.S. (eds). Pergamon Press: New York.
198. Carrington, P. (1982). 'Meditation techniques in clinical practice,' in *The Newer Therapies: a Sourcebook*, Abt, L.E. and Stuart, I.R. (eds). Van Nostrand: New York. And also Carrington, P. (1984). 'Modern forms of meditation,' in *Principles and Practice of Stress Management*, Woolfolk, R.L. and Lehrer, P.M. (eds). Guilford Press: New York.
199. Kishimoto, K. (1985). 'Self-awakening psychotherapy for neurosis: Attaching importance to oriental thought, especially Buddhist thought. *Psychologia*, 28, pp.90–100.
200. Singh, R. and Oberhummer, I. (1980). 'Behavior therapy within a setting of Karma Yoga.' *Journal of Behavior Therapy and Experimental Psychiatry*, 11, pp.135–41.
201. Mikulas, W.L. (1981). 'Buddhism and behavior modification.' *Psychological Record*, 31, pp.331–42.
202. de Silva, P. (1984). 'Buddhism and behaviour modification.' *Behaviour Research and Therapy*, 22, pp. 661–78. See also Shapiro, D.H. (1978), *Precision Nirvana*. Prentice-Hall: Englewood Cliffs, NJ.
203. Rahula, W. (1959). *What the Buddha Taught*. Grove Press: New York.
204. Morris, R. and Hardy, E. (eds). *Anguttara Nikaya*. Pali Text Society: London.
205. Katz, N. (1982). *Buddhist Images of Human Perfection*. Motilal Banarsidas: Delhi. See also Goleman, D. (1976). 'Meditation and consciousness: An Asian approach to mental health.' *American Journal of Psychotherapy*, 30, pp. 41–54. And Narada (1977). *The Buddha and His Teachings*. 3rd edn, Buddhist Missionary Society: Kuala Lumpur, Malaysia.

206. Rhys Davids, T.W. and Carpenter, J.E. (eds). *Digha Nikaya*. Pali Text Society: London.

207. de Silva, P. (1983). 'The Buddhist attitude to alcoholism,' in *Drug Use and Misuse: Cultural Perspectives*, Edwards, G., Arif, A. and Jaffe, J. (eds). Croom Helm: London.

208. Wolpe, J. (1958). *Psychotherapy by Reciprocal Inhibition*. Stanford University Press: Stanford, California.

209. Bandura, A. (1977). *Social Learning Theory*. Prentice-Hall; Englewood Cliffs, NJ.

210. cf. Wolpe, op.cit.

211. For example, Stuart, R.B. (1978). *Act Thin, Stay Thin*. Norton: New York.

212. cf. Mikulas, op.cit.

213. Skinner, B.F. (1966). *The Behavior of Organisms*. Prentice-Hall; Englewood Cliffs, NJ.

214. Bellack, A.S. and Morrison, R.L. (1982). 'Interpersonal dysfunction', in *International Handbook of Behavior Modification and Therapy*, Bellack, A.S., Hersen, M. and Kazdin, A.E. (eds). Plenum Press: New York.

215. Rachman, S. and Hodgson, R. (1980). *Obsessions and Compulsions*. Prentice-Hall: Englewood Cliffs, NJ.

216. Kazdin, A.E. (1974). 'Self-monitoring and behavior change,' in *Self-control: Power to the Person*, Mahoney, M.J. and Thoresen, C.E. (eds). Brooks Cole: Monterey, California.

217. cf. Wolpe, op.cit.

218. Cautela, J.R. (1967). 'Covert sensitization.' *Psychological Report, 74*, pp.459–68.

219. For example, Beck, A.T., Rush, A., Shaw, B. and Emery, G. (1979). *Cognitive Therapy of Depression*. Wiley: New York. And Ellis, A. (1970). *The Essence of Rational Psychotherapy*. Institute for Rational Living: New York.

220. de Silva, op.cit; de Silva, P. (1984). 'Early Buddhist and modern behavioral strategies for the control of unwanted intrusive cognitions.' *Psychological Record, 35*, pp.437–43; Mikulas, W.L. (1978). 'Four Noble Truths of Buddhism related to behavior therapy.' *Psychological Record, 28*, pp.59–67; and Mikulas, W.L. (1983). *Skills of Living*. University Press of America: Lanham, Md.

221. Norman, H.C. (ed.). *Dhammapada Commentary*. Pali Text Society: London.

222. Goleman, op.cit.

223. Rachman, S. and Wilson, G.T. (1980). *The Effects of Psychological Therapy*, 2nd edn, Pergamon Press: Oxford.

13   *Bankei — Seventeenth Century Japanese Social Worker?*

224. Brandon, D. (1976). *Zen in the Art of Helping*. Routledge & Kegan Paul: London.
225. Watts, A.W. (1962). *The Way of Zen*. Penguin: Harmondsworth.
226. Dumoulin, H. (1963). *A History of Zen Buddhism*. Random House: New York.
227. Fromm, E., Suzuki, D.T. and De Martino, R. (1974). *Zen Buddhism and Psychoanalysis*. Souvenir Press: London.
228. Storr, A. (1973). *Jung*. Fontana: London.
229. Suzuki, D.T. (1976). 'Dogen, Hakuin, Bankei — three types of thought in Japanese Zen,' Part II. *The Eastern Buddhist*, 9, p.7.
230. Waddell, N. (1973). 'The Zen sermons of Bankei Yotaku.' *The Eastern Buddhist*, 6, p.133.
231. Waddell, N. (1974). 'The Zen sermons of Bankei Yotaku.' *The Eastern Buddhist*, 7, p.127.
232. Waddell (1973), op.cit; p.140.
233. Waddell (1974), op.cit; p.101.
234. Waddell, N. (1974). 'A selection from Bankei Zen dialogues.' *The Eastern Buddhist*, 8, p.121
235. Ibid; p.119.
236. Waddell (1973), op.cit; p.148.
237. Ibid. pp.133—4.
238. Waddell (1974), op.cit; p.117.
239. Ibid; p.114.
240. Ibid; p.115.
241. Waddell (1974), op.cit; p.134.
242. Reps, P. (1971). *Zen Flesh, Zen Bones*. Penguin: Harmondsworth.

14   *Meditation: Psychology and Human Experience*

243. I am grateful to the meditators who participated in the interviews and to Julie Newsome for her careful and patient transcribing; finally, to Lesley Neal for help and for comments on earlier drafts of this chapter — *Namaskar*.

244. Das, N.N. and Gastaut, H. (1955). 'Variations de l'activité électrique du cerveau, du coeur et des muscles squelettiques au cours de la méditation et de l'extase yogique.' *Electroencephalography and Clinical Neurophysiology, 6,* pp.221–19.

245. Bagchi, B. and Wenger, M. (1957). 'Electro-physiological correlates of some yogi exercises.' *Electroencephalography and Clinical Neurophysiology, Supplement, 7,* pp.132–49.

246. Kasamatsu, A., Okuma, T., Takenaka, S., Koga, E., Ikeda, K. and Sugiyama, H. (1957). 'The EEG of "Zen" and "Yoga" practitioners.' *Electroencephalography and Clinicial Neurophysiology, 9,* pp.51–2.

247. Fenwick, P. (1960). 'Computer analysis of the EEG during mantra meditation,' Paper presented at conference on The Effects of Meditation, Concentration and Attention on the EEG. University of Marseilles.

248. Wallace, R.K. (1970). 'Physiological effects of transcendental meditation.' *Science, 167,* pp.1751–4.

249. Wallace, R.K., Benson, H. and Wilson, A. (1971). 'A wakeful hypometabolic physiologic state.' *American Journal of Physiology, 221,* pp.795–9.

250. Fenwick, P., Donaldson, S., Gillis, L., Bushman, J., Fenton, G.W., Perry, I., Tilsley, C. and Serafinowicz, H. (1977). 'Metabolic and EEG changes during transcendental meditation.' *Biological Psychology, 5,* pp.101–18.

251. Holmes, D.S. (1984). 'Meditation and somatic arousal reduction: A review of the experimental evidence.' *American Psychologist, 39,* pp.1–10.

252. Shapiro, D. and Walsh, R. (1984). *Meditation: Classic and Contemporary Perspectives.* Aldine: New York.

253. West, M.A. (1979a). 'Meditation: A review.' *British Journal of Psychiatry, 135,* pp.457–67. And West, M.A. (1983). 'Meditation and self-awareness: Physiological and phenomenological approaches,' in Underwood, G. (ed.), *Aspects of Consciousness, Volume 3, Awareness and Self-Awareness.* Academic Press: New York.

254. West, M.A. (1979b). 'Physiological effects of meditation: A longitudinal study.' *British Journal of Social and Clinical Psychology, 18,* pp.219–26.

255. Goleman, D.J. and Schwartz, G.E. (1976). 'Meditation as an intervention in stress reactivity.' *Journal of Consulting and Clinical Psychology, 44,* pp.456–66.

256. For reviews see West, M.A. (1980a). 'Meditation and the EEG.' *Psychological Medicine, 10,* pp.369–75. And Delmonte, M.M. (1984a). 'Electocortical activity and related phenomena associated with meditation practice: A literature review.' *International Journal of Neuroscience, 24,* pp.217–31.

257. Anand, B.K. Chhina, G.S. and Singh, B. (1961). 'Studies on Shri Ramanand yogi during his stay in an air-tight box.' *Indian Journal of Medical Research, 49,* 1, pp.82–9.

258. See note 249 above.

259. Hjelle, L. (1974). 'Transcendental meditation and psychological health.' *Perceptual and Motor Skills, 39,* pp.623–28. And also Ferguson, P. and Gowan, J. (1976). 'TM: Some preliminary findings.' *Journal of Humanistic Psychology, 16,* pp.51–60.

260. Williams, P., Francis, A. and Durham, R. (1976). 'Personality and meditation.' *Perceptual and Motor Skills, 43,* pp.787–92. See also Fehr, T. (1977). 'A longitudinal study of the effect of the TM program on changes in personality,' in Orme-Johnson, D. and Farrow, J. (eds), *Scientific Research on the Transcendental Meditation Program, Collected Papers.* MIU Press: Switzerland. And Delmonte, M.M. (1984b). 'Psychometric scores and meditation practice: A literature review.' *Personality and Individual Differences, 5,* pp.559–63.

261. Rogers, C. and Livingston, D. (1977). 'Accumulative effects of periodic relaxation.' *Perceptual and Motor Skills, 44,* p.690. See also West, M.A. (1980b). 'Meditation, personality and arousal.' *Personality and Individual Differences, 1,* pp.135–42. And Williams *et al., op.cit.*

262. See West (1979a), op.cit. for a review.

263. Benson, H., Frankel, F.H., Apfel, R., Daniels, M.D. Schniewind, H.E., Nemiah, J.C., Sifneos, P.E., Crasweller, K.D., Greenwood, M.M., Kotch, J.B., Arns, P.A. and Rosner, B. (1978). 'Treatment of anxiety: A comparison of the usefulness of self-hypnosis and a meditational relaxation technique.' *Psychotherapy and Psychosomatics, 30,* pp.229–42.

264. Woolfolk, R.L., Carr-Kaffashan, L. and McNulty, T.F. (1976). 'Meditation training as a treatment for insomnia.' *Behavior Therapy, 7,* pp.359–65.

265. Patel, C. and North, W. (1975). 'Randomised controlled trial of yoga and biofeedback in management of hypertension.' *The Lancet, 2,* pp.93–5. See also Blackwell, B., Bloomfield,

S., Gartside, P., Robinson, A., Hanenson, I., Magenheim, H., Nidich, S. and Zigler, R. (1976). 'Transcendental meditation in hypertension.' *The Lancet*, *1*, pp.223–6. And Pollack, A.A., Weber, M.A., Case, D.B. and Laragh, J.H. (1977). 'Limitations of transcendental meditation in the treatment of hypertension.' *The Lancet*, *1*, pp.71–3.

266. Shafii, M. (1973). 'Adaptive and therapeutic aspects of meditation.' *International Journal of Psychoanalysis and Psychotherapy*, *2*, pp.431–43. See also Carrington, P. (1977). *Freedom in Meditation*. Anchor/Doubleday: New York. And Shapiro, D. and Giber, D. (1978). 'Meditation and psychotherapeutic effects.' *Archives of General Psychiatry*, *35*, pp.294–302.

267. Jarrell, H.R. (1985). 'Meditation and psychotherapeutic effects.' *Archives of General Psychiatry*, *35*, pp.294–302.

267. Jarrell, H.R. (1985). *International Meditation Bibliography, 1950–1982*. The Scarecrow Press: London.

268. West (1980b) op.cit., and Delamonte (1984b) op.cit.

269. Markova, I. (1985). 'Is evolutionary methodology a suitable alternative in applied social research?' Paper presented at Annual Conference of the Social Psychology Section of the British Psychological Society. Cambridge, England.

270. Shapiro and Walsh (1984), op.cit.

271. West (1980b), op.cit.

272. Underwood, G. (ed.) (1983). *Aspects of Consciousness, Volume 3, Awareness and Self-Awareness*. Academic Press: New York.

273. Apter, M., Fontana, D. and Murgatroyd, S. (eds). (1985). *Reversal Theory: Applications and Developments*. University College Cardiff Press: Cardiff.

274. Mischel, T. (ed.) (1980). *The Self: Psychological and Philosophical Issues*. Basil Blackwell: Oxford.

275. Eiser, J.R. (1980). *Cognitive Social Psychology*. McGraw Hill: Maidenhead, England. See also Rosenberg, M. and Turner, R.H. (eds; (1981). *Social Psychology: Sociological Perspectives*. Basic Books: New York.

15   *The New Religions and Psychotherapy: Similarities and Differences*

276. Kilbourne, B. and Richardson, J.T. (1984). 'Psychotherapy

and the new religions in a pluralist society.' *American Psychologist*, *39*, pp.237—51. And Vaughan, F. (1983). 'A question of balance: health and pathology in new religious movements.' *Journal of Humanistic Psychology*, *23*, pp.20—41.

277. For example, Kilbourne and Richardson, op.cit.

278. Barker, E. (1985). *The Making of a Moonie*. Basil Blackwell; Oxford.

279. Conway, F. and Seigelman, J. (1978). *Snapping: America's Epidemic of Sudden Personality Change*. Delta: New York; Galanter, M. M. (1982). 'Charismatic religious sects and psychiatry: an overview.' *American Journal of Psychiatry*, *139*, pp.1529—48; and Rochford, E.B. (1982). 'Recruitment strategies, ideology and organisation in the Hare Krishna movement.' *Social Problems*, *29*, pp.399—410.

280. Frank, J. (1974). *Persuasion and Healing*. John Hopkins Press: Baltimore.

281. Goldfried, M.R. (1980). 'Towards the delineation of therapeutic change principles.' *American Psychologist*, *35*, pp.991—9; Sloane, R.B., Staples, F.R., Cristol. A.H., Yorkston, N.J. and Whipple, K. (1975). *Psychotherapy versus Behaviour Therapy*. Harvard Commonwealth Fund Books; and Strupp, H. and Hadley, S. (1979). 'Specific versus non-specific factors in psychotherapy: a controlled study of outcome.' *Archives of General Psychiatry*, *30*, pp.1125—36.

282. Schonfield, J., Stone, A.R., Hoehn-Saric, R., Imber. S.D. and Pande, S.K. (1969). 'Patient therapist convergence and measures of improvement in short-term psychotherapy.' *Psychotherapy: Theory, Research and Practice*, *6*, pp.267—71; and Strong, S.R. and Claiborn, C.D. (1982). *Change through interaction*, Wiley: Sussex.

283. Fielding, R.G. and Llewelyn, S.P. (1986). 'Applying the social psychology of groups in clinical settings.' *British Journal of Psychotherapy* (in press); and Kelman, H.C. (1963). 'The role of the group in the induction of therapeutic change.' *International Journal of Group Psychotherapy*, *13*, pp.399—432.

284. Bloch, S. and Crouch, E. (1985). *Therapeutic Factors in Group Psychotherapy*. Oxford University Press: Oxford; and Yalom, I.D. (1975). *The Theory and Practice of Group Psychotherapy*. Basic Books: New York.

285. Pilgrim, D. and Eisenburg, N. (1985). 'Should the special hospitals be phased out?' *Bulletin of the British Psychological Society, 38*, pp.281–84.

286. Galanter, M., Rabkin, R., Rabkin. F. and Deutsch, A. (1979). 'The "Moonies": a psychological study of conversion and membership in a contemporary religious sect.' *American Journal of Psychiatry, 136*, pp.165–169.

287. Deutsch, A. (1975). 'Observations on a sidewalk Ashram.' *Archives of General Psychiatry, 32*, pp.166–75; and Schwartz, L.L. and Kaslow, F.W. (1979). 'Religious cults, the individual and the family.' *Journal of Marital and Family Therapy, 5*, pp.15–26.

288. Levin, T.M. and Zegans, L.S. (1974). 'Adolescent identity crisis and religious conversion: implications for psychotherapy.' *British Journal of Medical Psychology, 47*, pp.73–82; and Levine, S. (1979). 'Adolescents, believing and belonging.' *Annals of the American Society for Adolescent Psychiatry, 7*, pp.41–53.

289. Levine, S. (1981). 'Cults and mental health: clinical considerations.' *Canadian Journal of Psychiatry, 26*, pp.534–9.

290. Etemad, B. (1978). 'Extrication from cultism.' *Current Psychiatric Therapy, 18*, pp.217–23.

291. Galanter (1982), op.cit.

292. See Galanter *et al.* (1979) and Levine (1981), op.cit.

293. Ross, M.W. (1981). 'Clinical Profiles of Hare Krishna devotees.' *American Journal of Psychiatry, 140*, pp.416–20. See also Levine (1981), op.cit.

294. Galanter, M. and Buckley, P. (1978). 'Evangelical religion and meditation: psychotherapeutic effects.' *Journal of Nervous and Mental Disease, 137*, pp.685–91; Galanter *et al.* (1979), op.cit; and Clark, J.G., Jr. (1979). 'Cults,' *Journal of the American Medical Association, 242*, pp.279–81.

295. Spitzer, I. (ed.) (1980). *Psychobattery: a chronicle of psychotherapeutic abuse.* Wiley: London; and Kilbourne and Richardson (1984), op.cit.

296. For example, Conway and Seigelman (1978), op.cit; and Maleson, F. (1981). 'Dilemmas in the evaluation and management of religious cultists.' *American Journal of Psychiatry, 138*, pp.925–29.

297. Galanter, M. (1983a). 'Engaged members of the Unification Church.' *Archives of General Psychiatry, 40*, pp.1197–1202; and Levine (1981), op.cit.

298. Galanter (1982), op.cit.

299. Levine (1981), op.cit., pp.534, 535.

300. Levine and Zegans (1974), op.cit. p.81.

301. Levine (1981), op.cit., p.537.

302. Singer, M.T. (1978). 'Therapy with ex-cult members.' *National Association of Private Psychiatric Hospitals' Journal*, *9*, pp.14–18; and Singer, M.T. (1979). 'Coming out of the cults.' *Psychology Today*, *12*, pp.72–80.

303. Conway and Seigelman (1978), op.cit.

304. Galanter, M. (1983b). 'Unification Church ("Moonie") dropouts: psychological readjustment after leaving a charismatic religious group.' *American Journal of Psychiatry*, *140*, pp. 984–9.

305. Smith, M.L. and Glass, G.V. (1977). 'Meta-analysis of psychotherapy outcome studies.' *American Psychologist*, *32*, pp. 752–60; and Strupp, H., Hadley, S. and Gomes-Schwartz, B. (1977). *Psychotherapy for Better or Worse: The Problem of Negative Effects*. Jason Aronson: New York.

306. Lieberman, M., Yalom, I. and Miles, M. (1975). *Encounter Groups: First Facts*. Basic Books: New York.

307. Llewelyn, S.P. (1986). 'Ethical issues in psychotherapy for women,' in *Ethics in Clinical Psychology and Behavioural Medicine*, Fairbairn, G. and Fairbairn, S. (eds). Routledge & Kegan Paul: London.

308. Temerlin, M.T. and Temerlin, J.W. (1982). 'Psychotherapy cults: an iatrogenic perversion.' *Psychotherapy: Theory, Research and Practice*, *19*, pp.131–41.

309. Hochman, J. (1984). 'Iatrogenic symptoms associated with a therapy cult: examination of an extinct "new psychotherapy" with respect to psychiatric deterioration and "brainwashing".' *Psychiatry*, *47*, pp.366–77.

310. Clark (1979), op.cit., p.280.

311. Cohen, S. (1972). *Folk Devils and Moral Panics*. McGibbon and Kee: London.

312. Vaughan (1983), op.cit.

16   *Psychotherapy and Techniques of Transformation*

313. As quoted by Bharti, M. (1981). *Death Comes Dancing*. Routledge & Kegan Paul: London.

314. Skynner, R. (1983). 'Psychotherapy and Spiritual Tradition,' in Welwood, J, *Awakening the Heart*. Shambhala: London.

315. Needleman, J. (1983). 'Psychiatry and the Sacred,' in Welwood, J. *Awakening the Heart*. Shambhala: London.

316. Vitz, P. (1979). *Psychology as Religion: The Cult of Self Worship*. Lion: Tring. See also Bobgan, M., and Bobgan D. (1979). *The Psychological Way/The Spiritual Way*. Bethany House: Minneapolis; Halmos, P. (1965). *The Faith of the Counsellors*. Constable: London.

317. Clare, A. and Thompson, S. (1983). *Let's Talk about Me*. BBC: London.

318. Ibid.

319. Bhagwan Shree Rajneesh, as quoted in *Rajneeshpuram* (1983), Rajneesh Foundation International: Oregon.

320. As quoted by Rhinehart, L. (1976). *The Book of est*. Holt, Rinehart & Winston: New York.

321. An excellent summary is provided by Finkelstein, P. *et al.* (1982). 'Large Group Awareness Training.' *Annual Review of Psychology*, pp.515–39.

322. As carried out by Heelas, P. Results to be published.

323. Kornfield, J. *et al.* 'Psychological Adjustment is not Liberation,' in Welwood, J. *Awakening the Heart*. Shambhala: London.

324. Henderson provides a useful guide: see Henderson, C. (1975). *Awakening Ways to Psycho-Spiritual Growth*. Prentice-Hall: New Jersey.

325. See Clare and Thompson, op.cit.

326. Mowrer, O. (1961). *The Crisis in Psychiatry and Religion*. Van Nostrand: London.

327. Lieberman, M. and Gardner, J. (1976). 'Institutional Alternatives to Psychotherapy.' *Arch. Gen. Psychiatry*, *33*, pp.157–62.

328. Schachter, S. and Singer, S. (1962). 'Cognitive, social, and physiological determinants of emotional state.' *Psychological Review*, *69*, pp.379–99.

329. Information collected by Cuney, J. and Heelas, P. whilst researching a book on Bhagwan's path.

330. See Turner, V. (1969). *The Ritual Process*. Routledge & Kegan Paul: London. The key term is 'communitas.'

331. As quoted by Rhinehart, (1976), op.cit.

332. Material gathered by P. Heelas, during a study of the seminar.

333. Rajen, S. (1984). 'An inside view of the spiritual therapy programs offered by Rajneesh International Meditation

University.' *The Rajneesh Times*, 17 February.

334. (1955) Hogarth: London. But see Rieff, P. (1979). *Freud: The Mind of the Moralist*. University of Chicago Press: Chicago, where he discusses the resemblance of psychoanalysis to Stoicism.

335. Freud, S. (1950). *Psychopathology of Everyday Life* in *The Basic Works of Sigmund Freud*. Modern Library: New York.

336. Freud, S. (1943). *Introductory Lectures*. Garden City Publishing Co.: New York. (Our emphasis.)

337. Freud (1950), op.cit.

338. Freud believed that he could understand his own dreams better than anyone else could. See Freud, S. (1953). *The Interpretation of Dreams* in *The Complete Psychological Works of Sigmund Freud*. Vol. *IV*, Hogarth Press: London. He also maintained that the dreamer never knows the meaning of his own dreams (see *Introductory Lectures*)!

339. Freud, S. (1949). 'Psychoanalysis and the ascertaining of truth in courts of law,' in *The Collected Papers of Sigmund Freud*. Vol. *II*, Hogarth Press: London.

340. Freud, S, (1949). 'Constructions in Analysis,' in ibid.

341. Freud (1953), op.cit.

342. Freud, S. (1953). On Psychotherapy,' in *The Complete Works*, Vol. *IV*, 'Recommendations on Treatment' in *The Collected Papers*. Vol.*II*, op.cit.

343. Frank, J. 'The Two Faces of Psychotherapy.' *The Journal of Nervous and Mental Disorders*. *164*, No. 1, pp.3–7.

344. Freud, S. (1930). *Civilization and Its Discontents*. Hogarth Press: London.

345. Jung, C. (1968). *Analytical Psychology: Its Theory and Practice*, Routledge & Kegan Paul: London.

346. Janov, A. (1973), *The Primal Scream*. Sphere: New York.

347. Maslow, A. (1968). *Toward a Psychology of Being*. Van Nostrand Reinhold Co.: New York.

348. McGowan, T. (1980). 'Conversion and Human Development,' in Richardson, H. *New Religions and Mental Health: Understanding the Issues*. The Edwin Mellen Press: New York and Toronto.

349. Erikson, E. (1959). *Young Man Luther: A Study in Psychoanalysis and History*. Faber: London; and (1970). *Gandhi's Truth: on the Origins of Militant Nonviolence*, Faber: London.

350. McGowan, op.cit.

351. Fromm, E. (1960). 'Psychoanalysis and Zen Buddhism,' in

Fromm, E., Suzuki, D.T. and De Martino, R. *Zen Buddhism and Psychoanalysis*. Allen & Unwin: London, pp.77–141.

352. Freud, S. (1950). 'Analysis, Terminable and Interminable,' in *The Collected Papers*. Vol.V, op.cit.

353. Fromm, op.cit.

354. Fromm, op.cit.

355. Fromm, op.cit.

17   Therapy and Beyond: Concluding Thoughts

356. Kelly, G.A. (1955). *The Psychology of Personal Constructs*. Norton: New York.

357. Welwood, J. (1983). 'Befriending emotion,' in J. Welwood (ed.), *Awakening the Heart*. Shambhala: Boulder, Colorado.

358. Schloegl, I. (1977). *The Zen Way*. Sheldon Press: London.

359. Trungpa, Chogyam Rinpoche (1967). *Meditation in Action*. Shambhala: Boulder, Colorado.

360. Laing, R.D. (1965). *The Divided Self*. Penguin: Harmondsworth.

361. Rogers, C.R. (1980). *A Way of Being*. Houghton Mifflin: Boston.

362. Welwood, op.cit.

363. Gendlin, E. (1974). 'Client-centred and experiential psychotherapy,' in Wexler, D. and Rice, L. (eds), *Innovations in Client-Centred Therapy*. Wiley: New York.

364. These questions are powerfully discussed by Brandon, D. (1976). *Zen in the Art of Helping*. Routledge & Kegan Paul London; and by Miller, A. (1983). *The Drama of the Gifted Child*. Faber: London.

365. Kelly, op.cit.

366. Rogers, op.cit.

367. Perls, F. (1972). *In and Out the Garbage Pail*. Bantam: Toronto.

368. Ellis, A. (1975). 'Rational-emotive psychotherapy,' in Bannister, D. (ed.) *Issues and Approaches in the Psychological Therapies*. Wiley: London.

369. Freud, S. (1965). *New Introductory Lectures on Psychoanalysis*. Norton: New York.

370. Wilber, K. (1984). *Quantum Questions*. Shambhala: Boulder, Colorado.